Freud on Schreber

The old charts
are not so wrong
which added Adam
to the world's directions

which showed any of us
the center of a circle
our fingers
and our toes describe

Letter 14
Charles Olson,
The Maximus Poems

Freud on Schreber

Psychoanalytic Theory and the Critical Act

C. Barry Chabot

The University of Massachusetts Press Amherst, 1982

Acknowledgments and Permissions

From *For Love: Poems 1950–1960.* Copyright © 1962 by Robert Creeley. Reprinted by permission of Charles Scribner's Sons. Published in Great Britain and the British Commonwealth by Marion Boyars Publishers Ltd.

From *Maximus Poems.* Copyright © 1960 by Charles Olson. Reprinted by permission of Corinth Books in association with Jargon Books.

From *Small Ceremonies* by Carol Shields. Copyright © McGraw-Hill Ryerson Limited, 1976.

From *Opus Posthumous,* by Wallace Stevens, ed. by Samuel Morse French. Copyright © 1957 by Elsie Stevens and Holly Stevens. Reprinted by permission of Alfred A. Knopf, Inc.

From *The Freud/Jung Letters: The Correspondence between Sigmund Freud and C. G. Jung,* ed. William McGuire, trans. Ralph Manheim and R. F. C. Hull. Bollingen Series 94. Copyright © 1974 by Sigmund Freud Copyrights Ltd. and Erbengemeinschaft Prof. Dr. C. G. Jung. Reprinted by permission of Princeton University Press and the Hogarth Press Ltd.

From *The Standard Edition of the Complete Psychological Works of Sigmund Freud,* trans. and ed. James Strachey. Vol. 2: *The Collected Papers of Sigmund Freud,* ed. Ernest Jones, M.D., authorized translation under the supervision of Joan Riviere. Vol. 3: *The Collected Works of Sigmund Freud,* ed. Ernest Jones, M.D., authorized translation by Alix and James Strachey. Vol. 4: *The Collected Papers of Sigmund Freud,* ed. Ernest Jones, M.D., authorized translation under the supervision of Joan Riviere. Reprinted by permission of Sigmund Freud Copyrights Ltd., the Institute of Psycho-analysis, the Hogarth Press Ltd., and Basic Books.

Quotations from Daniel Paul Schreber's *Memoirs of My Nervous Illness,* trans. and ed. with introduction and notes by Ida Macalpine and Richard A. Hunter, published by William Dawson and Sons Limited, Folkestone, England, 1955, are by the kind permission of Dr. Richard Hunter.

An earlier version of chapter three appeared as "Psychoanalysis as Explication." Copyright © 1978 by *Journal of the Philadelphia Association for Psychoanalysis.* Reprinted by permission of David Sachs, editor.

Printed in the United States of America LC 81–16476 ISBN 0–87023–348–3

Library of Congress Cataloging in Publication Data appear on the last printed page of this book.

To

Jeffrey and Justin

who would ask, "How long does it take to make a book, anyway,"

and to Susan who knew.

Acknowledgments

During the time I worked on this project I incurred numerous debts which I wish now to acknowledge, if not hereby discharge. The American University twice provided crucial assistance—first in the form of a grant to work on a more modest project which, with time, became this book; and then again later in aiding with the preparation of the final manuscript. My colleagues here consistently supported my efforts, even when I could give them little concrete reason to think that anything would come of them. This sort of trust is increasingly rare in the academic world; I am grateful for it, and hope that at least a beginning has been made toward earning it. Rudi von Abele, Charley Hardwick, and Tom Maddox kindly read various versions of what follows. I might not have persisted without their encouragement; and I would not have achieved even my present measure of success without their assistance. Thanks of a special sort are due Norman Holland, who introduced me not only to psychoanalysis, but also to how one might conduct a life of teaching and research. If in what follows I have the temerity to criticize his work on this or that specific point, I can only do so because he, more than anyone else, taught me how to think. A student's indebtedness can go no deeper.

An earlier version of chapter three was published in the *Journal of the Philadelphia Association for Psychoanalysis;* I thank its editor, David Sachs, for permission to republish materials originally published in its pages. A subsequent version of the same chapter was presented to the Kanzer Seminar for Psychoanalysis and the Humanities at Yale University; the various participants assisted me in understanding some of the implications of the position I was arguing.

Contents

Introduction: Contexts and Problems

1

Situated somewhere between clinic and salon, Daniel Paul Schreber's *Memoirs of My Nervous Illness* confronts the reader as a work that is at once clinical document and literary exercise. Schreber undertook his memoirs, which detail his extraordinary experiences during a severe and prolonged psychotic episode, in 1900, and the writing occupied him for more than two years. Having resolved to petition for his release from the Sonnenstein Asylum where he was being detained, Schreber originally intended *Memoirs* for a narrow audience, to provide his wife and immediate acquaintances with, in his own words, "an approximate idea at least of my religious conceptions, so that they may have some understanding of the necessity which forces me to various oddities of behavior, even if they do not fully understand these apparent oddities."[1] As he reviewed his experiences of the past six years while working on the manuscript, however, he came to suspect a greater relevancy for his new religious beliefs. Schreber eventually resolved upon publication of *Memoirs* both to promulgate his radically unique cosmology and to attract an "expert examination of [his] body and observation of [his] personal fate . . . [which] would be of value both for science and the knowledge of religious truths" (M, 3). Thus Schreber finally considers himself a prophet of sorts—indeed, he compares himself to Christ (M, 214)—destined to occasion a "fundamental revolution in mankind's religious views unequalled in history" (M, 215) and appears confident he will accordingly achieve enduring personal renown.

Fame has in fact come to Schreber, but in a manner he could only greet with horror. Not honored as a prophet, Schreber has become instead "the most quoted patient in psychiatry."[2] More cruelly, Schreber's fame is indirect, for he can only come to us now mediated by the commanding presence of Sigmund Freud, whose seminal essay on *Memoirs of My Nervous Illness* conferred upon text and author much of their subsequent import. Freud's ponderously entitled essay, "Psychoanalytic Notes on an Autobiographical Account of a Case of Paranoia (Dementia Paranoides)," remains central in psychiatry's understanding of paranoia; even differing theories of the disorder must define themselves in their departures from the formulations Freud offers in his commentary upon Schreber's *Memoirs*. Thus the fame Schreber anticipated is his, but it comes, ironically, only through his status as an exemplary mental patient, a designation *Memoirs* strenuously rejects.

Freud's essay is noteworthy not only because it contributed to our understanding of paranoia. Of at least equal interest, I think, is the fact that Freud never met Schreber, that his seminal essay was written almost exclusively from a careful and exhaustive reading of *Memoirs*. In his introduction Freud justifies this departure from common practice by observing that paranoids are uniquely accessible in this way: "Since paranoics cannot be compelled to overcome their internal resistances [hence free association proves most difficult], and since in any case they only say what they choose to say, it follows that this is precisely a disorder in which a written report or a printed case history can take the place of personal acquaintance with the patient."[3] Freud's rationale aside, this procedure makes his essay, whatever else it may in fact be, an exercise in literary criticism. This fact, of course, has been seized upon by several of Freud's detractors, much as if it were a scandal that prima facie deprives his work of seriousness.[4] As will become clear in the course of this book, I believe such criticisms completely unfounded; they derive from a mistaken, scientistic notion of the nature of psychoanalysis. In fact, I initially resolved to work with Freud's essay on *Memoirs* precisely because it reveals so unmistakably the nature of that discipline and its necessary reciprocity with literary criticism.

To argue today for some revolutionary joining of psychoanalytic and literary studies must occasion a certain amount of ennui. In one sense, of course, their very separation is a fairly recent historical phenomenon, simply one manifestation among many of the drift toward specialization or professionalism. We need only recall Aristotle's "catharsis," Keats's "negative capability," and Coleridge's imaginations and fancy to recognize that psychological assumptions and theories have historically served as the keystones to many an aesthetic. Be that as it may, now, on the other side of their sunderance, we can trace the dispiriting history of calls for their reunion back at least as far as Freud's 1897 letter to Wilhelm Fliess, in which he suggests now familiar reasons for the persistent power of Sophocles' *Oedipus Rex*. Indeed, the gesture toward the arts, especially literature, seems part of Freud's legacy to succeeding psychoanalysts; the frequency with which they turn to literary exercises suggests the vague feeling that they can only rightly claim their full patrimony by doing so. Too often these exercises respect the rigor of neither discipline, but content themselves with merely using features of literary texts as exemplars for one or another psychoanalytic theory or complex. One of two interests guides the more serious of such efforts. On the one hand, psychoanalysts and their literary colleagues have tried to derive from psychoanalysis an understanding of the creative process. Freud's "Creative Writers and Daydreaming," Ernst Kris's *Psychoanalytic Explorations in Art*, and Marion Milner's *On Not Being Able to Paint*, for example, investigate this process in a general way, whereas the many biographical studies, such as Bernard Meyer's *Joseph Conrad* and John Cody's *After Great Pain: The Inner Life of Emily Dickinson*, seek its workings in individual cases. More commonly, psychoanalysis has been employed to explicate individual texts or canons; Ernest Jones's *Hamlet and Oedipus* and Frederick Crews's *The Sins of the Fathers* are exemplary of this less ambitious, but still vital, tradition. If my own experience is at all indicative, much such work assumes that the verities of psychoanalysis—a "science" after all—will secure the interpretive process, control what otherwise seems a capricious activity. Actually, the operative assumption is more complex. Not only are psychoanalytic "facts" taken as though of a different order—one somehow more stable and more to the point than literary "facts"—but the interpretive process within psychoanalysis as well is assumed to be less arbitrary, more "objective." Or so I used to think.

The present essay takes a different tack. I have nothing explicit to say about the creative process; nor, except by way of exemplification, am I here concerned with the interpretation of any particular text. Rather, I go behind such activities to inquire into the nature of the interpretive process in psychoanalysis: primarily what it must assume, but also its affiliations with psychoanalytic theory, the steps it evolves through, its criteria for validity. The more I have worked with psychoanalysis the more the certainty I originally sought evaporated. If I previously hoped that psychoanalytic interpretation could secure literary studies, with time I have come to think that the interpretive situations in these disciplines are little different. The similarities are more than fortuitous, for whether we know it or not, whether we care to acknowledge it or not, we are engaged in a common enterprise: the understanding of another through an understanding of his or her language.[5] But that task presupposes a psychological theory capable of explicating an individual's relations with his or her language. If such is in fact the case, the estrangement of psychoanalyst and literary critic is more than usually pernicious, for they have much to learn from one another. I conceive of this book as an attempt to renew a dialogue between psychoanalysis and literary studies, a dialogue in which both parties can learn about their affiliations to one another and, hence, something about their own nature.

Of late claims of this sort frequently have a decidedly French accent. I refer, of course, to the increasing body of work taking its inspiration from Jacques Lacan. Because his name will appear most infrequently hereafter despite the many apparent parallels between our projects, a word or two by way of explanation seems in order. Like Lacan and his followers, I take seriously the fact that psychoanalysis uses as its object the language of an individual; and like them again, I pursue the implications of this fact primarily through a reading of Freud—in this instance, chiefly of his essay on Schreber. It is precisely at this point that our undertakings diverge. The Freud I read is Freud the clinician, whereas the Lacanian Freud is chiefly a metapsychologist. I want to understand what assumptions and moves Freud made when interpreting a piece of clinical language, whereas the Lacanian wants to unpack Freud's implicit understanding of the nature of the subject and its relations to its language.

Several further differences would seem to follow from these different points of departure. First, I claim that Freud's own interpretive practice assumes the radical cohesion of the individual life, a cohesion that finds theoretical justification, as I show in the fourth chapter, only in Freud's concept of transference. Working largely from metapsychological texts, Lacan and his followers, on the other hand, repeatedly stress the discontinuity within the individual life, a discontinuity based, in the last analysis, on that between the signifier and the signified. The disjunctive nature of an individual life is not anything that anyone even casually familiar with psychoanalysis (much less with life itself) would care to deny. However, the burden of my argument is that Freud's own interpretive practice, as given in his essay on Schreber, argues for understanding these breaks within the more fundamental assumption of a cohesive life, and that lacking such an assumption, there would be no reason to interpret something one way rather than another. I claim, furthermore, that Freud's interpretive practice implies a distinction between interpretive and theoretical discourse—that they are not continuous, that they cannot quickly be assimilated one to the other. Perhaps because they are primarily concerned with metapsychology, Lacanians have not made this distinction. It might even be said that the French Freud yields no interpretive discourse. An example in point would be Lacan's own famous essay on Poe's "The Purloined Letter." Lacan uses Poe's short story by way of analogy to make a theoretical point about the location of the subject. Essays by his followers that take this essay as an example of what psychoanalysis might contribute to literary studies find themselves reiterating this lesson tiresomely without ever getting to what could properly be termed interpretive discourse. In my view, therefore, their preoccupation with theoretical matters has severely limited the contributions Lacan and his followers might have made to the renewal of a dialogue between psychoanalysis and literary studies; worse, despite (and because of) their theoretical preoccupations, the Lacanians consistently misconstrue important issues in Freud's theory and interpretive practice.[6]

Because of these failings, it seems to me best to begin with the manner in which Freud deals with a piece of clinical language, and to follow him in the interpretive process. Thus I begin with readings of Schreber's *Memoirs of My Nervous Illness* and Freud's "Psychoanalytic Notes," for in this instance we have unique access to all the language with which Freud worked. In what remains of the Introduction I take up some of the difficulties inherent in any current reading of *Memoirs.* Chapters one and two are largely expository. Since I cannot justly presume a reader familiar with *Memoirs,* in chapter one I offer a summary, as unencumbered as possible by interpretation, of the concerns and issues that permeate that remarkable book. The second chapter takes up Freud's "Psychoanalytic Notes on an Autobiographical Account of a Case of Paranoia (Dementia Paranoides)"; it summarizes in some detail both aspects of the essay—Freud's fragmentary interpretation of Schreber, and his presentation of a theory of paranoia. Although they derive from the foregoing, the third and fourth chapters represent something of a theoretical interlude. Specifically, the third chapter investigates the nature of Freud's commentary upon *Memoirs;* it is concerned with the relationship within psychoanalysis between theoretical and interpretive discourse, the role of historical excavation in interpretation, the questions Freud asks in constructing an interpretation, and, finally, the criteria for validity entailed by those questions. The Schreber case history discloses these issues with a remarkable clarity, and it does so precisely because it reveals, as Freud's occasional essays on more traditional literary topics do not, the necessary reciprocity between psychoanalysis and literary studies. Chapter four seeks the theoretical groundings for what I come to call the enabling assumptions of psychoanalytic interpretation: the notion of the radically cohesive life. With the fifth chapter I return to Schreber and the realm of interpretive discourse in offering another reading of *Memoirs.* Finally, in the Epilogue I reflect back upon the interpretive process engaged in chapter five to join the argument of the essay in a polemic against the mutually debilitating estrangement of psychoanalysis and literary studies.

2

Memoirs of My Nervous Illness presents a thicket of difficulties for its readers. Some of these at least potential problems reside in the text's own problematics; others, no less serious, *Memoirs* may tend to engender in its reader's responses. Unless we keep these difficulties in mind we seriously risk misapprehensions of this most elusive of texts. The possibility that a text might remain hermetically sealed away from us, its secrets locked in some beyond we cannot penetrate, a possibility always before us in reading, seems especially acute with *Memoirs;* hence the need to proceed slowly, with extreme caution and self-reflection.

The text of *Memoirs* is convoluted, often cancels itself out. Again and again we come across contradictory assertions, sometimes separated by several pages, sometimes almost contained in the same sentence. A major source of these difficulties is the manner in which Schreber composed *Memoirs.* Several years into his ordeal he began preserving his experiences in the form of notes: these "consisted at first only of a few unconnected thoughts or words which I put down; later—beginning with the year 1897—I started to keep regular diaries in which I entered all my experiences. . . . I also started to sketch my future *Memoirs,* which I had already planned" (M, 159–60). Only in 1900, drawing upon these earlier notes and diaries, did he begin actually writing *Memoirs,* completing the volume two years later. Thus, although *Memoirs* presents itself to us at once, it was in fact contemplated and written over a period of many years, years during which Schreber's material circumstances improved dramatically:

> While at the beginning [i.e., 1900] I was living in almost prison-like isolation, separated from contact with educated people, excluded even from the family table of the Director (to which so-called boarders of the Asylum were admitted), never able to go outside the walls of the Asylum, etc., I have gradually been granted increasing freedom of movement, and contact with educated people has been made increasingly possible. Finally I was completely successful in winning the proceedings against my tutelage. . . . My legal capacity was thereby acknowledged and free disposition of my properties restored to me. (M, 31)

This increased freedom of movement, which undoubtedly corresponds to the authorities' perception of increased mental health, forced Schreber to recognize that some of his "earlier opinions need revision" (M, 31). Nonetheless, he leaves these internal contradictions extant, both because he deems these errors trivial and because he does not want to "prejudice the freshness of the original descriptions" (M, 32). Even here, however, we come upon still another of these contradictions, for he writes in a footnote to the ninth postscript, in regard to the possibility of libel: "Besides repeatedly revising my work after the termination of the proceedings regarding my tutelage, I cut out, altered and tried to tone down my expressions so much that I believe the question of insulting content no longer arises" (M, 243 n).[7] But do not such alterations "prejudice the freshness of the original descriptions?" Which, if indeed either, of these statements should the reader believe? Such questions confront the reader of *Memoirs* at every turn, for little of its narrative remains stable, unqualified, uncontroverted.

Moreover, writing *Memoirs*, an act that, as appended court reports demonstrate, played a role in his eventual release from Sonnenstein, was itself restorative. While describing his transformation into a woman, we find Schreber saying, "It occurred to me only much later, in fact only while writing this essay did it become quite clear to me, that God Himself must have known of the plan . . ." (M, 77). Thus Schreber's understanding of his experiences, however bizarre we may think it, evolved with his progress on the manuscript: the act of writing was for him an act of revision. This makes *Memoirs* almost a palimpsest: successive readings of events are embedded one upon the other; none is completely erased; the only warrant for the last is the fact it is the most recent. The experience typically precedes the final understanding by several years, and the reader should keep these two presents distinct.[8] Moreover, since, as we have seen, Schreber does not delete all the inconsistencies and errors he himself perceives during his revisions, he gives us a text internally at odds with itself. Thus in investigating *Memoirs* we must remain aware of the succession of Schreber's beliefs, of the contradictions their revision occasions, of the multiple time frame inscribed within the text.

The abrupt disjunction in *Memoirs of My Nervous Illness* between Schreber's often quite fantastic assertions of fact and his generally careful, dispassionate, reasoned tone holds another difficulty for the reader. How, we may wonder, can anyone so reasonable, so impressed by science, so concerned with objectivity, anyone capable of pleading successfully in court against his institutionalization harbor such frankly bizarre views?[9] Apparently this difficulty is one we share with Schreber's associates. Appended to *Memoirs* are various documents related to Schreber's successful petition for discharge from Sonnenstein. Among them are two reports to the court by Dr. Weber, the asylum's director. During meals with his family, Weber reports, "Whatever matters were discussed—naturally apart from his delusions—whether they touched on state administration and law, politics, art or literature, social life or anything else, in all Doctor Schreber showed keen interest, detailed knowledge, good memory and correct judgment, and in ethical matters as well an attitude which one can only agree with" (M, 279). These considerable testimonies to his sanity existed side-by-side with Schreber's grandiose beliefs; as one and now another come to the fore a radical discontinuity is introduced into his behavior.

If Schreber's delusions themselves were fixed, completely impervious to change, perhaps this inconsistency would not be so unsettling. However they are not. Schreber's apparent passion to tailor his beliefs to the circumstances as he understands them in fact gives the text its similarity to a palimpsest. In a postscript written in January 1901, for instance, Schreber observes that his greater freedom of movement has "made it undeniable that manifestations of life in human beings (and animals) are not exclusively caused by the influence of the rays [as he had previously believed and stated] . . . when I listen to a performance in the theater or to a sermon in Church I cannot really maintain that every word spoken by the actors on the stage or by the parson in the pulpit is caused by their nerves being influenced by miracles" (M, 221–22). These read more or less like the words of a reasonable man, or at least of a man open to the vagaries of the world. The appearance is momentary, however, for Schreber immediately goes on to attribute the quiet murmurs of the audience and the muffled coughs of the congregation to precisely such miraculous interference. Reasonable and bizarre by turns, *Memoirs* presents the reader with an apparently discontinuous portrait of its author; consequently, Schreber's narrative threatens to remain elusively just beyond our every attempt at synthesis.[10]

Of course we may not even attempt such comprehension. We are only too aware before we read the text, and the contradictions we encounter may only seem to confirm the fact, that the book we hold in our hands is the product of a madman. This recognition might tempt us simply to dismiss *Memoirs* as incoherent, hopelessly muddled, the outré product of a deranged mind. Madness, so this logic runs, is by definition incomprehensible, so why trouble ourselves with the thicket of difficulties we necessarily encounter as we turn the pages of Schreber's book? This possible difficulty resides not so much in the text itself, as in the anticipations and reactions it can engender in its readers. We can discriminate various degrees of such reactions; they can range from outright dismissal of the entire text, to the characterization of certain knottier passages as unintelligible word-salads, to the premature seizure of a transcendent solution that leaves the often baffling inconsistencies of the text far behind in a dimly perceived past. All such responses represent premature closures, and threaten in their varying degrees to bar understanding. Elaborate reasoning or admonitory sermonizing, however, are of little recourse here; we can only trust that we remain open to the multiple inscriptions of *Memoirs,* for only in their midst can we hope to ground an adequate understanding.

Another difficulty that faces any contemporary reader of *Memoirs* is perhaps the most elusive and indirect. For all its indirectness, however, its force is no less strong; I suspect it has bedeviled more than one innocent reading of the book. As I have said, we now come to Schreber indirectly; Freud's seminal essay, still so central to psychiatry's understanding of paranoia, both sends us to *Memoirs* and forever mediates the volume for us. Thus I suspect that the reader's attitudes toward Freud and his essay, be they favorable or not, inevitably shadow his or her reading of Schreber. Of course Schreber's *Memoirs* is not unique in this regard; as even a cursory review of psychiatric and psychoanalytic periodicals reveals, we are touching on a phenomenon that pervades the mental-health disciplines. The figure of Freud still looms over psychoanalysis, receiving willy-nilly reactions ranging from filial deference and devotion to patricidal displeasure and rage. Again, no simple illustration of the problem or dispassionate logic will quickly right the situation. Rather, as we read Schreber's *Memoirs* we must recognize that the figure of Freud can never be far from us, and that our attitudes toward the founder of psychoanalysis inexorably shadow our work.

Of course I too am implicated in this. In my turning back to reinvestigate *Memoirs of My Nervous Illness* and Freud's reading of it, I recognize something of the rambunctious son challenging paternal authority, perhaps even glimpse one of Harold Bloom's pale ephebes struggling with a weighty inheritance. Actually, I do not so much challenge Freud's authority as seek to extend its domain; I want to demonstrate no more than that the interpretive powers of Freud's discipline are greater than he sometimes knew. When Freud writes, "So long as the individual is functioning normally and it is consequently impossible to see into the depths of his mental life" (SE, 12:60), or when he suggests that paranoids are uniquely accessible through written documents, he unnecessarily circumscribes the implications of his work: psychoanalysis can lend understanding to "normality" and illness alike, and it can do so precisely by conceiving its objects through, and as, coherent written documents.

This enumeration of the problems attendant upon such an enterprise would not be complete if I failed to mention another of an altogether different order: I work almost exclusively from translations. In the case of Freud, this of course means James Strachey's standard edition; in that of Schreber, I have relied largely upon the translation of Ida Macalpine and Richard Hunter. With Freud this does not seem an insurmountable problem.The *Standard Edition* is almost universally regarded as a superlative achievement;[11] moreover, because I am not primarily interested in the density of Freud's texts, but in the interpretive strategies that permit them and in turn characterize the discipline they found, occasional local difficulties seem quite beside the point. As regards Schreber's *Memoirs,* however, the situation seems more serious, for in the pursuit of other aims I base a reinterpretation of Schreber upon the translation. I have proceeded as cautiously as possible: since substantial and crucial portion of *Memoirs* cited by Freud are independently translated by Strachey, I have benefited from the opportunity to compare the translations against one another; for questionable and important passages I have consulted the original German, utilizing dictionaries and at times requesting the assistance of colleagues. Nonetheless, the opportunities for substantive error in my interpretation remain more numerous than I would obviously prefer. However, insofar as the reading of *Memoirs* in chapter five serves as more than simply another reading of another text—that is, insofar as it serves as an exemplum of how such readings could and should be pursued, within both psychoanalysis and literary studies alike—occasional lapses, although regrettable, are not altogether debilitating. Simply, the emphasis throughout this essay is not upon Schreber but upon the nature of interpretations and of the interpretive process, be it literary or clinical. And to the extent that Freud's essay on Schreber's *Memoirs* demonstrates with a unique force how inextricably intertwined are the literary and the clinical, I feel the potential benefits of working with this particular text far outweigh the obvious risks.

1 : Schreber and His *Memoirs*

Schreber himself was well aware of the difficulties his text would present to readers. At one point, while describing a transitory belief that he was the last human left on earth, he breaks off the narrative to reassure his readers: "I am fully aware how fantastic all this must sound to other people . . ." (M, 86). Moreover, again and again he despairs of communicating his extraordinary experiences in mundane, everyday language. "I cannot of course count upon being *fully* understood," he says in the introduction, "because things are dealt with which cannot be expressed in human language; they exceed human understanding" (M, 41). And much later: "Again it is extremely difficult to describe these changes in words because matters are dealt with which lack all analogies in human experience and which I appreciated directly only in part with my mind's eye, in part only by their effects, so that I may have formed but an approximate picture" (M, 117). No doubt hoping to mitigate these difficulties, Schreber precedes the narrative of his perilous personal situation with brief remarks on the cosmology in which they attain significance. We shall follow his example.

1

"The human soul," Schreber tells us, "is contained in the nerves of the body"; external forces acting upon the individual account for the "total mental life of a human being" (M, 45). As individuals mature their nerves differentiate themselves according to function, receiving sensory impressions, mentation, and so on. The nerves, which are the soul of man, are nourished by the body; however, when the latter dies, the nerves and all the impressions they contain go "into hibernation as some lower animals do and can be re-awakened to a new life" (M, 46).

"God to start with is only nerve, not body, and akin therefore to the human soul" (M, 46). However, whereas both the number and life expectancy of man's nerves are limited, God's nerves are infinite and eternal. Moreover, God's nerves can transform themselves into anything He desires; "herein," says Schreber, "lies the essence of divine creation" (M, 46). "God *wills* that something should be, and by dispatching rays with this will, *what He wills immediately comes into existence*" (M, 184). Thus God created the universe simply by willing it into existence. God's creative power is not boundless, but "is somehow dependent" (M, 184) upon proximity to the creation. Nor is this spontaneous creation continuous; rather (except for the "conditions contrary to the Order of the World" that embroil Schreber), because the final goal of God's creation on earth was attained with the creation of man, God Himself has "retired to an enormous distance" (M, 191) from earth. Across this distance God generally does "not interfere directly in the fate of peoples or individuals" (M, 48).

"Regular contact between God and human souls occurred in the Order of the World only after death" (M, 48). After the body's death, God draws up men's souls to Him, thus bringing them to heavenly life. (For this reason Schreber voices serious reservations about cremation, which might destroy the nerves [M, 244].) Because it is "their destiny to be attached to God Himself and ultimately to become in a sense part of Him as 'forecourts of heaven' " (M, 49), the souls undergo purification, as distinct from punishment. The length and intensity of this cleansing process depends in each case upon how blackened by sin it is. Since a "greater part of the nerves of morally depraved men is probably useless" (M, 49) to God and must be exterminated, a hierarchy of states of Blessedness, determined by the number of pure nerves each soul retains, exists in the forecourts of heaven. During the purification rites the souls learn God's language, "the so-called 'basic language,' a somewhat antiquated but nevertheless powerful German" (M, 49—50). A peculiarity of this language is its extreme tendency toward euphemism, which extends to outright reversals of meaning; thus souls who had not yet been cleansed were called "tested souls," and those that had were designated "non-tested souls."

Once completely cleansed by this mysterious process of purification, the souls, nerves actually, ascended to heaven and "so gained the *state of Blessedness*. This consist[s] of uninterrupted enjoyment combined with the contemplation of God" (M, 51). A soul's happiness, Schreber tells us, "lies in continual revelling in pleasure" (M, 52), which he later, while relating his transformation into a woman, repeatedly calls "soul-voluptuousness." Unaccountably, Schreber makes a sexual distinction here: "The male state of Blessedness," he says, is "superior to the female state; the latter seems to [consist] mainly in an uninterrupted feeling of voluptuousness" (M, 52).[1] Finally, however, all souls transcend their earthly identities entirely and fuse together, forming higher entities aware only that they are "part of God" (M, 52).

Schreber perceives, then, a cyclical eternity at work in the Order of the World. In the act of creation God transforms part of Himself into the beings of the world; in their ascent toward Blessedness after the death of the body, the souls again unite with the Maker. Here is Schreber's description of the cycle: "In creating something, God in a sense divests Himself of part of Himself or gives different form to part of His nerves. This apparent loss is restored when after hundreds or thousands of years the nerves of departed human beings who, in their lifetime had been nourished by other created things and had attained to the state of Blessedness, return to Him as the 'forecourts of Heaven' " (M, 53 n).

To this smooth recurring cycle Schreber adds complications. God Himself dwells above the forecourts of heaven to which the souls of men ascend. Moreover, no doubt on the model of the trinity, God is "subject to a peculiar division, a lower God (Ariman) and upper God (Ormuzd) being distinguished" (M, 53). Schreber confesses to knowing little about this, in his word, "peculiar" division, except that Ariman "seems to have felt attracted to nations of originally brunette race (the Semites) and the upper God to nations of originally blonde race (the Aryan peoples)" (M, 53). Several pages later Schreber adds that Ariman's rays can unman humans, a process crucial to *Memoirs,* whereas those of Ormuzd can restore manliness if necessary (M, 74). As Schreber describes it, unmanning, or the transformation into a woman, is a process innate in the Order of the World when a human comes into continued contact with divine rays:

> This is connected on the one hand with the nature of God's nerves, through which Blessedness . . . is felt, if not exclusively as, at least accompanied by, a greatly increased feeling of voluptuousness; on the other hand it is connected with the basic plan on which the Order of the World seems to rest, that in the case of world catastrophes which necessitate the destruction of mankind on any star, whether intentionally or otherwise, the human race can be renewed. . . . In such an event, in order to maintain the species, one single human being

was spared—perhaps the relatively most moral—called by the voices that talk to me the *"Eternal Jew."* . . . The Eternal Jew (in the sense described) had to be unmanned (transformed into a woman) to be able to bear children. (M, 72–73)

Apparently, the much simpler route, the saving of a female, was not in accordance with the Order of the World.

Unlike the Christian deity, Schreber's God is neither omniscient nor omnipotent. In the Order of the World God has contact only with the souls of the dead. This, Schreber explains, is doubly felicitous. First, "the nerves of *living* human beings particularly when in a state of *high-grade excitation,* have such power of attraction for the nerves of God that He would not be able to free Himself from them again, and would thus endanger His own existence" (M, 48). Second, as Schreber's own circumstances amply attest, such contact also endangers the living and makes their lives a constant torture, for God does "*not really understand the living human being* and [has] no need to understand him, because . . . He [deals] only with corpses" (M, 75). Were God able to learn from experience such discomfort would be merely transitory; unfortunately, however, He is uneducable: "It seems to be impossible for God to draw a lesson for the future from . . . experience, perhaps because of some qualities innate in His nature" (M, 154). Curiously, then, in Schreber's cosmology God must remain eternally ignorant of the nature of His very creations; indeed, should He approach them, God risks not only their well-being but also His own autonomy.

Schreber himself observes that his cosmology radically departs from the Christian. Moreover, he confidently asserts that any comparison between them can only favor his own. He sets out two reasons. First, Schreber's deity, being neither omniscient nor omnipotent, does not "*continuously* [see] inside every individual living person, [perceive] every feeling of his nerves, that is to say at all times 'tried his heart and reins' " (M, 54). This decrease in divine vigilance obviously comforts Schreber. Second, Schreber's cosmology "lacks any of the features of severity, of purposeless cruelty imprinted on some of the notions of the Christian and in a still greater degree on those of other religions." Again the advantage comes by way of a negative, almost as if Schreber has constructed his imagined universe with an eye toward omitting the features of the one he inherited that most trouble him. In sum, according to Schreber, the "whole Order of the World . . . appears as a 'miraculous structure,' the sublimity of which surpasses in [his] opinion all conceptions which in the course of history men and peoples have developed about their relation to God" (M, 54). The trials he endured no doubt severely tested Schreber's faith in the beneficence of his idiosyncratic cosmology. In the end, though, its "miraculous structure" provided him with the confidence both to persevere during his tribulations and to achieve reconciliation with his apparent fate. More important for Schreber and his readers, his cosmology lends his experiences significance; in so doing it reduces the mundanely inexplicable to the divinely certain. Thus, following Schreber, we must place his own experiences within this general frame.

2

The "mental illness" during which Schreber received these revelations was his second requiring extended hospitalization. The first occurred in the autumn of 1884; it was occasioned, Schreber says, by "mental overstrain" (M, 61) as a result of candidacy for Parliament. This first illness centered on "certain hypochondriacal ideas . . . , primarily concern over loss of weight" and "passed without any occurrences bordering on the supernatural" (M, 62). Schreber spent nearly six months at this time in the Psychiatric Clinic of the University of Leipzig where its director, Professor Flechsig, was in charge of his treatment. Schreber expresses gratitude toward Flechsig for his recovery, but in a manner so hedged with doubts and reservations that it subverts the expressed appreciation. The theme uniting these reservations seems to be Flechsig's perceived depreciation of Schreber; that is, his failure to recognize his patient as "a human being of high intellect, of uncommon keenness of understanding and acute powers of observation" (M, 62). Schreber's wife apparently harbored no such reservations: "My wife felt even more sincere gratitude and worshipped Professor Flechsig as the man who restored her husband to her; for this reason she kept his picture on her desk for many years" (M, 63).

After discharge from Flechsig's clinic Schreber returned to a position of importance in the community as the presiding judge of an inferior court in Leipzig. In *Memoirs* he characterizes these years as "on the whole quite happy . . . , rich . . . in outward honors, and marred only from time to time by the repeated disappointment of our hope of being blessed with children" (M, 63). This muted reference to disappointment conceals the extent to which their desires for children were thwarted; we now know that between his marriage in 1878 and his hospitalization in November 1893, his wife had six spontaneous miscarriages.[2] These private frustrations were compensated by public successes, and in June 1893 the Minister of Justice informed him "in person" of his imminent appointment as *Senatspräsident,* presiding judge, of the Dresden Court of Appeals.

Schreber's worldly success was fleeting; in fact, as I shall discuss later, he seems almost to have feared the professional heights to which he had risen. Before assuming office, Schreber found his sleep troubled by dreams, one of which he thought significant in retrospect: "It was the idea that it really must be rather pleasant to be a woman succumbing [curious word] to intercourse. This idea was so foreign to my whole nature that I may say I would have rejected it with indignation if fully awake . . ." (M, 63). On actually taking up his office Schreber drove himself unmercifully to insure his achievement of "all the necessary respect." This task was complicated by the fact that the judges over whom Schreber presided were "much senior to me (up to twenty years)" (M, 63); further, unlike Schreber, they were all familiar with the procedures of the court. The new *Senatspräsident* badly overtaxed himself and, in his words, "at the very moment when I was able to feel that I had largely mastered the difficulties of settling down in my new office" (M, 64) he found it impossible to sleep. His deterioration was rapid; by early November he again found his way to Flechsig's clinic. After a brief attempt at out-patient treatment, during which Schreber in his desperation attempted suicide, he was admitted to the asylum.

Schreber was melancholic in the asylum. Despite various attempted remedies, sleep still proved elusive, and Schreber dwelled on the apparent hopelessness of his situation: "My will to live was completely broken; I could see nothing in the future but a fatal outcome, perhaps produced by committing suicide eventually; as to the plans for the future with which my wife tried again and again to raise my spirits, I could only shake my head in disbelief" (M, 68). His wife's continual presence, however, was undoubtedly salutary, for when she took a much-needed holiday in February 1894 he again worsened. His condition was now such that he prohibited visits upon his wife's return, because, in his words, "I could not wish my wife to see me again in the low state into which I had fallen" (M, 68). Schreber does not elaborate on his newly deteriorated condition, but he does relate another event that contributed to his rapid decline: "Decisive for my mental collapse was one particular night; during that night I had a quite unusual number of pollutions (perhaps half a dozen)" (M, 68).

This second, deeper swerve into illness proved momentous. "From then on," Schreber tells us in the immediately following sentence, "appeared the first signs of communication with supernatural powers, particularly that of nerve-contact which Professor Flechsig kept up with me in such a way that he spoke to my nerves without being present in person" (M, 68). Only now, three months into his hospitalization, as many as nine months after the first disturbing dreams, does Schreber receive the revelations that occasion these *Memoirs.* Only now does Schreber begin the involved elaborations of the delusions—for that is what they are—that lend his torn and fragmented condition meaning. His bizarre interpretations of his experiences transform him from a broken institutionalized man into a harried martyr upon whose survival the very existence of the world depends; no longer bereft of a future, Schreber comes to an extraordinary destiny: "If it be true that the continuation of all creation on our earth rests entirely on the very special relations into which God entered with me, the reward of victory could only be something very extraordinary for my loyal perserverance *[sic]* in the struggle for my reason and for the purification of God" (M, 215). Schreber's delusions, then, are desperate attempts to restore him to the world and the world to him.

3

As Schreber says, after his wife's holiday he recognized that "Professor Flechsig had secret designs against [him]" (M, 68). At different times Schreber offers two explanations for how this plot came about. In the *Memoirs* proper, thus in 1900, Schreber suggests that somehow Flechsig had learned how to put divine rays to his own uses. He learned, moreover, through either research or the agency of divine rays, about the tendency in the Order of the World for an unmanning to occur when divine rays come into contact with a human soul. Somehow Flechsig established contact with Schreber's soul, a contact that God was powerless to dissolve. He continues:

> In this way a plot was laid against me (perhaps March or April 1894), the purpose of which was to hand me over to another human being after my nervous

illness had been recognized as, or assumed to be, incurable, in such a way that my soul was handed to him, but my body—transformed into a female body and, misconstruing the above-described fundamental tendency of the Order of the World—was then left to that human being for sexual misuse and simply "forsaken," in other words left to rot.(M, 75)

Why Flechsig entered into this intrigue and the identity of this third person who threatens sexual abuse are questions Schreber does not elaborate upon at this time.

Concurrently, Schreber believed that Flechsig had somehow managed to ascend to heaven and become a leader of rays (M, 75). Moreover, because souls lack any capacity for self-sacrifice, "Flechsig's soul gained certain technical advantages . . . over those of God's nerves with which it first came into contact" (M, 78). Thus Flechsig presented God with a temptation that His rays, by their very nature, could not resist, for he offered them the possibility of soul-voluptuousness in Schreber's body. In so doing, of course, God is inadvertently entering upon a course of action *contrary* to the Order of the World; He is violating the very "miraculous structure" He created.[3] In thus placing Himself at odds with His creation, God only insures His inevitable failure:

. . . the Order of the World reveals its very grandeur and magnificence by denying even God Himself in so irregular a case as mine the means of achieving a purpose contrary to the Order of the World. . . . From this apparently so unequal battle between one real human being and God Himself, I emerge, albeit not without bitter sufferings and deprivations, victorious, because the Order of the World is on my side. (M, 78—79)

In this version of Flechsig's initial involvement in Schreber's trials, then, the professor is clearly a powerful and resourceful villain: he plots Schreber's sexual debasement, he even tempts God into joining in this unholy enterprise, a temptation unresistible to God.

The incongruence between these actions that Schreber attributes to Flechsig, and his affirmed respect for the professor's "person, *whose integrity and moral worth I have not the least right to doubt*" (M, 34), obviously troubled him. Only after completing his manuscript, however, does he come to "a new idea which might *possibly* lead to the correct solution of the problem" (M, 34). In an "Open Letter to Professor Flechsig," which is dated March 1903 and which prefaces *Memoirs,* Schreber still maintains that the origin of his contacts with the supernatural "consisted of *influences on my nervous system emanating from your nervous system*" (M, 34). But the motivation Schreber ascribes to Flechsig has now changed. At first Flechsig carried out hypnotic contact with his patient for purely therapeutic purposes. Then, discovering that others were also in contact with Schreber, for scientific reasons Flechsig may have stayed in contact with him until he finally became uneasy about the morality of his actions. But the termination may not have been complete:

> But it is possible that in this process a part of your own nerves—probably unknown to yourself—was removed from your body . . . and ascended to heaven as a "tested soul" and there achieved some supernatural power. This "tested soul" still endowed with human faults like all impure souls . . . then simply allowed itself to be driven by the impulse of ruthless self-determination and lust for power. . . . (M, 34)

This second explanation attributes to Flechsig little of the malignancy of motive that characterizes the first. Flechsig's initial impulses are here seen as therapeutic, not destructive; moreover, the actual agency of Schreber's difficulties is no longer Flechsig himself, but an independent fragment of his soul. Therefore, there is now no reason "to cast any shadow upon your person and only the mild reproach would perhaps still remain that you, like so many doctors, could not completely resist the temptation of using a patient in your care *as an object for scientific experiments* apart from the real purpose of cure . . ." (M, 34). Thus the absolution here is not complete, but Schreber, who we must now remember is at this point reconciled to his fate, does dramatically soften his charges against Flechsig.

Flechsig or his disembodied nerves, as the case may be, achieves this power over his victim through *nerve-language,* of which most humans are unaware. Schreber explains this concept by analogy with a congregation's silent prayers, in which an individual "causes his nerves to vibrate in the way which corresponds to the use of the words concerned, but the real organs of speech . . . are either not set in motion at all or only coincidentally" (M, 69). In most circumstances, of course, this can only happen at the will of the individual concerned, but for Schreber this is not a voluntary happening: "In my case, however, since my nervous illness took the above-mentioned critical turn, my nerves have been set in motion *from without* incessantly and without respite" (M, 69).[4] Flechsig's and, later, God's employment of the nerve language in their dealings with Schreber, then, represents a usurpation of his autonomy, an invasion of the victim's body which he finds himself helpless to resist.

This usurpation of Schreber's prerogatives images the act by which Flechsig plans to attain his intentions, soul murder. Everything is quite obscure here. Perhaps the conspiracy intends to deny the Schrebers children; perhaps its goal is only to deny the Schreber family close contact with God: Schreber himself only offers suggestions, nothing definite (M, 57). Moreover, we are never told unequivocally the nature of soul murder—"Apart from these hints I cannot enlarge on the essential nature of soul murder or, so to speak, its technique" (M, 58);[5] it is only obvious, as I shall elaborate later, that it entails one individual's subversion of another's autonomy. Schreber suggests, for instance, that the tradition in folklore—"that it is somehow possible to take possession of another person's soul in order to prolong one's life at another soul's expense" (M, 55)—derives from the practice of soul murder. In the "Open Letter to Professor Flechsig," written more than two years later, Schreber hypothesizes that the voices' incessant talk about soul murder "can be explained by the souls (rays) deeming it impermissible that a person's nervous system should be influenced by another's to the extent of imprisoning his will power . . ." (M, 34–35). In this tangle of uncertainties all that Schreber knows for certain is that a soul murder has been attempted —perhaps as the voices suggest in recent (i.e., 1900) times, by Schreber himself (M, 55)—and that it has caused the rent in the Order of the World.

One cause of these difficulties is easy to locate. Just as Schreber lowers his original estimation of Flechsig's personal responsibility for Schreber's present plight, we can see the same sorts of revisions being carried out here. In the text itself, Schreber displaces the responsibility from Flechsig to one of his ancestors. He offers an elaborate hypothesis that some "bearer of the name Flechsig" (M, 56) began the difficulties. As the hypothesis continues, however, it becomes increasingly clear that the present Flechsig fits the illustration perfectly (indeed, it parallels the analysis offered in the "Open Letter" [M, 34–35]), yet for some reason Schreber finds it impossible to implicate him directly (M, 56–59). The "Open Letter" attenuates Flechsig's responsibility even further. Perhaps all this talk about soul murder was only the souls' imperfect way, "because of their innate tendency to express themselves hyperbolically" (M, 35), of referring to hypnosis. Thus not only is Flechsig himself not responsible for the crime, perhaps there is no crime, or only a most minor one. (Schreber's discomfort about his own assertions, his need to retract or at least mitigate them, is a subject to which we shall return.)

Perhaps Schreber's new appreciation of Flechsig's role in his fate is only appropriate. With Schreber's removal from Flechsig's clinic in June 1894 much of the latter's power passed to von W., Schreber's new attendant and tormentor, even though von W. generally "recognized the leadership of Flechsig's soul, which remained as before the spiritual leader of the whole rebellion against God's omnipotence" (M, 110). Moreover, with the passage of years Flechsig's soul has "progressively lost its intelligence so that now hardly a trace of awareness of its own identity remains" (M, 117), thus making him increasingly ineffectual. Flechsig's ever diminishing importance is matched by God's gradual participation in the conflict, and it soon becomes apparent in *Memoirs* that the crucial struggle is between Schreber and God, both of whom are contending for their personal autonomy.

The motivation given in *Memoirs* behind God's initial involvement with Schreber is as bedeviled by hedges, doubts, and contradictory suggestions as Flechsig's. We can choose among several: perhaps God did not recognize the gravity of Flechsig's actions at first and was drawn in unawares (M, 58); perhaps the forecourts of heaven entered into a covert conspiracy with Flechsig unknown to Ariman and Ormuzd (M, 57); perhaps Flechsig held some mysterious power over God's rays (M, 75); or perhaps, most dark of all, God Himself instigated this plot against Schreber, and the professor was merely one of His pawns (M, 77). Whatever the reason, God's active role in his struggles was for Schreber an incontestable fact. Moreover, once, through Flechsig's agency, divine rays were in contact with Schreber, God found Himself imperiled, for, as we have discussed, the nerves of living human beings hold such powers of attraction that He could not disentangle Himself from His host (M, 48). Thus against His will God was attracted to Schreber by an indescribable force; and His complete ignorance of living humans only compounded their mutual dilemma.

The result of this impasse on God's part was, in Schreber's words, a "*policy of vacillation* in which attempts to cure my nervous illness alternated with efforts to annihilate me as a human being who, because of his ever-increasing nervousness, had become a danger to God Himself" (M, 75). Various strategies to cancel Schreber's attractiveness were tried, none of which was finally successful. At one point God tried to unman Schreber, planning then to allow his "body to be prostituted like that of a female harlot" (M, 99). But this achieved exactly the reverse effect, for the "gradual filling of [his] body with nerves of voluptuousness (female nerves)" (M, 99) only increased his soul-voluptuousness and, hence, power of attraction. At other times God tried to murder Schreber. For a while scorpions were repeatedly placed on his head, no doubt to "carry out some work of destruction," but this too failed because the scorpions, recognizing the "purity of [Schreber's] nerves and the holiness of [his] purpose" (M, 99), withdrew. This having failed, God plotted to blacken Schreber by depositing in his body the blackened nerves of the deceased. Again, however, His efforts were futile and in time these blackened nerves vanished without affecting their reluctant host, leaving his power of attraction undiminished (M, 100).

The strategy to which God reverted upon His earlier failures was the attempted destruction of Schreber's reason. This was the course he most feared. Once, for example, there was an attempt by two "little men"—"Little Flechsig" and "little von W."—to pump out his spinal cord: "The effect of the pumping out was that the spinal cord left my mouth in considerable quantity in the form of little clouds. . . . One can imagine the apprehension with which such events filled me," says Schreber, "as I did not then know whether or not any part of my reason would thus in fact vanish into the air" (M, 135). At another time God attempted to pull the nerves out of his head (M, 135); at others "flights of rays" attacked his head, trying "to tear it asunder and pull it apart in a fashion comparable to quartering" (M, 136). Like the others, this strategy failed too, but we find interesting analogues to it, although reversed ones, in later misunderstandings that arise between Schreber and his uneducable God.

All of God's frustrated attempts to annihilate Schreber's power of attraction were carried out by miracles. Now, miracles do not ordinarily occur within the Order of the World, in part because of God's great distance from the earth. However, because of the increased soul-voluptuousness and attractiveness of Schreber's feminized nerves, God has been drawn closer to the earth, subjecting it once again to miracles: "As God was forced to draw nearer the earth again and remain permanently relatively close to it . . . the earth has once again become the permanent scene of divine miracles" (M, 196). This is especially true of Schreber's immediate environment, where his every action, every thought, every muscle seem subject to miracles many times over daily. In their number and variety they prohibit detailed discussion, so I shall simply list several: compulsive thinking (M, 70); "the so-called *putrification of the abdomen*" (M, 135); the *com-*

pression-of-the-chest-miracle ("one of the most horrifying") (M, 133); the *cursed creation of a false feeling* (M, 129); the bellowing miracle (M, 165); *birds created by miracle,* which "daily heaped upon [his] body" the poison of corpses (M, 167); the head-compressing machine (M, 138); the *coccyx miracle* (M, 139). The list could be much extended. These numerous miracles are aspects of what the voices told Schreber was "the cursed-play-with-human-beings"; that is, the attempt to create "interferences" or diversions necessary for God to free Himself from Schreber's voluptuous nerves and to withdraw again from earth. Throughout his institutionalization one or another of these miracles constantly plagued Schreber, making his every action and thought a continuous nightmare.

Despite God's efforts, Schreber's power of attraction increased daily. Indeed, through the years the forecourts of heaven gradually depleted themselves as more and more of the purified souls were drawn into Schreber's body. "This process frequently ended with the souls concerned finally leading a short existence on my head in the form of 'little men'—tiny figures in human form, perhaps only a few millimeters in height—before finally vanishing" (M, 83). Although greeted there by soul-voluptuousness, many of the souls resisted their dissolution in Schreber's body, as he proves "by the continual cries for help which I daily hear in the sky from those parts of the nerves which have become separated" (M, 61). Knowing this, Schreber for a time warned the souls against approaching him, "but the souls could not at first believe that I had such a dangerous power of attraction" (M, 84).

Of course the constant absorption of these nerves only hurried Schreber's unmanning, or transformation into a woman. As this was happening, two delusions developed. First, at some time prior to June 1894 he came to believe that he was "the last real human being on earth" (M, 85). This "idea was partly of a gruesome nature, partly of an indescribable sublimity" (M, 86), and was unshaken when he was moved from Flechsig's clinic to Dr. Pierson's private asylum in June: ". . . I did not know whether to take the streets of Leipzig through which I travelled as only theater props, perhaps in the fashion in which Prince Potemkin is said to have put them up for Empress Catherine II of Russia during her travels through the desolate country, so as to give her the impression of a flourishing countryside" (M, 102). Second, Schreber for a while interpreted all humans with whom he came in contact as "fleeting-improvised men" created by miracle

(M, 85). These fictitious creatures, who only compounded Schreber's bedevilment, were intended in the Order of the World for the maintenance and provision of the Eternal Jew selected to bear God's children (M, 74). Taken together, then, these delusions—and so Schreber himself came to recognize them (M, 221)—create the conditions necessary in the Order of the World for an unmanning. In a way, they provide its justification, or at least a means by which Schreber might come to accept his fate as God's elected bride.

Schreber's increasing feminization was of course met by countermeasures by Flechsig and God. One of these is Flechsig's partition of souls. Here is Schreber's description of the phenomena:

> Flechsig's soul introduced the partition of souls mainly in order to occupy the whole heavenly vault with parts of souls so that divine rays, following some power of attraction, met resistance on all sides. The picture which I have in my mind is extremely difficult to express in words; it appears that nerves . . . were strung over the whole heavenly vault, which the divine rays were not able to surmount. . . . I was for them only a means to an end to capture the divine rays brought nearer by the power of attraction with which they adorned themselves, like a peacock with strange feathers, so attaining the gift of miracles. (M, 109–10)

Schreber reasoned that if he could rid the earth of these fragmented souls, who only desired "to assert themselves in their usurped heavenly position" (M, 117), then, with only him and God remaining, a rapid resolution of his dilemma would follow. One night several years after his transfer to Sonnenstein, therefore, he "succeeded with immense mental effort in temporarily drawing down to [himself] all impure (tested) souls" (M, 118). His recovery seemed at hand, for Schreber now required only one purgative sleep for its restoration.

But Flechsig recognized this new danger and introduced another expedient, *mechanical fastening*. In its final form this resulted in the many tested souls "tying to some distant stars . . . which from then on excluded the possibility of a complete dissolution in [Schreber's] body in consequence of [his] power of attraction; on the contrary withdrawal was safeguarded through the mechanical fastening so established" (M, 118). At first God considered this so contrary to the Order of the World that he prohibited it; later, however, even He, confronted with Schreber's ever-increasing voluptuousness, resorted to mechanical fastening:

> In this way "tying-to-celestial-bodies" became a permanent institution continuing to the present day. . . . I realize that such a conception, according to

which one must think of my body on our earth as connected to other stars by stretched out nerves, is almost incomprehensible to other people considering the immense distances involved; for me however as a result of my daily experiences over the last six years there can be no doubt as to the objective reality of this relation. (M, 118–19)

If all the other miracles give evidence of God's inordinate concentration upon Schreber as a continued menace to His own survival, *mechanical fastening* provides a figurative demonstration. Schreber's description of his situation pictures him as the center of the universe, around which all the heavenly bodies and spirits align themselves.

My description of the conflict between Schreber and God thus far might suggest that the author of *Memoirs* was a willing participant in his unmanning, that only God resisted his increased soul-voluptuousness. Nothing could be further from the truth, for Schreber too was initially horrified by the changes he perceived occurring daily in his body. He writes:

Having, as I thought, definitely come to realize this abominable intention, one may imagine how my whole sense of manliness and manly honor, my entire moral being, rose up against it. . . . Completely cut off from the outside world, without any contact with my family, left in the hands of rough attendants with whom, the inner voices said, it was my duty to fight now and then to prove my manly courage, I could think of nothing else but that any manner of death, however frightful, was preferable to so degrading an end. (M, 76)

For some time Schreber met the palpably growing voluptuousness of his body with a vigilant suppression motivated by his "sense of manly honor and . . . the holiness of [his] religious ideas" (M, 120). Except for occasional lapses of his "will power," particularly when in bed (M, 120), Schreber fought with God against his transformation into a woman, with the attendant dangers to God's well-being and injury to Schreber's "sense of manly honor" that implies.

Indeed, despite his recognition that God was now acting contrary to the Order of the World, and despite the miracles that plagued him constantly, Schreber considered this a "*holy* time" (M, 79), and the "holiness of [his] religious ideas . . . occupied [him] almost exclusively" (M, 120). During one period at Sonnenstein Schreber appeared catatonic, because he had come to consider "absolute passivity almost a religious duty" (M, 127). As usual, Schreber offers several motivations for his behavior, none of which seems to have any clear priority over the others, but all of which have to do with his "religious" ideas. In the first place, he suggests that the rays demanded his immobility, perhaps hoping that God's ignorance of living humans might be overcome if Schreber's condition approached that of a corpse (M, 127). Then, too, Schreber believed that rays would be irrevocably lost should he move about, and fearing that the supply was limited, he took it upon himself to preserve their existence. Moreover, he thought that his immobility would facilitate the drawing down to him of the tested souls and thus more quickly rid the heavens of them. "I therefore made the almost incredible sacrifice of desisting from every movement and of course from every occupation for several weeks and months" (M, 129). Obviously, this is overdetermination with a vengeance. But it gives an example of the complexity of motive and result with which Schreber clothed his world, and of the lengths to which he would go to fulfill these apparently bizarre demands his divinity seemingly placed upon him. Even now, about a year into his institutionalization, he "could not get [himself] to believe that God harbored really evil intent towards [him]" (M, 129).

4

What emerges from *Memoirs of My Nervous Illness* is a depiction of a world hopelessly at odds with itself; for whatever reason, the smooth, benevolent cycle of eternity that Schreber describes in the opening chapters is now broken. None of the major figures in Schreber's drama is either content with his present condition or free to change it. God finds Himself drawn toward earth, his preeminence endangered, but, despite the variety of miracles He enacts, His every attempt to extricate Himself is frustrated. Flechsig's soul originates the machinations against Schreber, but the concatenation of events he sets in motion is beyond his control and ironically reduces him, in the end, to a thin shadow of his former self. Finally, events entrap Schreber too in circumstances he can barely understand, much less alter. As the incessant target of miracles, he is bedeviled by the heavens. Moreover, Schreber feels his body undergoing a transformation into that of a woman, a process his "manly honor" and God's miracles—for here they are aligned—are powerless to change. In sum, the beneficence of the universe has turned itself inside out; now that very universe victimizes its hapless inhabitants.

Obviously something must happen to resolve this impasse. In November 1895, Schreber effects a radical change in stance toward his experiences. Prior to this date he was of course aware of the insidious feminization he was undergoing. He repeatedly refers to his increased soul-voluptuousness; he even tells us that "several times (particularly in bed) there were marked indications of an actual retraction of the male organ" (M, 132). By late 1895 these developments no longer could be simply shrugged aside:

> During that time the signs of transformation into a woman became so marked on my body, that I could no longer ignore the imminent goal at which the whole development was aiming. . . . Soul-voluptuousness had become so strong that I myself received the impression of a female body, first on my arms and hands, later on my legs, bosom, buttocks and other parts of my body. (M, 148)

These physical changes suggested to Schreber that the process was too far gone, that no matter how violently outraged by feminization, his "manly honor" was now impotent to reverse the inevitable. Various strategies open to meet this new development and Schreber is forced to choose among them. Rather than heroically resisting the inevitable, knowing that the universe doomed the exertions of his manly courage to failure, or quietly, passively, accepting his transformation into a woman, Schreber aligns himself with and embraces this future, even finds within its apparent damnation a form of redemption. In so doing he resisted the "hypocritical" cries of the rays, who ridiculed his new stance by incessantly repeating phrases to him, such as " 'Are you not ashamed in front of your wife?' " The issue was clear: "it was *common sense,*" he tells us, "that nothing was left to me but [to] reconcile myself to the thought of being transformed into a woman" (M, 148).

Schreber's embrace of this stance introduces a radical shift in his behavior. No longer does he resist the transformation; rather he now acts to speed its progress: "Since then I have wholeheartedly inscribed the cultivation of femininity on my banner, and I will continue to do so as far as consideration of my environment allows, whatever other people who are ignorant of the supernatural reasons may think of me" (M, 149). He insists that this new attitude is neither a voluntary nor a perverse insistence upon gratification: "I consider it my right and in a certain sense my duty to cultivate feminine feelings" (M, 207–8). Indeed, his unique relationship with God has reversed the usual prescripts of morality: voluptuousness now "has become 'God-fearing,' that is to say it is the likeliest satisfactory solution for the clash of interests arising out of circumstances contrary to the Order of the World" (M, 210). As we see, Schreber recognizes that others might perceive his behavior as deviant, but he attributes the causes or motivation behind that deviance to cosmic forces beyond his control. His behavior has been "forced" upon him; "God demands *constant enjoyment*" (M, 209), which Schreber is duty bound to provide. Thus just when Schreber reconciles himself to his apparent fate, he disavows responsibility for the decision. Of course *he* does not desire such sensuality, God does. And if Schreber derives "a little sensuous pleasure" in the process of fulfilling his obligations, he feels himself "entitled to it as a small compensation for the excess of suffering and privation that has been [his] for many years past" (M, 209).

Schreber develops various techniques for his divinely dictated cultivation of feminity. One of these, which he only alludes to in passing, consists of standing before a mirror, dressed in "feminine adornments" (M, 207). Dr. Weber, in his report to the court, elaborates: ". . . it only remains to mention that . . . in his pleasure in feminine toilet articles, in small feminine occupations, in the tendency to undress more or less and to look at himself in the mirror, to decorate himself with gay ribbons and bows, etc., in a feminine way, the pathological direction of his fantasy is manifested continually" (M, 273). Perhaps useful while before the mirror is another means of heightening his femininity, *picturing.* Schreber explains: "Perhaps nobody but myself, not even science, knows that man retains all recollections in his memory, by virtue of lasting impressions on his nerves, *as pictures* in his head. Because my inner nervous system is illuminated by rays, these pictures can be voluntarily reproduced; this in fact is the nature of 'picturing' " (M, 180). Thus Schreber can often entertain himself and the rays by "picturing" that his "body has female breasts and a female sex organ" (M, 181). This of course greatly increases his feeling of soul-voluptuousness, which heightens his power of attraction over the divine rays, which in turn, as they find dissolution in his body, speeds his transformation into a woman.

If Schreber was now resigned to his fate, God was not. He persisted in his efforts "to avoid the fate of having to perish in my body with more and more parts of His totality, and indeed one was not very particular in choosing the means of prevention" (M, 150). Thus God continued His efforts to destroy Schreber's reason, hoping thereby to bring about the possibility of a withdrawal. Due to God's ignorance of the ways of living humans, this produced curious strains for His victim. For instance, God mistakes relaxation for madness; thus Schreber must constantly be doing or thinking something, for at the first indication that he is not in "complete possession of his mental powers" (M, 165 n) God will withdraw. The *"compulsive thinking"* demanded of Schreber "denied [him] man's natural right to give the nerves of his mind their necessary rest from time to time by thinking nothing" (M, 70). Obviously this was troublesome; moreover it was only one among many irksome demands made upon Schreber, but struggle as He might, God was unable to reverse the process decreed necessary by the very Order of the World.

Despite God's opposition, then, by 1900 Schreber imagined his transformation into a woman to be quite far along. He saw signs of it everywhere, particularly in his body. By now his "whole body [was] filled with nerves of voluptuousness from the top of [his] head to the soles of [his] feet" (M, 204); in fact, this process was now clearly visible to anyone:

> . . . my breast gives the impression of a pretty well-developed female bosom; this phenomenon can be *seen* by anybody who wants to observe me *with his own eyes*. . . . I venture to assert flatly that anybody who sees me standing in front of a mirror with the upper part of my body naked would get the undoubted *impression of a female trunk*—especially when the illusion is strengthened by some feminine adornments. (M, 207)

Schreber asked Dr. Weber for such verification, only to be told that science did not recognize the existence of female nerves of voluptuousness. This does not shake Schreber's convictions, however, and he offers as proof his knowledge that these nerves "are by origin nothing but erstwhile nerves of God, which can hardly have lost their qualities as nerves through having entered [his] body" (M, 206–7). Thus side-by-side with science's denigrations of his beliefs, we find his appeals to it for validation. It presents a curious image of a man who finds it impossible to survive in the everyday world but equally impossible to live without that world's standards.

As his feminization approaches completeness, several other changes occur, almost as though they were corollaries. Most obvious, the more rays his body absorbed the less the voices and other miracles troubled Schreber. The miracles persist, but "the longer they last the more they take on the character of a comparatively harmless prank" (M, 219) because of his increased soul-voluptuousness. For the same reason, the tempo and volume of the voices he has heard constantly since his first nerve contact with God has diminished, so that "the hissing of the voices is now best compared to the sound of sand trickling from an hour glass" (M, 226).

More dramatic and less obvious changes also occurred. Soon

after Schreber embraced his unmanning, he questioned his status as the last surviving human: "I could no longer doubt that a real race of human beings in the same number and distribution as before did in fact exist" (M, 163). However, at the same time he acknowledged that others did in fact exist, he refused to consider his previous beliefs as delusions or hallucinations. This naturally opens up an unbridgeable gap between mutually contradictory assertions; and Schreber recognizes his dilemma even if he is unable to resolve it. "This difficulty remains even today, and I must confess that I am faced with an unsolved riddle, one which is probably insoluble for human beings" (M, 164). Schreber does not expressly link his new attitude toward his unmanning to this new appreciation of the existence of other humans, but the proximity of the changes, both in his dating of their occurrence and his placement of them in the narrative, strongly suggests some oblique connection. Perhaps, his transformation apparently all but accomplished, and now made legitimate as his duty in accordance with the Order of the World, Schreber no longer required the apocalyptic rationale for accepting it that these (now discarded) beliefs had formerly provided.

Equally puzzling is a reversal in the behavior of Ariman and Ormuzd that Schreber reports. In the Order of the World, as you may recall, Ariman holds the power to unman humans, should the necessity arise. Until November 1895 only Ariman seemed to have become caught up with Flechsig in the plot against Schreber; Ormuzd's behavior remained properly respectful of Schreber's autonomy: "Now this relationship was reversed. The lower God (Ariman) as stated, did not object to losing himself with part of his nerves in my body, because he almost always met soul-voluptuousness there; he severed the close relations which apparently had existed between him and Flechsig's 'tested' soul; the latter . . . formed a sort of hostile alliance against me with the *upper* God" (M, 150–51). As evidence for this realignment of heavenly forces Schreber cites the nature of the miracles that incessantly emanated from both Ariman and Ormuzd. The voices of the latter are hostile and abusive, and those of the former contain much "neutral nonsense," which is much easier to tolerate (M, 151). Schreber recognizes the "tangle of contradictions" (M, 152) that this reversal occasions (for instance, only Ariman is supposed to have the power to unman), but fails to elaborate on this curious and puzzling conjunction of events: his reversal of attitude toward his unmanning and the concurrent reversals of the Gods' actions toward him. A link must exist, but it never finds articulation.

Whether his adversary is Ariman or Ormuzd, however, finally matters little. Their resistance, no matter how powerful, will prove futile, and Schreber seems secure in his destiny. In the final pages of *Memoirs* Schreber puts aside his narration of injustices done him to look to the future. Just as the torments of the Gods had diminished with the passage of years, the "circumstances of [his] outward life have [also] lately changed markedly for the better" (M, 201), a process he hopes will culminate in his release from Sonnenstein, as it eventually does. More to the point, the transformation will continue its course: "From all this I believe I can predict for the not too distant future that in my lifetime I will enjoy in advance that Blessedness granted to other human beings only after death" (M, 240). There is some doubt here; he suspects now and then that he may not live to see the process through, "that to the end of [his] days there will be strong indications of femaleness, but that [he] shall die as a man" (M, 212). The process will continue; the only uncertainty, and that is but occasional, centers on the possibilities for its completion.

If Schreber can doubt the details of his fate, he allows himself none as to his ultimate destiny. His tribulations will find ample reward: "I have the impression," he says, "that in my future life some *great* and *magnificent satisfaction* is in store for me—not provided by human beings but somehow as a logical development arising out of the situation itself" (M, 214). Perhaps, as he suggests, his *Memoirs* will be the vehicle for a profound revolution of mankind's religious beliefs. In any event, he receives as a certainty the notion that the "reward of [his] victory could only be something very extraordinary for [his] loyal perserverance *[sic]* in the struggle for [his] reason and for the purification of God" (M, 215).

I have summarized the progress of Schreber's beliefs at some length for several reasons. First, I suspect that many are simply not familiar with either Schreber's *Memoirs* or Freud's essay. Moreover, I fear that many of Freud's readers have for one reason or another ignored his admonition to "make themselves acquainted with the book" (SE, 12:11) in order to better follow his exposition. Of course both the German and English versions of *Memoirs* are comparatively hard to come by. However, the subsequent commentary on *Memoirs* and Freud's analysis of it returns with distressing regularity exclusively to those passages in *Memoirs* first cited by Freud. Finally, my extended summary provides the necessary minimal context for both my investigation in chapters two and three of Freud's procedures as he seeks the meaning of Schreber's delusions and for my own rereading of them in chapter five. If, as I shall shortly argue, psychoanalysis and literary criticism share certain enabling assumptions, given their nature no other procedure seems possible.

2 : Freud and Schreber's *Memoirs*

Havelock Ellis has sent me the sixth volume of his studies: *Sex in Relation to Society.* Unfortunately my receptivity is consumed by my nine analyses. But I shall set it aside for the holidays along with the wonderful Schreber, who ought to have been made a professor of psychiatry and director of a mental hospital.[1]

September is not the right time of year to enjoy the beauty here [in Rome]. My travelling companion is a dear fellow, but dreamy in a disturbing kind of way, and his attitude towards me is infantile. He never stops admiring me, which I don't like, and is probably sharply critical of me in his unconscious when I am taking it easy. He has been too passive and receptive letting everything be done for him like a woman, and I really haven't got enough homosexuality in me to accept him as one. These trips arouse a great longing for a real woman. A number of scientific notions I brought with me have combined to form a paper on paranoia. . . .

I have succeeded where the paranoiac fails.[2]

Despite his rhetorical admission that a physician in private practice faces difficulties in understanding paranoia, Freud brought to his reading of *Memoirs* in 1910 a rather well-developed theory of the phenomenon. The structure of the essay suggests that he did not, moving as it does from a summary of *Memoirs,* through the humbly entitled "Attempts at Interpretation," to finally the general propositions in "On the Mechanisms of Paranoia." In the concluding paragraphs, however, a Freud who no longer needs to bring his readers gently along, who, in fact, is now denying that his theory rests on this singularly convenient case, brings forth witnesses "that I had developed my theory of paranoia before I became acquainted with the contents of Schreber's book" (SE, 12:79).[3] Thus Freud's reading of Schreber did not occasion his theorizing about paranoia; rather,

Memoirs provided him an unexpected vehicle for presenting his theory to the psychiatric community. Not only did *Memoirs* apparently validate Freud's thinking, but it also, because it was already in the public domain, relieved him of the obligation to falsify and perhaps thereby distort the case's details in order to preserve the anonymity of his subject. Since it surely directs his commentary on *Memoirs,* I want first to sketch the theory of paranoia Freud then possessed before I turn to his reading of Schreber.

1

We first see Freud meditating on the complexities presented by paranoia in his correspondence with Fliess in January 1895, some eight years prior to the publication of *Memoirs,* more than fifteen years before he wrote the essay that confers on Schreber whatever immortality he now possesses. "Now it is in fact the case that chronic paranoia in its classical form is *a pathological mode of defense.* . . . People become paranoic about things that they cannot tolerate—provided always that they have a particular psychical disposition."[4] Although he goes on in "Draft H" to comment definitively on some features of paranoia, the intolerable "things" receive no gloss. At some point before his reading of Schreber in the summer of 1910 he came to suspect an intimate and necessary linkage between a revulsion against homosexuality and paranoia;[5] thus, in relation to Schreber, he writes: "We should be inclined to say that what was characteristically paranoic about the illness was the fact that the patient, as a means of warding off a homosexual wishful fantasy, reacted precisely with delusions of persecution of this kind. . . . [We] are in point driven by experience to attribute to homosexual wishful fantasies an intimate (perhaps an invariable) relation to this particular form of disease" (SE, 12:59).

Itself complex and controversial, homosexuality should not deflect our attention, but we should notice three factors. First, Freud locates the roots of homosexuality in fixations occurring during the narcissistic stage, a phase "the development of the libido . . . passes through on the way from auto-eroticism to object love" (SE, 12:60). Second, because of the kinship Freud espies between homosexuality and paranoia, he hypothesizes that "we are driven to suppose" that paranoids undergo fixations and hence suffer vulnerabilities during an analogous phase, i.e., prior to object love (SE, 12:62). Finally, I want to emphasize that Freud does *not* say paranoids are homosexuals or vice versa. Indeed, according to Freud paranoia arises because of an individual's inability to accept homosexual ideas; a vigorous rejection of homosexuality generates paranoia.

Freud does not initially present this linkage dogmatically; he recognizes it as a working hypothesis requiring "the investigation of a large number of instances of every variety of paranoic disorder" (SE, 12:63). Such an investigation, he acknowledges, might strictly delimit the relevance of his present analyses to a single variety of paranoia. He hesitates only momentarily, however, for with a dismissing "nevertheless" he asserts anew that "the familiar principal forms of paranoia can all be represented as contradictions of the single proposition: '*I* (a man) *love him* (a man),' and indeed that they exhaust all the possible ways in which such contradictions could be formulated" (SE, 12:63). The possibilities of error or fragmentary knowledge recognized, Freud sets out one of his most impressive analyses.

Having implicated homosexual fantasies among the causal factors of paranoia, Freud turns, in his own words, "to the two factors in which we expected from the first to find the distinguishing marks of paranoia, namely, the mechanism *by which the symptoms are formed* and the mechanism *by which repression is brought about*" (SE, 12:65). The formative mechanism is projection. As Freud describes it in the Schreber essay, projection is a process through which "an internal perception is suppressed, and, instead, its content, after undergoing a certain kind of distortion, enters consciousness in the form of an external perception" (SE, 12:66). In delusions of persecution this distortion involves a reversal of affect; what should be perceived internally as love is seen externally, attributed to someone else, as hate. Projection, Freud recognizes, plays a fundamental and necessary role in the development of paranoia, but its presence does not, in and of itself, guarantee the production of paranoid ideas. Indeed, projection occurs in all development and possesses "a regular share assigned to it in our attitude towards the external world" (SE, 12:66). Because of this complication, Freud postpones a definitive discussion of symptom-formation in paranoia, but his subsequent writings fail to return to the subject.

If we carefully collate Freud's discussions of paranoia and projection, however, we can carry the investigation somewhat further. In his first discussion of paranoia, the "Draft H" mailed to Fliess in 1895, Freud details the functions of projection in the case of a female patient:

To start with it had been an internal reproach; now it was an imputation coming from outside. The judgment about her had been transposed outwards: people were saying what she would otherwise have said about herself. Something was gained by this. She would have had to accept the judgment from inside; but she could reject the one from outside. *In this way the judgment, the reproach, was kept away from the ego.*

Thus projection relieves the woman from the burden of guilt. What makes it pathological in this case is that the woman refuses conscious awareness of an internal change: "If we forget it, and if we are left only with the leg of the syllogism that leads outwards, then we have paranoia, with its exaggerations of what people know about us and of what people have done to us—what people know about us, what we have no knowledge of whatever, what we cannot admit. *This, then, is a misuse of the mechanism of projection for the purposes of defense.*"[6]

With this in mind let us return to Freud's discussion of the contradictions paranoia effects on its repudiated basic proposition, "*I* (a man) *love him* (a man)." Obviously, this baldly states the homosexuality that paranoia seeks to erase. The first contradiction reverses the verb, converting the love to hate, producing, "I do not *love* him—I hate him." The paranoid carries this two steps further. First he reverses the subject and object, producing "he hates me." Then he projects this altered proposition onto the external world, branding its inhabitants with his own misconstrued emotions. The entire process thus transforms the unacceptable inner desires into their opposite, and then locates them outside the individual. One important result of this process is the justification it provides for the now reversed feelings: "I do not *love* him—I *hate* him, because *he persecutes me.*" Finally Freud suggests that the paranoid does not designate his persecutor haphazardly; rather he locates as the agent of his victimization the very person who is the object of his repressed desire: "Observation leaves room for no doubt," Freud writes, "that the persecutor is someone who was once loved" (SE, 12:63).

This complicated process transforms undeclared love into delusions of persecution. Obviously, as Freud quite rightly observes, a central feature of the process is the projection outward of ideas and feelings the individual finds unacceptable. But his analysis also reveals that the transformatory process is more complicated. Actually, four maneuvers are present, though Freud explicitly labels only the third. The potential paranoid first *negates* or *represses* his own feelings: I (love him). (Throughout this analysis the parentheses enclose the negated or repressed thoughts.) Then he *reverses* the feelings, still without acknowledging their existence, producing I (hate him). Third, he *projects* this proposition outward, thereby inverting its subject and object: he (hates me). Finally, in this form the proposition *attains consciousness;* this erases the parentheses, leaving us with "he hates me." Only at the end of the process can the feelings reversed in the second stage become conscious; and they can precisely because the subsequent location of an external persecutor validates their intensity: "I hate him *because* he persecutes me." As this analysis demonstrates, then, Freud masks his rigorous dissection by only labeling a single significant phase of the process. By itself projection does not generate delusions of persecution; rather, these paranoid ideas derive from a complicated process involving *repression, reversal* of feelings, *projection,* and a *coming to consciousness* that validates the paranoid's own hatred of his supposed victimizer.[7]

Freud goes on to discuss three more contradictions of the initial proposition, each equally complex, but we need not subject them to equally detailed analysis. If the first rewriting contradicts, in Freud's terms, the verb (and we now realize the deceptive simplicity of putting it this way), a second transforms the object. Thus the initial proposition, through much the same process, gives way to "I do not love him—I love her, because *she loves me*" (SE, 12:63). Freud terms this condition erotomania, an exaggerated sense of one's own desirability as a heterosexual love object, which masks the original homosexual impulses.[8] Delusional jealousy, the third transformation, contradicts the subject. Thus the proposition for jealousy—"It is not I who love the man—she loves him" (SE, 12:64)—displaces the forbidden love onto another, masking the homosexual fantasy twice—by making the love heterosexual, by locating the love elsewhere. Finally, Freud mentions a fourth contradiction, one that negates the entire proposition and produces megalomania: " *'I do not love at all—I do not love anyone.'* And since, after all, one's libido must go somewhere, this proposition seems to be the psychological equivalent of the proposition: 'I love only myself' " (SE, 12:65). Although any one of these transforming processes can dominate in an individual case, a mixture usually occurs. In particular, his observations make Freud expect at least elements of megalomania in all cases of paranoia.

The stern corollary of megalomania demands a withdrawal of attention and affect from the outside world. Rather than turning outward toward the world, Freud posits, in such cases libido turns inward and backward, returning to earlier fixations. It is here that Freud finds a second defining feature of paranoid disorders. That is, as with all other psychic disorders, paranoia displays unique and defining points of fixation in the developmental process:

> From this [the concurrence of paranoia and megalomania] it may be concluded that in paranoia the liberated libido becomes attached to the ego, and is used for the aggrandizement of the ego. A return is thus made to the stage of narcissism (known to us from the development of the libido), in which a person's only sexual object is his own ego. On the basis of this clinical evidence we can suppose that paranoics have brought along with them *a fixation at the stage of narcissism,* and we can assert that the length of the *step back from sublimated homosexuality to narcissism* is a measure of the amount of *regression* characteristic of paranoia. (SE, 12:72)

Withdrawn from a world to which he is seemingly indifferent, the paranoid constructs in the freedom of his solitude the delusions that so characterize his condition. Far from intensifying his isolation, however, the delusions announce his reentry into the world:

> *The delusion formation, which we take to be the pathological product, is in reality an attempt at recovery, a process of reconstruction.* Such a reconstruction after the catastrophe is successful to a greater or lesser extent, but never wholly so. . . . But the human subject has recaptured a relation, and often a very intense one, to the people and things in the world, even though the relation is a hostile one now, where formerly it was hopefully affectionate. We may say, then, that the process of repression proper consists in a detachment of the libido from people—and things—that were previously loved. It happens silently; we receive no intelligence of it, but can only infer it from subsequent events. What forces itself so noisily upon our attention is the process of recovery, which undoes the work of repression and brings the libido again on to the people it had abandoned. In paranoia this process is carried out by the method of projection. It was incorrect to say that the perception which was suppressed internally is projected outwards; the truth is rather, as we now see, that what was abolished internally returns from without. (SE, 12:71)

The contortions of a paranoid's delusions, therefore, represent the only terms upon which he can engage his world, whatever the anguish these terms exact. Finding his affectionate relationship intolerable because it is homosexual, the paranoic denies such desires in himself and his world. Thus we find that the first phase in the production of paranoid ideas, negation, corollates with the withdrawal of libido from the external world. This is the repression proper, and it affects both internal and external worlds. Finally, with both the feelings and the actors' roles reversed, the paranoid projects his delusions and clamorously reenters his environment. Thus the projection itself at once shields against unacceptable ideas and undoes the repression, restoring the paranoid to his world.

As we have seen, when the paranoid projects his delusions outward he invariably selects as his persecutor the former object of his desire or a substitute for him. The selections are not haphazard but intensely motivated. This is as far as Freud had carried his understanding of projection by the time he came upon Schreber's *Memoirs.* In a sense, the paranoic victimizes the person whose victim he perceives himself to be. Often innocent of evil intent, a person suddenly, surprisingly, finds himself the object of startling, outrageous accusations. In a 1922 essay, "Some Neurotic Mechanisms in Jealousy, Paranoia and Homosexuality," Freud significantly amends this depiction:

> We begin to see that we describe the behavior of both jealous and persecutory paranoics very inadequately by saying that they project outwards on to others what they do not wish to recognize themselves. Certainly they do this; but they do not project into the blue, so to speak, where there is nothing of the sort already. They let themselves be guided by their knowledge of the unconscious, and displace to the unconscious minds of others the attention which they have withdrawn from their own. (SE, 18:226)

For example, Freud discusses a husband whose intense jealousy was aroused by noticing the many slight, unconscious flirtatious mannerisms of his wife. "His abnormality really reduced itself to this, that he watched his wife's unconscious mind much more closely and then regarded it as far more important than anyone else would have thought of doing" (SE, 18:226). This amendment makes the theory considerably more subtle.[9] Thus the paranoic assigns to the trivial actions of those close to him and to the accidental happenings in his environment—all of which he closely scrutinizes—a momentous, disproportionate significance. His problem is not a lack of attention to his world but an excessive reading of it. This undoubtedly contributes to the unshakeable quality of his delusions; in a sense, he is always right: the signs *are* there, he differs only in his suspicious reading of them.[10] The very importance of his supposed persecutor demands this scrutiny; however, no one could sustain the rigid, total loyalty the paranoid expects. And every deviation, however slight, the paranoic takes as further evidence that his affection is not warranted, his suspicions only too just. Thus the paranoid thrusts himself into his world and upon his persecutor with a vengeance. Exposed and vulnerable, he then scrutinizes every detail of his environment in a determined effort to locate the potential dangers or possible slights he rightly anticipates.

2

Freud's early theory of paranoia obviously guides his interpretation of Schreber's *Memoirs*. He opens his interpretation by quoting extensively from Dr. Weber's reports to the court concerning his patient's evolving status: "The medical officer," Freud writes, "lays stress upon two points as being of chief importance: the patient's *assumption of the Role of the Redeemer*, and his *transformation into a woman*" (SE, 12:18). Whereas Weber considers the former the core of his patient's delusional system and the latter only the bizarre means to its accomplishment, Freud reverses this emphasis: "... a study of the *Denkwürdigkeiten* compels us to take a very different view of the matter. For we learn that the idea of being transformed into a woman (that is, of being emasculated) was the primary delusion, that he began by regarding that act as constituting a serious injury and persecution, and that it only became related to his playing the part of Redeemer in a secondary way" (SE, 12:18).

Freud offers four pieces of evidence for his reversal. First, there is a genetic reason; that is, Schreber's idea that he is God's elected lover grows out of, and in a sense is dependent upon and a continuation of, his earlier belief that he was suffering sexual persecution at the hands of Flechsig, his doctor. Second, Freud calls our attention to the fact that the voices Schreber incessantly hears "never treated his transformation into a woman as anything but a sexual disgrace, which gave them an excuse for jeering at him" (SE, 12:20). Thus even during the time Schreber thinks his feminization is for some higher purpose, the voices reflect his previous fears, demonstrating their temporal priority. The dream Schreber recalls from before his hospitalization, the dream in which he speculates on a woman's pleasure in "succumbing" to intercourse, also suggests the early motivating force of the emasculation fantasy. Finally, at the other end of Schreber's ordeals, after his release from Sonnenstein, Freud locates a fourth piece of evidence. "It also proved to be the one part of it that persisted after his cure, and the one part that was able to retain a place in his behavior in real life after he recovered. . . . In contrast to the way in which he put his emasculation fantasy into action, the patient never took any steps towards inducing people to recognize his mission as Redeemer, beyond the publication of his *Denkwürdigkeiten*" (SE, 12:21). Together, Freud concludes, these observations force us to acknowledge the primacy of the emasculation fantasy and concurrently to recognize the secondary nature of his exalted religious life.

In doing this, Freud is emphatically not minimizing Schreber's religious ideas nor assigning them a peripheral role in his illness. Indeed, immediately after locating them as secondary formations, he enters upon an extended explication of Schreber's theological conceptions similar to the one offered in the previous chapter. As an index to Freud's sense of their import we can take the following assertion, which concludes his discussion of the theology found in *Memoirs:* "No attempt at explaining Schreber's case will have any chance of being correct which does not take into account these peculiarities in his conception of God, this mixture of reverence and rebelliousness in his attitude towards Him" (SE, 12:28–29). Thus by relegating Schreber's Redeemer delusions to a secondary role, Freud refers mainly to their late appearance, their replacement of his original hypothesis that he was being sexually debased, and does not consign them to irrelevance.

After lamenting the censorship that excised from the text those familial passages he feels "would in all probability have thrown the most important light upon the case" (SE, 12:37), Freud turns to Schreber's relations with his first doctor, Flechsig. Schreber credited Flechsig with his recovery from an earlier nervous illness, so, when another breakdown threatened, he naturally found his way back to him. Of course this time the results were not so felicitous. Rather than providing a cure, Schreber perceives his doctor as instigating an ignominious persecution which would eventually terminate in Schreber's being "forsaken," that is, "left to that human being for sexual misuse and . . . [then] left to rot" (M, 75). Initially Schreber saw only Professor Flechsig as his tormentor; at the time God seemed Schreber's natural ally. However, he gradually came to number God among his persecutors (perhaps even as the instigator of the entire plot) and with this change God more and more usurps Flechsig's role. In fact, long after Flechsig's persecutions had lapsed into mere nuisances, God, says Schreber, continued to visit painful miracles upon him. Thus in the course of the delusions, God replaces Flechsig as Schreber's chief persecutor, thereby granting His hapless victim a higher, if still unenviable, status.

Previous clinical experience with such delusional persecutions provides Freud with a "simple formula" for understanding the relationship among Schreber, Flechsig, and God:

> It appears that the person to whom the delusion ascribes so much power and influence, in whose hands all the threads of the conspiracy converge, is, if he is definitely named, either identical with some one who played an equally important part in the patient's emotional life before his illness, or is easily recognizable as a substitute for him. The intensity of the emotion is projected in the shape of external power, while its quality is changed into the opposite. The person who is now hated and feared for being a persecutor was at one time loved and honored. (SE, 12:41)

The paucity of information, especially as to the nature and causes of the first illness for which Flechsig treated Schreber, hampers Freud at this point. He speculates about Schreber's likely attitude toward his physician as he feels his world again giving way, offering a series of possibilities that all, finally, point to the same conclusion: "The exciting cause of his illness, then, was an outburst of homosexual libido; the object of this libido was probably from the very first his doctor, Flechsig; and his struggles against the libidinal impulse produced the conflict which gave rise to the symptoms" (SE, 12:43). At this point, then, Freud essentially reverses Schreber's projections; the hate is now perceived as love, and Schreber, not Flechsig, is revealed as its source.

Despite the obvious scandal of this interpretation, and after meeting many objections to it, Freud notes that "this hypothesis harmonizes with a noteworthy detail of the case history, which remains otherwise inexplicable" (SE, 12:45). As you recall, Schreber suffered a decisive collapse after his hospitalization when his wife took a needed brief vacation. She had visited with him for several hours each day, but after her return his circumstances were so altered he prohibited her visits, not wanting her to witness "the low state into which I had fallen." Schreber offers only one detail about this deepening of his illness: "Decisive for my mental collapse was one particular night; during that night I had a quite unusual number of pollutions (perhaps half a dozen)" (M, 68). Freud accounts for this momentous turn in Schreber's condition, for this collapse initiated the dreaded nerve-contact, by postulating that "the mere presence of his wife must have acted as a protection against the attractive power of the men about him" (SE, 12:45). With her removal, however, Schreber's homosexual fantasies break through, causing his nocturnal emissions. Without his otherwise outrageous interpretation, Freud argues, this must remain a discordant happening in Schreber's narrative; and to the extent it lends Schreber's experiences intelligibility, it gains, as we shall see, probability.

But Freud's interpretation cannot explain the precise timing of Schreber's decline into a second hospitalization. All people constantly oscillate between hetero- and homosexual feelings, but the absence of more detailed knowledge of Schreber's circumstances immediately prior to his breakdown makes it impossible to locate confidently the explanation for this decisive fluctuation. However, Freud does call our attention to a possible somatic factor: the male climacteric. He returns even more speculatively to this problem later in the essay. If wishful fantasies always derive from some frustration, perhaps we can connect his delusions to some privation. Here Freud calls our attention to the Schrebers' inability to have children, in particular to their lack of a son "who might have consoled him for the loss of his father and brother and upon whom he might have drained off his unsatisfied homosexual affections" (SE, 12:57). Given this failure, which Schreber himself says "marred" (M, 63) the happiness of his marriage, Freud conjectures that "Dr. Schreber may have formed a fantasy that if he were a woman he would manage the business of having children more successfully; and he may have found his way back into the feminine attitude towards his father which he had exhibited in the earliest years of his childhood" (SE, 12:58). Perhaps, therefore, the issue of Schreber's relations with his God would in part rescue him from his childlessness. Even if true, and the lack of data prohibits any meaningful validation, this interpretation still cannot account for the exact timing of Schreber's collapse. Both the male climacteric and this fantasy may be operative, but even together they are neither necessary nor sufficient. Thus Freud's interpretation leaves the question open; this is a subject to which we shall return in chapter five.

Freud soon modulates his interpretation. It may be that Schreber's homosexual yearnings were directed not solely at Flechsig himself; perhaps the doctor mediates between Schreber and others:

> The patient's friendly feeling towards his doctor may very well have been due to a process of "transference," by means of which an emotional cathexis became transposed from some person who was important to him onto the doc-

tor who was in reality indifferent to him; so that the doctor will have been chosen as a deputy or surrogate for someone much closer to him. To put the matter in a more concrete form: the patient was reminded of his brother or father by the figure of the doctor, he rediscovered them in him; there will then be nothing to wonder at if, in certain circumstances, a longing for the surrogate figure reappeared in him and operated with a violence that is only explained in the light of its origin and primary significance. (SE, 12:47)

Thus familial homosexual feelings the young Schreber repressed long before erupt to disturb his relationship with Flechsig; his delusions of persecution, then, represent a renewed flight from his unacknowledgeable affections.

As we have seen, however, Flechsig is not alone the perpetrator of Schreber's sufferings, for he is soon replaced by the superior figure of God. Two chains of associations link and explicate this replacement, one manifest and the other latent. First, the *Memoirs* "show us that in the patient's mind 'Flechsig' and 'God' belonged to the same class." Again Freud offers two demonstrations. "In one of [Schreber's] fantasies he overheard a conversation between Flechsig and his wife, in which the former asserted that he was 'God Flechsig' " (SE, 12:49); they are associated further in that both Flechsig and God undergo radical decompositions. This replacement does not simply perpetuate Schreber's travails, however, much less simply escalate them, for it initiates the "solution of the conflict":

It was impossible for Schreber to become reconciled to playing the part of a female wanton towards his doctor; but the task of providing God Himself with the voluptuous sensations that He required called up no such resistance on the part of his ego. . . . By this means an outlet was provided which would satisfy both of the contending forces. His ego found compensation in his megalomania, while his feminine wishful fantasy made its way through and became acceptable. The struggle and the illness could cease. (SE, 12:48)

With voluptuousness no longer a private sin but a public duty, the very sign of his devotion to God, Schreber can now openly acknowledge it, thereby foregoing disavowal and consequent renewed symptom-formation: in their present form his homosexual longings need not be resisted.

On the latent level, when God replaces Flechsig Schreber's illness likewise undergoes a significant transformation. If Flechsig mediates between Schreber and a lost object of his love, God's involvement must signal the reawakening of a more significant relationship.

Whereas Freud previously lumped brother and father together, he now discriminates between them: "The feminine fantasy, which aroused such violent opposition in the patient, thus had its roots in a longing intensified to an erotic pitch, for his father and brother. This feeling, so far as it referred to his brother, passed, by a process of transformation, on to his doctor, Flechsig; and when it was carried back on to his father a settlement of the conflict was reached" (SE, 12:50). Whereas Flechsig stands for his brother, God images Schreber's father, and the persecution He visits upon His hapless subject caricatures, through the processes of projection, Schreber's forbidden love for his father.

Lest this bold interpretation too seem unwarranted, Freud enumerates several grounds for it. First, Schreber's father was an extremely prominent physician and educator, who attracted considerable attention and following.[11] This fame, says Freud, renders him "by no means unsuitable for transformation into a God in the affectionate memory of his son" (SE, 12:51).[12] Second, Schreber's relationship to God, which initially seems so singular, in fact replicates the commonplace; that is, the "mixture of reverent submission and mutinous insubordination that we have found in Schreber's relation to his God" (SE, 12:52) merely lifts to a higher register the infantile attitudes of boys toward their fathers. There was a third reason that Freud thought of especial significance: "But the circumstance that Schreber's father was a physician, and a most eminent physician, and one who was no doubt highly respected by his patients, is what explains the most striking characteristics of his God and those upon which he dwells in such a critical fashion." Not only does the common profession prepare for association from *Dr.* Flechsig-brother to God-*Dr.* Schreber, but it also becomes the vehicle for much of Schreber's hostility: "Could more bitter scorn be shown for such a physician than by declaring that he understands nothing about living men and only knows how to deal with corpses?" (SE, 12:52). Moreover, the treacherous miracles of Schreber's God cast aspersions upon the "miracles of medicine," and, in the words of their patients, the "miraculous cures" effected by doctors.[13] Finally, as a fourth circumstance affirming his introduction of Schreber's father, Freud calls attention to his subject's unique relation to the sun. Schreber tells us that the voices speaking to him identify God with the sun (M, 95). The sun speaks to him and he occasionally makes it the target of his bellowed vituperations; moreover, Schreber can stare unblinkingly into its glare. Freud's interpretative procedures shift here; he finds the sun a "sublimated symbol" (SE, 12:54), more or less universal, for the father. Therefore, rather than looking to the details of Schreber's *Memoirs* for confirmation as he does elsewhere in the essay, he turns instead to the similar fantasies of other patients and, especially in the postscript, which was added subsequent to the original publication, to folklore and mythology. Thus Freud finds an explanatory parallel to Schreber's delusions in the behavior of a mythic eagle:

> The eagle . . . who makes his young look into the sun and requires of them that they shall not be dazzled by its light, is behaving as though he were himself a descendant of the sun and were submitting his children to a test of their ancestry. And when Schreber boasts that he can look into the sun unscathed and undazzled, he has rediscovered the mythological method of expressing his filial relation to the sun, and has confirmed us once again in our view that the sun is a symbol of the father. (SE, 12:81–82)

Even this very different interpretative strategy, then, brings Freud to the same conclusions: that Schreber struggles with, and is inevitably delusionally reconciled to, his love for his father, who sprawls as an unacknowledgeable presence throughout *Memoirs of My Nervous Illness.*

If, as Freud says early in his essay, he rarely can come into prolonged contact with paranoia in his practice, he here domesticates its otherness by locating within it "the familiar ground of the father-complex. . . . None of the material which in other cases of the sort is brought to light by analysis is absent in the present one: every element is hinted at in one way or another" (SE, 12:55). The father (and his surrogates) inhibits the child's satisfaction; the voices, we recall, announce to Schreber that his hospital attendant, von W., gave "false evidence about me in some State enquiry, either on purpose or through carelessness, and [seems] particularly to have accused me of masturbation" (M, 107).[14] This is territory only too familiar to psychoanalysis: desires, threats, accusations, subterfuge retributions, fugitive fulfillments. From these commonplaces, however, Schreber achieved a startlingly unique gratification; says Freud, "In the final stage of Schreber's delusion a magnificent victory was scored by the infantile sexual urge; for voluptuousness became God-fearing, and God Himself (his father) never tired of demanding it from him. His father's most dreaded threat, castration, actually provided the material for his wishful fantasy (at first resisted but later accepted) of being transformed into a woman" (SE, 12:55–56).

Thus the fantasies Freud posits as active in Schreber's illness, as he himself acknowledges, are resolutely mundane; they are a constant presence in all psychic life. Alone the "father-complex" cannot, just because of its pervasiveness, account for the particular shape of Schreber's illness. What singles Schreber out, then, is not the father-complex but rather the fate it undergoes. I refer of course to the negation, reversal, projection, and coming to consciousness characteristic of paranoia. We are now in a position to summarize Freud's interpretation of Schreber's *Memoirs.* When, for a variety of reasons, Schreber feared a second breakdown and again sought out Flechsig, he responded to the doctor with an intense homosexual longing. There is good reason to suppose that behind the figure of Flechsig stands Schreber's older brother (and ultimately father), for whom he initially felt this longing. However, Schreber repudiated these feelings, refusing them conscious articulation. This had two consequences. First, he disowned his feelings by projecting them onto his environment so that they became inverted. Now rather than loving Flechsig he felt persecuted by him. Second, Schreber withdrew libidinal interest from his world and cathected in its stead his own ego. In this maneuver we see the reasons for his fantasy that the world had been destroyed. "The end of the world is the projection of this internal catastrophe [i.e., the withdrawal of libido]; his subjective world has come to an end since his withdrawal from it" (SE, 12:70). When God enters Schreber's delusions as Flechsig's ally, behind him we can discern Schreber's father. This initially appears to heighten the conflict, but in actuality it prepares for its "resolution." When Schreber finds his way to the proposition that voluptuousness or passive sensuality is his solemn obligation, he ceases to resist it—indeed, he now cultivates his feminine longings. Where he could not sanction such an attitude toward his doctor, the elevated figure of God allows its adoption. With this turn of events, Schreber's delusions settle into a kind of fixity; and apart from this singular delusional relationship, Schreber increasingly engages his world. Now, says Freud, "his ego found compensation in his megalomania, while his feminine wishful fantasy made its way through and became acceptable. The struggle and the illness could cease" (SE, 12:48). And eventually, although the Royal Superior Country Court of Dresden would harbor "no doubt that [Schreber] is insane" (M, 342), they also found him "capable of dealing with the demands of life" (M, 355) and removed his tutelage, thereby preparing for his release from Sonnenstein.

3 :
Psychoanalysis as Literary Criticism / Literary Criticism as Psychoanalysis

If . . . one had to found a college of psychoanalysis, much would have to be taught in it which is also taught by the medical faculty: alongside of depth-psychology, which would always remain the principal subject, there would be an introduction to biology, as much as possible of the science of sexual life, and familiarity with the symptomatology of psychiatry. On the other hand, analytic instructions would include branches of knowledge which are remote from medicine and which the doctor does not come across in his practice: the history of civilization, mythology, the psychology of religion and the science of literature. Unless he is well at home in these subjects, an analyst can make nothing of a large amount of his material.[1]

. . . psychoanalysis in its early development, intimately linked to the discovery and study of symbols, was on the way to participating in the structure of what was called in the Middle Ages, "the liberal arts."[2]

One way for psychoanalysis and literary studies to situate themselves vis-à-vis one another would be to account for the seemingly anomalous inclusion of Freud's essay on Schreber's *Memoirs of My Nervous Illness* among the canonical five case histories. Is this a scandal, the result of some oversight, a regrettable lapse in taxonomy? Should not this essay, whatever its theoretical importance, be collected with *Delusion and Dream*, "Creative Writers and Day-Dreaming," "The Uncanny," "Dostoevsky and Parricide"; that is, should it not be collected with Freud's occasional reflections—effusions, one might almost call them—on art and the artistic process? Is there not, finally, a sheer divide between the rigorous heart of psychoanalysis, located in its metapsychology and clinical practice, and its applications, however locally interesting, beyond its proper domain?

I think not. In fact, I shall argue that the inclusion of "Psychoanalytic Notes on an Autobiographical Account of a Case of Paranoia

(Dementia Paranoides)" among the case histories signals the fundamental relationship between the seemingly disparate domains of psychoanalysis and literary studies. They are not merely analogous disciplines, adjacent series of assumptions and moves that parallel one another; they take the relationship of outside to inside. All interpretation, whether of individual texts or of patients, is essentially a textual exercise; understanding strings of words, with their metaphors and their sequence, word-after-word, is the objective of both; both can only do so within the securing context of a psychological theory that explicates the relationships of those words to their speaker and to one another. Psychological theory, then, is a necessary preliminary to, or a condition for, the interpretive process in either discipline, a process that is itself linguistic to the core, whether the object of attention is a sonnet or a patient.

Therefore "Psychoanalytic Notes," which openly declares this relationship while retaining, as Freud's other literary exercises do not, the rigor of the case histories, possesses a unique strategic importance for any attempt to grasp the relations between psychoanalysis and literary studies. In this chapter I shall focus neither upon the specifics of Freud's interpretation, as in chapter two, nor upon the probable validity of that interpretation; rather, I shall investigate how Freud went about constructing that interpretation, the sorts of interests he brought to the task, the questions he asked, his implicit criteria for validity. In a general way, it might be accurate to say that I want to reconstruct the sort of rationality operative in psychoanalytic interpretation, the principles and criteria of its operation. No doubt few practicing analysts will immediately recognize the characterizations of their everyday activities—there is no discussion of the play of transference and counter-transference, none of the crucial therapeutic issue of the timing of interpretive interventions. Nonetheless, what follows should not be thought of as irrelevant to these more immediately accessible issues; it simply seeks to clarify in an abstract way the implicit logic of interpretation in psychoanalysis.

1

Before turning to these crucial issues, however, I want briefly to consider two factors, both external to our concerns, which nonetheless decisively shape Freud's essay. First, Freud's very fragmentary knowledge of Schreber's life limits his interpretations. The essay is unique among the five major case histories in that Freud never met its subject, but worked almost exclusively from his reading of *Memoirs of My Nervous Illness*;[3] even "Little Hans," whom Freud himself did not analyze, was brought periodically to the professor for consultations. This of course is the reason for our interest in the essay, for it reveals the irreducibly textual nature of psychoanalytic interpretation. However, the text from which Freud worked had been censored before publication. Its third chapter, which opens by announcing the twinned topics of "soul murder" and Schreber's family of origin, was almost completely deleted, as was an earlier passage of uncertain length pertaining to "soul murder." The resultant unavailability of material he thought "would in all probability have thrown the most important light upon the case" forced Freud into a "policy of restraint" (SE, 12:37). Therefore, Freud's interpretation of Schreber's *Memoirs* seems unusually tentative, fragmentary, altogether lacking in the rich density we find in, say, the triumphant case history of Rat Man.

Given this severe limitation, one may reasonably ask why Freud elected to write about Schreber at all, especially because he chose to write up relatively few of the many clinical histories his daily practice obviously made available. I suggest that Schreber attracted Freud on two quite different grounds. First, because *Memoirs of My Nervous Illness* was already in the public domain, Freud was relieved of the responsibility for either breaching the confidentiality of the consulting room or falsifying, and thereby perhaps irreparably damaging, the clinical data in preparing it for publication. This alone may have attracted him, but I suspect another consideration played its part. Most of Freud's case histories have some pedagogic or polemic aim beyond the simple presentation of yet another clinical history, and this aim refocuses the material. For instance, in "From the History of an Infantile Neurosis," his study of Wolf-Man, Freud takes up a polemic against the theoretical revisions attenuating the existence and importance of infantile sexuality put forth by Adler and Jung. Therefore he does not present a more or less complete case history; in fact he barely mentions the illness that brought Wolf-Man into therapy. Rather, Freud confines himself largely to explicating the much earlier, infantile neurosis, with its clear sexual determinants, thereby refuting his wayward colleagues. In the present instance, Freud seems to have seized upon Schreber's *Memoirs* as an opportunity for presenting his already formulated theory of paranoia. After returning from the trip to Italy during which he read *Memoirs,* Freud writes to Jung: "During my trip I was able to amplify this theory [i.e., "that paranoics are unable to prevent the re-cathexis of their homosexual leanings"] a little, and now I mean to test my progress against Schreber's case history and various other publications on paranoia. . . . In any case the outcome will be a study of Schreber and people will think I designed my theory with the book in mind."[4] Thus, although Schreber himself undoubtedly interests Freud, he shares the focus of the essay that he occasions with more theoretical concerns. The resultant bifurcation of interest subtly affects the case history itself, rendering its tenuousness still more so: not only does the unavailability of information inhibit the possibility of a comprehensive interpretation, but the primary status of the case history as an exemplum of larger theoretical concerns makes such comprehensiveness unnecessary as well. Thus the two concerns of the essay are disproportionate; insofar as the Schreber material serves chiefly to illustrate the larger theoretical issues, it assumes an ancillary role, and even, I would hold, ceases being a case history in any rigorous sense of the word. We must take Freud's title seriously; these are "Notes" toward an interpretation he never wrote, even though the essay suggests the manner in which an interpretation might be derived.

2

Already we touch on the first of the theoretical issues that concern us, the two levels on which Freud argues in the Schreber essay. He presents both extensive notes toward an interpretation of Schreber and a general theory of paranoia. The former concerns me here, not the latter. That is, my focus is upon how Freud might have elaborated an interpretation and not upon the general psychological theory that might influence that construction. This severance may appear artificial, pedantic, perhaps even erroneous. Surely a counter-argument might run, the former is derived from the latter; to the extent that the latter lacks validity so too must the former. Even clinically, however, as Marshall Edelson has pointed out, "knowledge of general law, as explanation of human behavior, is not a sufficient foundation for clinical skill," for general psychological propositions and individual interpretive statements make different explanatory commitments.[5] Michael Sherwood argues this discontinuity in his important *The Logic of Explanation in Psychoanalysis:*

Our point is simply that the explanation in an individual case does not make any commitment to general theoretical statements but only to assertions about the individual patient; the explanation is not deduced from a general theory of human behavior in conjunction with statements of initial conditions. The role of general theory, including both theoretical generalizations and higher level theoretical statements, can be characterized as *directive* in the sense of pointing out to the analyst the areas that should be investigated and the sorts of factors likely to be found operative. . . . Nevertheless, the fact that his theory directed him to [an] important event does not mean that when he uses this point as part of an explanation he is logically obliged to invoke the theory.[6]

Suppose, for instance, that in the course of an analysis the patient displays a seemingly inordinate concern with orderliness. He believes everything has its proper place and becomes disturbed when that order is disregarded; he carries out even the smallest tasks with the most scrupulous concern for details that others might reasonably overlook as inessential; his honesty is, shall we say, unbesmirched. Having been presented with such material, the analyst might call to mind Freud's 1908 essay, "Character and Anal Eroticism," with its famous discussion of the obsessive triad—"*orderly, parsimonious* and *obstinate*" (SE, 12:169)—and anticipate the presence of the latter traits. In such an instance Freud's theoretical remarks serve a directive role; they orient the practicing analyst to issues that may prove relevant in the particular case at hand and suggest the lines along which these issues may be related. Whatever the eventual interpretation, the analyst need not invoke Freud's theoretical statements, nor does the validity of either entail that of the other, for the specific interpretation and the theory that directed the analyst to it exist within different realms of discourse.

An important consequence of this discontinuity, one I shall discuss further in the Epilogue, is that interpretive discourse need not—indeed, should not—utilize a heavily theoretical vocabulary. Think for a moment of the numerous studies that employ a heavily psychoanalytic vocabulary yet seem so tangential to their subjects. Their authors confuse the levels; assuming the validity of Freud's theory, they suppose that its deployment alone assures the validity of their interpretations.[7] Unfortunately, such is not the case. The twenty-four volumes of the Standard Edition cannot shield us from interpretive error in any particular interpretive situation, for there is no reciprocal relation between the adequacy of specific interpretations and the theories that suggest them: adequate interpretations do not logically depend upon, nor do they alone validate, adequate theories and vice versa. In the instance at hand, therefore, we could not evaluate Freud's interpretation of Schreber's *Memoirs* simply by measuring its conformity to his theoretical statements in the same essay. We would have to locate other criteria, a point to which we shall return. The theory obviously serves as a pointer in his understanding of Schreber, but the two are logically distinct. If we keep this discontinuity in mind, as we shall see Freud himself did, we perhaps can avoid some of the grosser errors into which psychoanalytic criticism recurrently falls.

3

My reading suggests that this discontinuity is most frequently obscured in regard to another issue prominent in "Psychoanalytic Notes"; I refer to the pervasive genetic or historical bias of psychoanalytic theory. When faced with some puzzling phenomena, the analyst often enough seeks resolution by uncovering the sequence through which the present was constituted. Several of Freud's statements in the Schreber essay reflect the supposed importance, both theoretical and therapeutical, of historical constructions in psychoanalysis. "It will be an unavoidable part of our task," says Freud, "to show that there is an essential *genetic* relation between [Schreber's delusions of being turned into a woman and his favored relation to God]" (SE, 12:34). In two other passages Freud loosely yokes historical reconstructions of Schreber's various delusions with their meaning. Confronted with such extraordinary material, he says, a psychoanalyst "will wish to go more deeply into the details of the delusions and into the history of its development" (SE, 12:18). And later, while countering likely criticisms of his suggestion of Schreber's repressed homosexuality, Freud writes that "our only concern is with the meaning and origin of this pathological idea [i.e., Schreber's unmanning]" (SE, 12:43). Although these passages join history and meaning, they do not equate them, which would convert the latter into the totality of the former. Rather, they suggest a bifurcation of interest: history *and* meaning, not history as meaning. They do, however, underscore the extraordinary attention Freud lavishes both here and elsewhere upon historical constructions.

These genetic concerns in psychoanalysis are subject to several criticisms. In *Gandhi's Truth* and elsewhere Erik Erikson has stigmatized as

> *originology* the habitual effort to find the "causes" of a man's whole development in his childhood conflicts. By this I meant to say that beginnings do not explain complex developments much better than do ends, and originology can be as great a fallacy as teleology. But in addition, the psychiatric origins of our approach have trained us to think in traumatological terms, that is, to discern not only in origins but traumatic ones at that—trauma meaning an experience characterized by impressions so sudden, or so powerful, or strange that they cannot be assimilated at the time and, therefore, persist from stage to stage as a foreign body seeking outlet or absorption and imposing on all development a certain irration causing stereotypy and repetitiveness.[8]

As I understand Erikson, he quarrels with a tendency in psychoanalysis to gloss over crucial events in adolescence and adulthood and to locate solely in childhood, and there exclusively in certain sorts of events, the determinants of all later behavior. In place of this limited, preclusive schema, Erikson erects his epigenetic theory of developmental phases extending from birth to old age: each stage both builds upon preceding ones and introduces new normative crises which the individual must resolve. Thus the life history itself holds no lesser position in Erikson's theory; he envelops the entire history with the same causal significance psychoanalysis apparently reserves for childhood, by scattering the determinant events throughout the human life cycle. His criticism is not only that psychoanalysis has overestimated the causal significance of childhood, but also that it too often systematically neglects other important issues and phases. To that limited extent, therefore, Erikson dislodges the primacy of a certain kind of historical construction in psychoanalysis.

But the point I want to make is subversive of the very possibility of this historical research as usually conceived: by its own relentless logic the historical excavation in psychoanalysis inevitably and necessarily opens upon an infinite regress. Erikson, no more than Freud in his more positivistic moments, never questions the very possibility of this historical enterprise: the past of course exists (or did); therefore so too must a possibility of its effective resurrection. However, in an admirable essay, "Freud and the Myth of Origins," David Carroll effectively traces Freud's successive compromises of what he initially takes as the effective primal event constitutive of a subsequent neurotic complex. In his early work with Breuer on hysteria, Freud posits an original traumatic event as its hidden center which, when located, will dissolve the baroque, neurotic manifestations that replaced it in consciousness. But as Freud's investigations continued he came to doubt both his ability to reconstruct this real, historical event and finally even its determinant occurrence. Carroll argues chiefly from Freud's 1918 emendation to his Wolf-Man essay, in which the additions displace the primal scene Freud originally reconstructed as the effective nexus of Wolf-Man's subsequent suffering. "At the very place where the origin is supposed to be," writes Carroll, "a multiplicity of origins is found: the reality of the scene, what was perceived by the child, turns out to be not an event in itself but a whole series of associations of events, scenes within scenes." That is, the psychically real for Freud becomes originally, at the very moment of its occurrence, permeated with, even constituted by, fantasy, memory, the unreal—"reality itself becomes a construct."[9] Thus our alternatives are not between working on the one hand with the troubling convolutions of neurosis and on the other with a clear, orderly sequence of real events, for these events are themselves inextricably infused with, and constituted by, the unreal. Nothing simply happens for the first time. It is always construed through earlier associations and becomes the occasion for subsequent ones. There is always something antecedent, extending from the moment before to, says Freud, the phylogenetic inheritance; thus the historical task, if conceived simply as the recovery of the psychically real, can never achieve completion.

Of course, the same problematic besets psychoanalytic therapy. Psychoanalysis expends much time and energy unearthing and gathering up a patient's fragmentary remembrances and reconstructing from them a clinical history. The "basic rule" of psychoanalytic therapy, that the patient free associate, say whatever comes to mind without censorship or distortion, is the vehicle for retrieving much of this purported historical material as well as for delineating the nexuses that bind it. This is a laborious process, for the patient, at times unwittingly, resists, withholding or camouflaging material by turns, and offers at best a revised edition of his or her history. The "true" history is only revealed—or, as I would prefer, constructed—as the therapy itself nears completion.

So the gathering of a history consumes many of the hours of the therapeutic enterprise. But that history itself, whatever its importance, is *not* the vehicle for change. Transference is. We shall discuss this phenomenon at length in chapter four; for the present it suffices to say that in its most restrictive sense transference is a clinical happening. In the postscript to the 1905 case history of Dora, Freud defines transferences: "They are new editions or facsimiles of the impulses and fantasies which are aroused and made conscious during the progress of the analysis; but they have this peculiarity, which is characteristic for their species, that they replace some earlier person by the person of the physician" (SE, 7:116). Essentially, then, the transference recapitulates within the therapeutic relationship the conflicts and ideas constitutive of the original neurosis, together with all their subsequent accretions. The analyst works with this new edition of the problem as it now exists apropos of himself, trying to bring the patient to a curative understanding of the disadvantageous ways in which he has been and still is perceiving and interacting with his world.

Recouping the past, therefore, is not in and of itself therapeutic; rather, the analyst must bring the patient to a curative understanding of his *present* modes of interaction. Since psychoanalysis posits that the past is active in the present—that, after all, is the reason for transference—it is plausible to argue that the role of the laboriously gathered clinical history is often misconstrued. What is essential, finally, is not the construction of the patient's purported history, but a sufficiently subtle grasp of his present. And that present contains that past, if we could only see it. Therefore, it seems possible to say, as Henry Ezriel does, that the distinction between past and present in psychoanalysis becomes chimerical:

> There is thus no difference between analyzing the content of the material produced by the patient [i.e., historical materials], and eliciting new material by analyzing his "here and now" relations with the analyst in which the patient's unconscious structures (the precipitates of unresolved conflicts with persons of his childhood environment) manifest themselves. . . . It thus seems possible to treat *all* material as transference material and hence to use it for "here and now" interpretations.[10]

How, then, does the history function within the analytic situation? I suggest that it fulfills several instrumental roles. First, when, as in much Kleinian analysis, all interpretations concern the present interaction between patient and analyst, the latter can appear demonic, threatening, as possessive and powerful as Flechsig's disembodied soul. In such situations the history gives that patient something of his own to hold out, as it were, against the analyst, some claim to integrity; moreover, the history provides a (seemingly) neutral ground for the interpretations, one (again, seemingly) remote from the potentially vampirish figure of the analyst. Second, the constructions of past interactions give the patient an arena in which to test out his developing understanding of the dynamics of his interaction in the present with the analyst. Finally, the clinical history provides both parties of the therapeutic transaction with a significant sample of the patient's purported desires and actions within which they can together discern a pattern. Quite simply, such a pattern may emerge with greater clarity and conviction from a larger bank of information. The present may be in principle sufficient, but its very narrowness can hinder our attempts at understanding.

The knot between past and present, clinical history and transference, possesses another convolution. The history constructed at every stage of the therapeutic process is more a function of the analyst's and patient's present understanding and present relationship than a mere reflection of the actual events (themselves problematic, as we have seen) that figure the past. In a sense, this simply transfers our previous analysis of the elusive quality of the "real" to the therapeutic context. As the analysis progresses, as the analyst and patient deepen their appreciation of their dynamics within the consulting room, so too do their constructions of the patient's history evolve and deepen. Just as the present finds itself figured by and therefore hostage to the past, one's present circumstances determine the shape one gives that past. Writes J. G. Schimek:

> What Freud (1899) said about conscious childhood memories—namely, that they are only memories "relating to our childhood," which do not simply re-emerge in the present, but are "formed at that time"—should apply as well to the reconstruction of the past through the psychoanalytic process. In our clinical work, we hope that the patient-analyst interaction will help the patient construct a new representation of his past, a more complete and integrated personal history, with a sense of continuity of the motives that make him an active agent in his present life, neither helpless nor omnipotent. And precisely to the extent that this new construction is more objective and realistic, it cannot be a faithful duplicate of the past as it was originally lived or experienced.[11]

Past and present, therefore, mirror and support one another; any failure to acknowledge this mutual dependency prohibits understanding of the subtleties psychoanalysis moves within.

On three grounds, then, I question the received notion of the centrality of historical constructions within psychoanalysis: (1) not only is the present in principle sufficient, but also (2) the past is hopelessly elusive, and (3) itself curiously dependent upon the present it figures. This does not mean I consider historical concerns altogether expendable. We have just seen that within the therapeutic (or more broadly, the interpretive) situation historical constructions can play several instrumental roles in assisting the patient and analyst to an effective understanding of their dynamics. Moreover, historical concerns obviously play an important role in the construction of theory, as opposed to understanding an individual's desires and actions. (Of course this is the wedge driven between psychoanalytic theory and individual interpretation seen from another perspective.) Understanding the aetiology of various normal and abnormal mental states has a considerable theoretical interest, as it is no doubt essential for formulating efficacious general mental health strategies. But this theoretical utility does not detract from our central demonstration: at the level of the individual, of interpretive discourse, historical construction is not *necessary* for an understanding, nor certainly is it *sufficient.*

Psychoanalytic criticism frequently mistakes the role of such historical constructions. It often substitutes a construction of the author's purported history (often gathered in the most fragmentary manner, on the most dubious grounds) for an analysis of the text in question. Whatever analogues that history contains to the dynamics of the poem are then seen as causal, in and of themselves explanatory of the latter phenomenon. When this practice is applied to literary characters, that is, when psychoanalytic critics construct clinical histories of fictional characters who palpably have none, the void upon which the entire enterprise rests yawns. The results would honor Borges were they offered with the slightest irony, but, alas, they are not. Indeed, they most frequently hold themselves quite seriously—they are Science, after all!—for they assume that the validity of psychoanalytic theory immunizes them from error. Such procedures not only seriously misconstrue the complex causality posited by psychoanalysis, but they also attenuate the interdependence of past and present that psychoanalysis discovers. To transfer our argument for a moment to the literary situation: the text is in principle self-sufficient—it contains within it the material for its own interpretation. However, just as the analyst makes instrumental use of historical data to help in detailing the relationship within the consulting room, so too might the critic. However, he must recognize the mediated nature of the data he employs (it is no more "real" than the text, perhaps less so; it is itself historical, hostage to current critical preoccupations), and use it merely as suggestions of issues perhaps relevant to the case at hand. Finally, however, in psychoanalytic criticism as in psychoanalysis proper, these biographical excursions neither necessarily nor sufficiently constitute an understanding.[12]

Of course literary critics are not alone in confusing the relationship between historical construction and interpretation. Given the theoretical emphasis psychoanalysis places upon genetic concerns, this stress almost inevitably leaks into the interpretations of individual patients. We can see this clearly in much of the literature that has accumulated around Schreber's *Memoirs.* Several of the significant and potentially useful studies have retrieved information on Schreber's father and his likely early relations with his son. Since the material consists largely of an examination of Dr. Daniel Gottlob Moritz Schreber's published views on pedagogy and child rearing, it was generally available to Freud; indeed, Morton Schatzman implicitly takes Freud to task for ignoring it.[13] Usually such investigations take the form of setting passages in the books of father and son side-by-side, seeing the former as both cause and explanation of the latter. A single example should suffice. Schatzman writes that the elder Schreber devised something called a

> *Schrebersche Geradhalter* (Schreber's straight-holder) to force children to sit straight. . . . This was an iron crossbar fastened to the table at which the child sat to read or write. The bar presses against the collar bones and the front of the shoulders to prevent forward movements or crooked posture. He says the child could not lean long against the bar "because of the pressure of the hard object against the bones and the consequent discomfort; the child will return on his own to the straight position." "I had a Geradhalter manufactured which proved its worth time and again with my own children. . . ."[14]

Beside this Schatzman sets a passage from *Memoirs* describing one of the "miracles" to which Schreber was repeatedly subjected: "One of the most horrifying miracles was the so-called *compression of the chest miracle* . . . ; it consisted in the whole chest wall being compressed, so that a state of oppression by the lack of breath was transmitted to my whole body" (M, 133). Schatzman considers this passage from *Memoirs* a "transform"[15] of the former; simply put, the former occasions and causes the latter, which is its sure echo.

I do not want to minimize the brutality of the elder Schreber's odd contrivances (could he witness my posture as I type these sentences I am confident he would, to my profound distress, set about fastening a *Geradhalter* to my desk). By this point, however, we should be sufficiently aware of the insufficiency of Schatzman's reasoning. What seems to be happening here is the displacement of the problematics and uncertainty of *Memoirs of My Nervous Illness* by the apparent lucidity and tangibleness of actual historical events. But there are several objections to this procedure. First, the certitude of this historical construction is not nearly as secure as it seems; the backward glance necessarily opens upon an infinite regress that prohibits our location of *the* determinant event, because all shaping events are themselves constituted by an admixture of desires and previous events, and become in turn the locus of subsequent associations. Second, this procedure ignores the potential self-sufficiency of the present (here, of the text) that psychoanalysis implies, if so rarely honors. If the present always embodies the past, as psychoanalysis posits, in principle no necessity exists to go beyond or behind it to excavate what turns out upon inspection to be an equally problematic past. Finally, the aetiology of a particular symptom, delusion, or entire mental set neither necessarily nor sufficiently offers an interpretation of it. There is always something left over, and that remainder is precisely the meaning we are trying to elucidate.[16]

Let me be quite clear. I am not reconstituting here Claude Lévi-Strauss's celebrated critique of the diachronic in the final chapter of *The Savage Mind.* I do not propose that we banish historical concerns from the entire realm of psychoanalysis. They legitimately enter in two disparate areas. First, as I have said, genetic and historical concerns are largely constitutive of the *theoretical* realm. In the last instance most theoretical discourse must concern itself with the relations through time of different psychological phenomena: what sorts of conditions follow upon other determinant conditions. Moreover, if the mental health professions are to establish for themselves any clear, programmatic objectives, they can only do so on the basis of such theoretical knowledge. Second, historical concerns can function effectively within the therapeutic or interpretive situation, that is, in the realm of *technique.* Gathering historical material can defuse the potentially explosive therapeutic alliance, for it gives the patient something meaningful (seemingly) beyond his own mystifications to contribute, as well as offering an arena for interpretation (again, seemingly) outside the immediate dyad. Also, the historical constructions provide more material within which to glean the patient's habitual perceptions of and interactions with his environment. For reasons already discussed, such constructions are necessarily hedged all around by tentativeness; as often as not they reflect more the present phase of the therapy than the actual events constitutive of the past. The authenticity of historical constructions within the analytic enterprise is, by the inner logic of psychoanalysis, necessarily suspect, but this does not deprive them of utility in the realm of psychoanalytic technique. Indeed, I shall shortly argue that within the quite different realm of psychoanalytic *interpretive* discourse, that is, at the level of understanding an individual's desires and action, any interpretation must take the form of a coherent narrative; however, we must not construe this narrative as some more or less accurate representation of a sequence of actual events. Nor should we construe the authority of such narratives as being due largely to its demonstrable derivation from psychoanalytic theory. The three realms—theory, technique, and individual interpretation—are quite distinct in psychoanalysis and much of the present confusion in the discipline results precisely from mistaking the attributes and methods of one for those of another.

4

Considering the preponderance of historical constructions in most psychoanalytic expositions, surely including Freud's essay on Schreber, a reader could construe my argument as emasculating the explanatory power of psychoanalysis quite as relentlessly as Schreber believes his situation unmans him. What after all remains? Let me return to two of the passages that inaugurated my critique of historical constructions in psychoanalysis: psychoanalysts, says Freud, "will wish to go more deeply into the details of the delusion and into the history of its development" (SE, 12:18); and "our only concern is with the meaning and origin of this pathological idea" (SE, 12:43). Freud's syntax in neither passage equates meaning with a historical construction; rather, it accords it a status equal to, and distinct from, a concern with origins. "Details of the delusion" and "meaning" constitute, then, the other, and for our purposes, more crucial locus of methodological concern.

Other passages in "Psychoanalytic Notes" signal that Freud operates under the assumption that coherence and comprehension serve to evaluate psychoanalytic interpretations. At one point Freud pauses to reflect that some may think it a "dubious hypothesis" that a revival of homosexual feelings toward his doctor occasioned Schreber's decisive second illness. He argues:

> But I do not think we should be justified in dismissing such a hypothesis merely on account of its inherent improbability, if it recommends itself to us on other grounds; we ought rather to inquire how far we shall get if we follow it up. For the improbability may be of a passing kind and may be due to the fact that the doubtful hypothesis has not yet been brought into relation with any other pieces of knowledge and that it is the first hypothesis with which the problem has been approached. (SE, 12:46)

Immediately thereafter Freud hits upon such a piece of knowledge, for he discovers that his "hypothesis harmonizes with a noteworthy detail of the case history which remains otherwise inexplicable [i.e., Schreber's collapse during his wife's vacation]" (SE, 12:45). Again, now a few pages later, after he has tentatively suggested that Schreber had associated his elder brother with Flechsig, and his father with both Flechsig and God, Freud's argument takes a similar tack: "We shall not feel that we have been justified in thus introducing Schreber's father into his delusions, unless the new hypothesis shows itself of some use to us in understanding the case and in elucidating *details of the delusions* which are as yet unintelligible" (SE, 12:50–51, my emphasis). The movement of these and similar passages harbors far-reaching implications for any attempt to understand the interpretive logic of psychoanalysis and its relation to that of literary studies. Such passages imply a hermeneutic or explanatory principle that does not go behind or beyond the enigma itself to locate its meaning, as does the genetic method. Rather, this other principle locates within the mystery the material for its resolution. Thus it does not send us away from our immediate difficulties but, on the contrary, demands that we hover about them. Put another way, this hermeneutic honors the potential self-sufficiency of any present therapeutic (and by analogy, of any literary) interpretive situation. Since the consequences are of such moment, I want to extrapolate from these passages carefully.

Consider the situation. Certain material puzzles Freud. In response to the question, How can I account for this situation? he arrives at a possible answer. At this point another question necessarily presents itself: What is the adequacy or validity of my solution? The passages I have quoted address the second question. In gauging the adequacy of his answer, Freud does not make recourse to his general psychological theory: this is so because such is always the case. Nor does Freud here necessarily engage in a historical excavation: Y, the present condition, evolved out of and was caused by X, an antecedent condition. Rather, Freud argues that we must evaluate the hypothetical answer by measuring its efficacy in achieving understanding of "details of the delusion which are as yet unintelligible." That is, we must take our possible answer back to the context of the puzzling material and gauge its effectiveness in elucidating it. By implication the criteria here are almost quantitative: the best answer encompasses and lends meaning to the largest amount of the material at hand. I say "almost" because reflection upon my own interpretive practice reveals that I implicitly privilege the odd and manifestly discordant data. In the first place such data press upon me the need to consciously interpret the phenomenon at hand. But the odd, the outré, the patently discontinuous are privileged also in a more fundamental sense; they are focal to the interpretive action, which seeks constructions that at once honor their distance from, yet bring them into line with, the rest of the available information.[17] Freud also consistently privileged the seemingly discontinuous; thus, although in the case at hand an outbreak of homosexual longings might initially seem an implausible answer, its ability to render understandable Schreber's "otherwise inexplicable" lapse at the time of his wife's vacation grants it a modicum of legitimacy.[18] Other things being equal, if other hypothetical answers cannot incorporate this detail, then the one that can is superior.

A crucial prior assumption of this evaluative method is that the materials at hand—the actions, desires, and beliefs of a particular individual—possess an extraordinary degree of interrelatedness and coherence. Without such an assumption we could not reasonably make recourse to actions X, Y, and Z to confirm our understanding of action A. Thus beyond its obvious concern with the discontinuities of any life, with the disjunction between conscious and unconscious, between primary and secondary thought processes, psychoanalysis also posits the radical continuity of that life. At this point that assumption may seem merely a heuristic necessity; in the following chapter I shall demonstrate its justifications within psychoanalytic theory. For our present purposes, however, it is sufficient only to call attention to the necessary presence of this too often neglected interpretive assumption.

W. W. Meissner and Michael Sherwood have put the case somewhat differently in their important analyses of Freud's interpretive strategies. After an extensive investigation of Freud's methodology Meissner comes to the conclusion that psychoanalysis "is based on the uniqueness and individuality of meaning of the individual's life history and experience."[19] Therefore, the "whole direction of the therapist's effort is toward elaboration of the full context of meaning in which the whole range of data that he has gathered about the patient falls into a consistent, coherent, and intelligible pattern. . . . This pattern of meaning at its highest level of generalization encompasses the entire life experience of the patient."[20] In *The Logic of Explanation in Psychoanalysis* Sherwood offers a similar conclusion: "It is our contention that the core of the psychoanalytic explanation . . . lies in a general, over-all account of the patient's life history and 'life-style,' the peculiar modes and patterns of behavior which mark that history."[21]

Although they in one sense confirm the heuristic necessity of what we can call the assumption of cohesion, in another sense, by enlarging the context to the whole of an individual's life, Meissner and Sherwood apparently undercut another side of my argument. Specifically, their (correct) stress upon the cohesion of the entire life seemingly reestablishes the primacy of historical constructions, although I have argued that they are, in principle at least, expendable, and that clinical interpretation only requires understanding of the dynamics within the consulting room. How are we to resolve this apparent contradiction? I grant the formative, causal role of the historical past, that in any life it organizes all subsequent events in certain, determinant, pervasive patterns. Having granted so much, however, it seems to me essential to recognize that the very dynamic that contours the present around the past prohibits, in principle, our effective reconstruction of an "original" determinative scene. We must remember that in psychoanalysis the "real" is never solely empirical, the hard and fast facticity of specific places, times, things, and people. The "real" is always constituted partially by fantasy, and it is this side of the "real," its constitution by desire, that accounts for the coherence of any life. We might say, therefore, that the "real" never occurs, just as Freud's early patients were never actually seduced by their parents. Moreover, no sooner is an event constituted, assimilated to the existent associative chain, than it becomes in turn the locus for associations from subsequent events, and in effect is reconstituted. A pervasive borrowing and lending of attributes occurs along the entire chain of associations that is impossible to parse accurately. No single event or series of events can be cleanly disengaged; the past can never be reconstructed "as it really happened." Thus the "consistent, coherent, and intelligible pattern" Meissner describes, or the "over-all account of the patient's life history" Sherwood calls for, does not necessarily reproduce the life as lived.

Recognition of the drift of attributes along the associative chain need not occasion interpretive despair. Such slidings are no more haphazard or arbitrary than the paranoid's selection of a persecutor; indeed, the latter is an instance of the former. Nor is the associative chain itself "free." Rather the chain images the determinative influence of past on present and of present on past that psychoanalysis posits; its links illustrate the ways in which the patient construes events through one another; finally, each link, due to the pressure of the past upon the present, shares a common structure with all the others. Thus if the chain of associations in one sense renders the past inaccessible, beyond recuperation, in another it opens it up before us, for we can be confident that it possesses a structure homologous with that of the present. The drifts and slippages that inevitably occur along the chain, that are in fact what bind the various links, connect similar constitutive elements of the repetitive structure. We have, then, a chain of recurrences, a chain in which we cannot locate a definitive first link, a chain in which attributes slide forward (which we call "transference") and slip backward (which we call "deferred action"), a chain always already constituted and also always in the process of being constituted. We might even say that the past is doubly alive: not only does it figure the present but it is also being continually revised by it. Given such a structure, a psychoanalytic interpretation must take as its object the chain itself, not the discrete events embedded in it. This, I take it, is what Meissner and Sherwood rightly stress when they variously insist upon the primacy of the "consistent, coherent, and intelligible pattern" or the "over-all account of the patient's life history." In the therapeutic situation, itself a determinant link in the chain, the analyst of necessity takes as his point of departure the present therapeutic interaction. However, his understanding of the dynamics within the consulting room and the construction of a coherent narrative of the patient's history, of the repetitive history of his desire, emerge simultaneously for they are mutually determinative. In the sense that its parts achieve clarity at the same time, that any one part must be grasped in terms of the others, that the associative net leads ever backward and forward from any one point, in that sense, however much grounded in the present interaction, in the last instance the interpretive commitment in psychoanalysis is necessarily totalizing.

This overarching commitment takes on an important corollary. An interpretation of a particular symptom, dream, or other action is subservient to and dependent upon this more comprehensive commentary. Indeed, we might go as far as to argue that isolated from this over-all interpretation the action in question lacks meaning, or at least that its meaning cannot be established. Meissner puts it this way: "[The] meaning of any fragment depended upon the meaning of the whole. The full interpretation of the dream or fragment of the analysis had to wait for the completion of the analysis in order that an approach be made to its understanding. Similarly the meaning of a single symptom cannot be understood except in the context of the full analysis."[22] Thus the psychoanalyst does not interpret discrete actions sequentially, and his final interpretive narrative does not comprise simply a string of such isolated interpretations. That is, the process is not additive; the over-all understanding is not dependent upon the understanding of smaller details, such as an individual dream. The analyst, often haltingly, with many false starts and new beginnings, confronts the totality of his data and attempts to bring it, at once, with a single, economic hypothesis, to understanding. The data may resist, forcing him to abandon one hypothesis for another, but he struggles to articulate a comprehensive narrative that honors the complexity of his data and within which that data achieves meaning.

Common sense and daily practice might suggest otherwise. Does not the practicing analyst every day come to some understanding of the singular dream or parapraxis? Must he not begin from some local understanding and trust that it can be generalized to incorporate the whole? Surely such often seems to be the case; I at least frequently find myself striving for understandings in this fashion. Here, however, as in so many instances, our intuitive sense of the interpretive process in psychoanalysis is inadequate. Even when the analyst or critic seems to be interpreting incrementally, moving bit-by-bit through the data, he is, if working correctly, doing something quite different. If he reflected back upon such experiences, he would likely recognize that his first, local understandings of a particular dream or the like have most often been radically transformed by the time of termination. It is not so much that the initial interpretations were flatly wrong as that they retrospectively appear inadequate to the density of the material at hand. Thus the initial understandings, however instrumental they may prove in the course of the analysis, inevitably appear inadequate once the analyst begins to sense the role and place of this incident within the context of the entire life.

The vexing problem of symbolism, of course, presents the one major area in which psychoanalysis apparently deviates from this strict contextual or holistic interpretive commitment. Freud invokes symbols in his interpretation of *Memoirs of My Nervous Illness.* "The sun," he declares, "is nothing but another sublimated symbol for the father" (SE, 12:54); he obviously thought this of some importance, for in a postscript added the following year Freud plunders the mythological archive for confirmation of this ascription (SE, 12:80–82). This is neither an appropriate occasion, nor have I the competence, to resolve this apparent anomaly with any finality, but the problem should at least be clear. If, as I have been arguing, all meaning in psychoanalysis is contextual, if it derives solely from some holistic interpretation of the individual life, the very existence of more or less universal symbols proves an embarrassment. Symbols claim a meaning independent of the context, one they import into it. Thus they suggest another, radically different interpretive method, one in which we simply sum the discrete figures our codebooks yield us. Yet in a passage added to *Interpretation* in 1914 Freud obscures these differences and at least suggests the primacy of the contextual hermeneutic we have been developing. Symbols, writes Freud, frequently "have more than one or even several meanings, and, as with Chinese script, the correct interpretation can only be arrived at on each occasion from the context" (SE, 5:353). The father-sun equation Freud establishes in his interpretation of Schreber, therefore, derives its cogency not alone from the mythological tradition, though that contributes, but as well from the contextual evidence that almost necessitates such a reading.[23]

Nevertheless, I cannot legitimately argue for the exclusion of symbols and their decoding from the psychoanalytic field solely for the sake of maintaining the consistency of its interpretive procedures. The necessity for their inclusion is exclusively an empirical decision. If symbols exist—and I'm not altogether certain they do, at least in the univocal sense—they must of course be interpreted in a manner appropriate to their nature. I resist them partially because they tend to be imperialistic; once admitted they are found everywhere, and the most common and fruitful interpretive strategy in psychoanalysis accordingly becomes obscured. Even if their existence is eventually grounded empirically, however, symbols would not completely subvert the contextual basis of psychoanalytic interpretation. Two questions would become relevant. First, assuming that the representation might have taken the more usual form, we might ask why a symbol was utilized in this instance, perhaps suspecting that they are being utilized by the resistance. Second, because, as Ernest Jones has noted, the referents of symbols recur with monotonous frequency, we might ask why this rather than that equivalent symbol was elected in this case.[24] Freud broaches this issue in *Interpretation:* "If a dreamer has a choice open to him between a number of symbols [between, shall we say, a cigar and a gun], he will decide in favor of the one which is connected in its subject-matter with the rest of the material of his thoughts—which, that is to say, has individual grounds for its acceptance in addition to the typical ones" (SE, 5:352–53). Thus even the existence of symbols does not finally rend the holistic commitment so basic to psychoanalytic interpretation.

Obviously, however, much existent psychoanalytic criticism ignores this commitment so crucial to the explanatory model upon which it ostensibly builds. To take a common occurrence, say the critic deciphers an oedipal relationship among several characters in a text. In elucidating this pattern he frequently commits errors of three sorts. First, he may ignore the distinction between theory and individual interpretation, arguing solely from the former in a futile effort to establish the legitimacy of his reading: these relationships exist among people, so that is what must be going on here. Second, he may substitute a purported history of the relationship among the characters, or alternatively one of that among the author and significant persons in his or her life, for an analysis of the dynamic of the relations in question. Besides committing himself to a logical absurdity in the case of the fictional characters, this procedure simply evades the potential sufficiency of the material at hand by aspiring to the mirage of something firmer, less dense. Finally, too often the critic isolates fragments he chooses to work with (here, the oedipal relations, but also possibly a symbol) from the rest of the text. The rationale seems to be that he is contributing his mite to some cumulative, embracing interpretation of the text. However, as we have just seen, psychoanalytic understandings do not develop in this manner; indeed, quite the reverse is true. The analyst, frequently with much stammering, moves from a hypothetical total narrative back to the understanding of individual instances. Moreover, separated from this securing context, the meaning of individual images, incidents, and the like is maddeningly elusive, for only within a holistic understanding can they emerge with any clarity. Thus unless psychoanalytic criticism itself aspires to this overarching interpretive commitment, it must impale itself on its own premises.

We inexorably return to where we began, the problem of evaluating psychoanalytic narratives. Sherwood locates two distinct sorts of criteria: the first concerns the adequacy of the interpretation, the second, its accuracy.[25] In the first group we find three distinct but overlapped standards: self-consistency, coherence, and comprehensiveness. That is, if psychoanalytic interpretations are to be judged adequate, they must, first, avoid making contradictory statements; second, they must draw our understanding into a coherent whole; and third, they must account for as much of the data, especially the odd and discordant, as possible. These are roughly the very standards we saw Freud invoke when he proposed weighing what seemed initially a dubious hypothesis against its utility in providing understanding of otherwise inexplicable details of Schreber's *Memoirs*. Notice how the third criterion silently approaches the quantitative; self-consistency and coherence being equal, that interpretation is best that extends understanding to the greatest portion of the puzzling data. Ideally nothing whatever would remain outside its orderly accounting. The second group, the standards of accuracy, are clearly distinguishable one from the other. First, does the offered interpretation honor the facts of the case as they are known or have simple empirical errors been committed? Second, is the interpretation consistent with psychological theory? We have seen that general theoretical propositions do not sufficiently constitute a psychoanalytic interpretation and that such interpretations are not logically derived from them. However, the extent to which interpretations comply with them—that is, seem plausible given our present understanding of mental functioning—is an important criterion of their accuracy. For the sake of convenience I have followed Sherwood in discriminating between the standards of adequacy and those of accuracy, but it should be clear that the latter are derivable corollaries of the former. The first standard of accuracy restates that of comprehensiveness, for any lapse of the latter is perforce a lapse in empirical comprehensiveness. The second standard of accuracy, compliance with general psychological theory, simply extends the demands for self-consistency and coherence, with the resultant demand that any interpretation be not only self-consistent and internally coherent, but also consistent and coherent in its relation to general psychological theory. These, in sum, are the demands of a coherence theory of truth, and it is such a theory, not, as is often thought, one of simple correspondence, that governs interpretive activity in psychoanalysis. Actually, however, that stark dichotomy inadequately catches the situation: psychoanalysis does not so much ignore correspondence—we have just seen its role among the evaluative criteria—as it assumes the radical cohesion of the data, the individual life, to which it must correspond.

5

Whether trained in literary studies or psychoanalysis, the reader may be struck by a curious result of my discussion of interpretive procedures in psychoanalysis. I may have seemed to domesticate Freud's discoveries, to have robbed them of their easy and natural proclivities for the bizarre, the subversive, the disjunctive. And I have. However, the preceding analysis focuses on the more formal and methodological aspects of psychoanalytic interpretation; the uniqueness of the discipline, with its concentration upon the fleshy adventures of desire, resides in its theoretical location of the nexuses that figure any individual's actions. That is, when we shear the interpretive act from the general psychological theory, as I argue we must if we are to understand the nature of either, the former emerges clothed in its essential commonplaceness.

The inclusion of "Psychoanalytic Notes" among the five canonical case histories prepares for the recognition that, whatever else it may in fact be, psychoanalysis at its core, in the consulting room, is an exercise in explication. Although unique in the sense that Freud never met its subject, the Schreber essay is not therefore different in kind from the other case histories, for there too Freud works with and through language. Like a critic with his sonnet or novel, the psychoanalyst takes as his object the discourse of a patient. Their common task is understanding: understanding these words, their relations among themselves, their relations, simple or convoluted, to their authors. More than a critic, perhaps we should say that analyst functions as editor, for his task does not stop with understanding the strings of words offered him; he must go on to suggest revisions—untangle knotted passages, cut the extraneous, fill the moaning gaps—so that by the time of termination the patient-author is in possession, often for the first time, of his own story. Be that as it may, his object is language *(parole),* his task, understanding; hour upon hour, day upon day, the psychoanalyst, like the literary critic, fulfills his vocation in the explication of a pained language.

Not only are the tasks similar, so too are the methods. As we have seen, psychoanalytic interpretation has a holistic interpretive commitment; any peculiarity of text or life has significance only insofar as it comes in contact with an overarching interpretation. Says Sherwood: "The explanation of, say, a particular dream or a transient compulsive idea is based upon and subservient to some framework of general principles within which the whole life history of the individual is organized and made meaningful."[26] Two otherwise quite different literary theorists can illustrate this commitment in literary studies. E. D. Hirsch, Jr., whose *Validity in Interpretation* constructs a model for all interpretive acts, insists on their intrinsically holistic nature: "An interpretation stands or falls as a whole. As soon as a judge begins to pick and choose elements from several hypotheses, he simply introduces new, eclectic hypotheses, which must in turn stand or fall as wholes. Belief in the possibilities of mere eclecticism is based on a failure to understand that every interpretation necessarily refers to a whole meaning."[27] Thus for Hirsch the literary critic does not simply sum the discrete readings of equally discrete images and the like; rather, he or she reaches above or beyond them to some holistic reading, which in turn lends meaning to the entire text simultaneously. Likewise, John Ellis argues that interpretive statements are necessarily "combinative."[28] That is, he argues that our intuitive prehension of the entire text, not of discrete elements within it, both determines the sorts of facts we shall perceive and has a logical priority over them. In both disciplines, therefore, interpretations are necessarily holistic; the meaning of any particular segment of a whole, be it rhyme scheme or a dream, is dependent upon an overarching interpretive commitment and not vice versa. (In psychoanalysis we have actually seen this twice over: not only do the relations of part to whole take this form but so do those of past to present.)

Likewise, psychoanalysis and literary studies share the criteria against which individual interpretive acts are evaluated. Since neither proceeds deductively, we cannot logically speak of verifying or confirming interpretations; validation must be our common goal.[29] Therefore, too, both disciplines often find themselves in the embarrassing position of arbitrating among various competing, often mutually exclusive, interpretations. In both cases the criteria of self-consistency, coherence, and comprehension apply. Other things being equal, that interpretation that accounts for the greatest amount of the available data, especially for the odd and seemingly discordant, can and should be judged superior. In our frequent professional reluctance to apply these criteria, from either ignorance or something else, literary criticism again, if this time inessentially, parallels psychoanalysis. In neither case, however, does this negligence alter the criteria to be employed in making such discriminations.

At this level, therefore, at the level of the discrete interpretive act, the vocations of psychoanalysis and literary criticism are indistinguishable. Of course these interpretive acts have different necessities and distinct fates: in the one a need to appropriate and so pass on a cultural heritage, in the other a more immediately therapeutic ambition, the easement of personal suffering. Nonetheless, I want to insist that both analyst and critic of necessity fulfill their vocations only by attending to language and that their interpretive strategies accordingly replicate one another. To the extent that they recognize that they work with language, it seems to me that literary critics possess an incalculable advantage over psychoanalysts. Their training attunes them to the accretions of metaphors, the significance of narrative sequence, the nuance of tone, the logics of case and voice. Of course psychoanalysts acquire these skills too, but as far as I know rarely in their formal training, which tends to by-pass the verbal nature of their discipline; these are most often considered ancillary, at best matters of technique, rather than the necessary prerequisites of successful practice. Freud himself was aware of the cogency of these issues, but his suggestions in "The Question of Lay Analysis" about the optimal content of analytic education have largely gone unheeded.[30] One ambition for this essay is that it can go some little way toward restoring the force of Freud's suggestions, for as soon as psychoanalysis forgets the irreducibly verbal nature of its evidence, it immediately lapses into something quite different, either biology or a positivistic sociology, and mystifies the nature of its interpretive activity.

On the other hand, analysts forge interpretations of their patients' lives within the securing context of a general psychological theory. Although the theory does not simply dictate the contours of any particular interpretation, it does suggest issues and contexts that might prove relevant; it does rule out the psychologically impossible. Thus however poorly articulated and internally inconsistent the present state of this theory, it nonetheless provides crucial assistance in, and control of, the interpretive act; moreover, as we have seen, correspondence with the theory is a criterion for evaluating individual interpretations. Most literary investigations lack this securing context, because literary studies lack even this ramshackle theoretical superstructure. Moreover, what general theory that literary studies do possess, explicitly, even systematically, avoids general psychological propositions. However literary critics find themselves willy-nilly dealing with psychological issues: Is there a relationship between an author's life and his work? If so, what is its nature? What, precisely, are the relationships among an author's various books? How do we, as readers, construe either an individual text or the relations among several? Confronted by such questions the literary critic sorely feels, or at least should feel, his lack of a general psychological theory; its absence manifests itself dramatically in the often self-contradictory or patently erroneous responses the critic makes to these and related questions. But we need not look to such large issues to locate the critic's need for general psychological theory; because they exist only in language, all literary texts have speakers, either the author directly or some fictive narrator who mediates between author and work. Much literature, moreover, concerns itself primarily with the human response to events, natural and social, or with the interactions among several characters. The critic cannot begin grasping the nature of fictive characters, or the affiliations among author, narrator and characters, or the relations among several characters without an adequate psychology.

Let me be programmatic: if the critic is to perform effectively he absolutely requires, among other things, a securing psychological theory. It may be objected that the presence of such a psychological theory will surely distort the critic's reading, stand somehow between critic and text. Two responses would be in order. First, it must be recalled that theory only fulfills a *directive* function; it suggests correlative issues that may prove relevant and the lines along which they might be related; it alone cannot provide warrant for any particular interpretation. More crucial, however, is that the objection seems to assume the possibility (indeed, the desirability) of reading without the intervention of some psychological theory. That assumption possesses no warrant; no reading can be innocent of psychological assumptions. If a critic elects to go it alone he or she simply, if covertly, erects a home-brewed psychology to fill the resultant gap. "The unfortunate thing for psychology," laments Jean Piaget, "is that everybody thinks of himself as a psychologist."[31] Whatever its present limitations, the very existence of psychoanalytic theory secures the analyst's interpretive activities in a way literary critics must envy. Thus again we see the centrality of Freud's essay on Schreber's *Memoirs of My Nervous Illness:* despite its departures from interpretation per se, its interpretive strategies, like their location within the context of a general psychology, constitute a model for all literary interpretation. And it is instructive that we find this model not in one of Freud's occasional essays on literary subjects but at the heart of psychoanalysis, in its canonical case histories; its location helps us appreciate, as perhaps we could not otherwise, the profound reciprocity between these two apparently disparate disciplines.

4 : Groundings in Theory: The Cohesive Life, The Whole Story

It is naturally impossible to carry out analysis if the patient's relations with other people and his thoughts about them are excluded.[1]

In the individual's mental life someone else is invariably involved, as a model, as an object, as a helper, as an opponent; and so from the very first individual psychology, in this extended but entirely justifiable sense of the words, is at the same time social psychology as well.[2]

It is above all necessary to avoid once more establishing "society" as an abstraction over against the individual. The individual *is* the *social being*. His vital expression—even when it does not appear in the direct form of a communal expression, conceived in association with other men—is therefore an expression and confirmation of social life.[3]

Breathing, waking, and sleeping; our lives are steamed and shaped into stories.[4]

The previous chapter demonstrates that psychoanalytic interpretation silently assumes the radical cohesion of any individual's life; it begins in the assumption that the same desires and displacements recursively figure any life, in illness and health alike. The assumption allows no exceptions: all of any particular life coheres because all lives cohere. I would insist that this assumption is more than a heuristic device, a temporary interpretive convenience, as is sometimes implied[5]—that psychoanalytic theory itself legitimates the assumption as it builds upon it. Immediately, however, what I am calling the enabling assumption of psychoanalytic interpretation generates anomalies. Does not psychoanalysis privilege as its objects precisely the discontinuous—the parapraxis, the dream, the symptom? And does it not read these phenomena guided by a theory that stresses the distance between conscious and unconscious, between secondary and primary processes, between manifest and latent meanings? Finally, does not my characterization of its enabling assumption neglect the essential contributions of psychoanalysis and return us, much impoverished by the transit, to a pre-Freudian concern with continuities?

Outside psychoanalysis proper, moreover, the notion of the cohesive life bears too obvious affinities with such celebrated notions as the "self" and "identity," intellectual categories that are under strenuous attack at the very time I may seem to be putting them forward in a different guise. This attack takes many forms, among them denigrations of entire fields within which such notions are central. In *Tristes Tropiques,* for instance, Claude Lévi-Strauss explains that he early dismissed the pretensions of phenomenology because it "postulated a kind of continuity between experience and reality." As for existentialism:

> . . . it seemed to me to be anything but a legitimate form of reflection, because of its indulgent attitude towards the illusions of subjectivity. The raising of personal preoccupations to the dignity of philosophical problems is far too likely to lead to a sort of shop-girl metaphysics, which may be pardonable as a didactic method but is extremely dangerous if it allows people to play fast-and-loose with the mission incumbent upon philosophy until science becomes strong enough to replace it: that is, to understand being in relation to itself and not in relation to myself.[6]

More extravagantly, Michel Foucault declares that as an intellectual category "man is an invention of recent date"—the curious epiphenomenon of a historical "change in the fundamental arrangement of knowledge"; should that arrangement shift again, "then one can certainly wager that man would be erased, like a face drawn in the sand at the edge of the sea."[7] For neither Lévi-Strauss nor Foucault, then, does the concept of the individual—much less the continuity of the individual life—possess enduring interest; it is a distraction, forever beside the point.

With Foucault this is something other than an empirical issue, for he equates the emergence of man as an intellectual category with the dawning of the bourgeoisie. Thus systems of thought that valorize identity, or that consider man or the self as irreducible categories become ideological legitimations for capitalism, with its emphasis upon free trade, individual initiative, and the contract freely entered into between individuals. Within this context, commentary on the current insufficiency of the individual, of his imminent passage from the historical stage, becomes explicitly ideological. This is so whether the end of man is decried, as it is among certain of the Frankfurt School,[8] or celebrated as a phase in the movement "to liquidate the last vestiges of bourgeois individualism itself and to prepare the basis for some new post-individualistic thought mode to come."[9]

Within the context of much contemporary thought, therefore, the reconstruction of the generative interpretive assumption of psychoanalysis offered here may seem to render the entire discipline problematic, as either a flaccid ancillary of some "shop-girl metaphysics," or worse, an anachronistic vestige of bourgeois individualism. Moreover, if this assumption is as crucial as I claim, how is it that Freud can pass over it in silence? Nowhere in the twenty-four volumes of the *Standard Edition*, nor even in the several volumes of letters, does Freud explicitly articulate this assumption. The clatterings of the attacks upon apparently cognate notion and the silence of Freud both dictate that I demonstrate the necessary pressure of this notion of the cohesive life upon psychoanalytic theory. That is the task of this chapter. I propose to undertake it by first investigating certain recent developments in psychoanalysis, in particular the work of Erik H. Erikson and Heinz Lichtenstein, which taken together retrospectively legitimate this interpretive assumption. Within the context of that discussion, I shall then turn to Freud's own writings, especially to those concerned with free association and transference, to demonstrate that the cohesive life is an inescapable corollary to —indeed, the very ground of—Freud's theories. In brief, Freud recognized the discontinuities of the life, whose first and most perspicacious student he was, as the folds or wrinkles of a nonetheless cohesive whole; and only by doing so was he able to read, and hence restore, the mutilations of that life.

1

Although the term "identity" entered psychoanalytic discourse relatively early (in 1919), it remained largely an empty counter for nearly thirty years.[10] In a series of papers and books Erik H. Erikson has redeployed the term within psychoanalysis and today his name is linked, I suspect irrevocably, with it. Erikson employs the concept variously by, as he says, "letting the term 'identity' speak for itself. . . . At one time, then, it will appear to refer to a conscious *sense of indi-*

vidual identity; at another to an unconscious striving for a continuity of *personal character;* at a third, as a criterion for the silent doings of *ego synthesis;* and, finally, as a maintenance of an inner solidarity with a group's ideals and identity."[11] Although we may distinguish these four threads (and we might add a fifth, referring to the "crisis of identity" he posits for the fifth developmental stage) in the abstract, the problem proves more intractable in actual practice. For instance, Erikson writes that the "conscious feeling of having a *personal identity*" rests in good part upon "the immediate perception of one's selfsameness and continuity in time" (23). Thus the first meaning, conscious personal identity, depends upon the second, continuity of personal character, which itself is only barely distinguishable even in the abstract from the third, the "silent doings of ego synthesis." Mindful of this difficulty, it remains possible to effect a crude analytic distinction along traditional lines. A "sense of personal identity," together with certain aspects of a person's alignment with a particular ideology, must be largely conscious;[12] but the "silent doings of ego synthesis" and the striving for a continuity of personal character are, by definition, unconscious. I shall discuss Erikson's concept along the lines of this rough approximation in an effort to discover the extent to which it provides adequate grounding for the psychoanalytic assumption of the cohesive life.

For Erikson the *conscious* awareness of possessing a personal identity is of the greatest importance; without it interaction produces only strain, derived either from the fear of engulfment by a stronger other, or from a desire for isolation that preempts the very possibility of interaction: "True 'engagement' with others is the result and the test of firm self-delineation" (124). Two simultaneous observations, according to Erikson, form the bases for cognizance of one's personal identity. The individual must recognize his or her continuity in time, must discern a continuity between what one was in the past, is in the present, and hopes to become in the future. Alone this recognition cannot sustain itself. That is, for an individual to feel a continuity over time, that continuity must be acknowledged, and that feeling legitimated, by significant other people with whom he or she interacts.

The development and maintenance of a firm sense of personal identity is a lifelong task; it is never achieved once-and-for-all; it is always dependent upon present circumstances; it is extremely corrodible. Constant changes in one's personal and social circumstances—

new relationships with others, the loss of other relationships, new responsibilities, one's successes and failures in varying spheres—all these necessitate continual alteration. Likewise, the maintenance of a "sense of personal identity" depends upon the more or less successful resolution of each of the successive psychosocial crises Erikson posits as inherent to the human life cycle. Thus trust, autonomy, initiative, industry, and so on through the life cycle must emerge in some positive ratios to their opposites for a stable personal identity to arise. A problematic resolution of one (or more) of these crises impedes, and possibly arrests, the developing conscious awareness of identity, leaving it to some degree impaired.

If maintaining a conscious sense of personal identity is the task of a lifetime, it assumes special import during adolescence. Adolescence marks for Erikson the fifth psychosocial crisis, that of "identity vs. identity diffusion"; it is the time during which the individual must emerge beyond the family constellation and peer groups to a fuller integration into society at large. The tasks of "adolescing" (Erikson is fond of neologisms) include containing the growing intensity of impulses invested in a rapidly maturing body, consolidating achievements in line with available work opportunities, and resynthesizing childhood identifications in a way that harmonizes them with the possible roles in the larger society just now available. Most societies ease the completion of these formidable tasks by offering "institutionalized *psychosocial moratoria,* during which a lasting pattern of 'inner identity' is scheduled for relative completion." When he finally locates a social place the "young adult gains an assured sense of inner continuity and social sameness which will bridge what he *was* as a child and what he is about to become, and will reconcile his *conception of himself* and his *community's recognition* of him" (111).

Thus the conscious "sense of inner identity" embraces much. Identity originates in a basic trust in the integrity of one's existence, an "ontological security," to borrow R. D. Laing's analogous term. The child's growth—first within the family constellation, later within society at large—predicates this basic *"I am,"* gives it a *"what,"* a social definition, one that both meets personal needs and is socially sanctioned. "At its best," writes Erikson, "it is a process of increasing differentiation, and it becomes ever more inclusive as the individual grows aware of a widening circle of others significant to him, from the maternal person to 'mankind.' "[13] Thus the process that begins with the "psychological birth" of the infant within the undifferentiated mothering person-child matrix ends, ideally, with his insertion into a social matrix, but now possessing an "inner identity" recognized by him and acknowledged by others.

With the enmeshing of the individual with society we move almost imperceptibly to Erikson's fourth definition of identity; that is, "maintenance of an inner *solidarity* with a group's ideals and identity" (102). For Erikson, ideology has none of the value-laden connotations usually appended to it, but refers simply to a "coherent body of shared images, ideas, and ideals which . . . provides for the participants a coherent, if systematically simplified, over-all orientation in space and time, in means and ends" (157).[14] An ideology offers the neophyte a depiction of an ideal future with which he can coordinate his past and present, "a geographic-historical framework for the young individual's budding identity" (146).

"Identity and ideology," says Erikson, "are two aspects of the same process" (157): the latter being a collective version of the former. No less than identities, of course, ideologies can become outdated; only by maintaining implicit correlations in its system of values to the main concerns of the adolescent ego's development can a particular ideology perpetuate itself through an infusion of youthful adherents. The benefits that accrue from this mutual recognition are likewise mutual. The individual finds in an ideology at a crucial moment in development wider recognition and validation of his particular concerns, together with a posture promising their resolution. He finds there, too, a vision of the future consistent with his past and present, as well as legitimation of his "inner identity." On the other hand, the ideology, whether or not it is fully institutionalized, finds similar recognition and legitimation in the neophyte's expression of allegiance. More important, only through the continual infusion of youthful energies can any particular "world-view" or system of values become actualized. The young require the coherence, sanction, and protection of the older generation; the ideology, the sanction and energy of the youth. Thus Erikson locates the process of identity formation both *"in the core of the individual* and yet also *in the core of his communal culture,"* and in the process that "establishes, in fact, the identity of these two identities."[15]

In his discussion of ideology Erikson's usage of "identity" begins an all but imperceptible drift in reference. To be sure, an individual aligns himself to and expresses his solidarity with a particular ideology purposively and consciously. But Erikson suggests that the allegiance of youth to an ideology works on other levels as well. In fact, *Young Man Luther* specifically defines "ideology" as an "*unconscious tendency* [underlying] religious and scientific as well as political thought; the tendency at a given time to make facts amenable to ideas, and ideas to facts, in order to create a world image convincing enough to support the collective and individual sense of identity."[16]

In classic psychoanalytic structural theory, the ego mediates among the often conflicting desires of the id, demands of the superego (which we may here transcribe as the demands of both parents and their successors, finally of a particular ideology), and the exigencies of the environment, social and natural, in an attempt to create a reconciliation. Although this task of the ego possesses preconscious and conscious aspects, the resultant syntheses are actually the products of unconscious activity. When Erikson refers to the formation of ego identity he refers not only to the "subjective experience" of self-existence and self-sameness, but also to the "dynamic fact" (23) of unconscious ego synthesis: "Identity formation," he writes, "is a lifelong development largely unconscious to the individual and to his society" (113). The ego integrates the psychosexual and psychosocial aspects at any given stage of development in a manner that reconciles the many conflicting demands pressing upon it at that time. However, since situations constantly shift, due partially to the physical maturing and altering social position of the individual, partially to steady realignments in the supportive milieu, new elements must be continually integrated and others displaced, that is, new syntheses achieved.[17]

Just as an individual's "inner identity" or subjective experience of self-sameness reaches a normative crisis at the end of adolescence, so too does his particular ego synthesis. At this time the individual, says Erikson, must subordinate his syntheses of various childhood identifications and projections to a new configuration that takes into account not only the ethos of the family but also that of the larger society beyond the walls of the home, a society he must now engage in new ways. Again, ideology performs an important function. The wide range of political, religious, ethical, and philosophical ideologies available to a young person offers the ego a variety of socially sanctioned syntheses. Therefore, beside providing youth the means for entering society and achieving its recognition, ideologies ideally provide the justification for, and the objectification of, particular reconciliations of the divergent demands placed upon the ego.[18] What emerges—again, ideally—from this interaction of ego and ideology is "an *evolving configuration*—a configuration which is gradually established by successive ego synthesis and resyntheses throughout childhood; it is a configuration gradually integrating *constitutional givens, idiosyncratic libidinal needs, favored capacities, significant identifications, effective defenses, successful sublimations,* and *consistent roles*" (116).

Striking parallels, then, exist between the conscious and unconscious phenomena Erikson melds in the concept of identity. Both reach normative crises during adolescence, both are intimately concerned with the relations between an individual and his or her social milieu and, hence, ideology performs a necessary role in both. Nonetheless, I cannot help but feel that Erikson's inclusive definition generates unnecessary ambiguities that finally attenuate whatever utility the concept possesses for psychoanalytic theory. The term drifts uncertainly in his prose; at many points even the most discriminating reader cannot decide whether it refers to conscious or unconscious phenomena.

Moreover, the yoking of conscious and unconscious phenomena by calling attention to their manifest similarities obscures an even more crucial difference. When Erikson denotes by identity a person's "conscious sense of identity," or the "subjective experience of continuity and selfsameness," or when he writes of a person's "inner identity," he is using "identity" basically as a descriptive term, for unlike phenomenology, he offers no model of consciousness generally. As such, he may use other adjectives to further characterize it—may call it strong or weak, firm or tenuous, healthy or even nonexistent—but that is all. In contrast, when Erikson means by identity the "silent doings of ego synthesis" he refers, as we have seen, to a configuration that emerges as the product of unconscious ego syntheses. This configuration is a mental structure and as such both it and its constitutive elements can be described; its various balances and tensions can be graphed. Moreover, this configuration both temporally precedes the particular "sense of individual identity" it evokes and governs it. In other words, the subjective experience depends upon the structure of the particular configuration it emanates from, even when, as is the case with certain schizophrenic conditions, no sense of inner identity exists. We are left, therefore, with an apparently paradoxical, but entirely psychoanalytic, position: we can delineate in any detail only those aspects of Erikson's concept of identity that refer to phenomena that exist outside consciousness—that is, those aspects that are systematic or structural, rather than merely descriptive.

Another difficulty emerges within Erikson's concept when we consider the interplay he describes between identity and ideology. We have heard Erikson say, "identity and ideology are two aspects of the same process" (157), a process concerned with the social formation of the individual. Thus in this aspect of his work Erikson moves beyond Freud—who often saw the relationship between the individual and society as an irreconcilable conflict—to consider the resources society makes available to its members. I think we must see this as a necessary and admirable amplification of psychoanalytic theory, an attempt to account for social formation without, as with similar attempts by the neo-Freudians, regressing to an essentially pre-Freudian, unpsychological position.[19] Erikson recognizes that the ego (of which identity is a "subsystem" [149]) is a thoroughly social product. Although he grants that once it might have been helpful to conceptualize "certain intrinsic antagonisms" between the individual and society, he warns that "the implicit conclusion that an individual ego could exist against or without a specifically human 'environment,' i.e., social organization, is senseless" (150–51). Erikson does not in this way deny the biological substrate of the ego per se. He continues the tradition begun when Freud assigned to the ego the function of "reality-testing," which has resulted in its being perceived, at least within ego psychology, as the repository of varying cognitive processes; however, Erikson insists that these processes do not unfold naturally, uninfluenced by a shaping cultural context. His famed studies of the Sioux and Yurok cultures represent efforts to document the manifold ways in which they, like all cultures, shape the cognitive processes (and hence the egos) of their members.[20]

Although Erikson thus recognizes that the ego, and not just the superego, is socialized to its very core, many of his descriptions of the dialectical interplay between identity and ideology apparently suppress this recognition. We witness this especially in his descriptions of the normative crises in adolescence, during which, he says, the individual must become fully socialized. Too often—as when he states that ideologies offer on the one hand a "seeming correspondence between the internal world of ideals and evils, and, on the other, the outer world with its organized goals and dangers in real space and time" (146)—Erikson subverts the dialectic he is developing by reverting to crude oppositions that suppress the fact that the ego is not irreducible, that it is already (and always) socialized.[21] I suspect that the origins of this slippage can be traced to Erikson's frequent reliance upon phenomenological descriptions—such hard and fast oppositions may feel irreducible; be that as it may, to the extent that such formulations persist, Erikson undercuts the truth he had gained and unfortunately sustains the erroneous notion that the ego unfolds asocially, even biologically, and is only socialized subsequently. Nonetheless, Erikson's recognition, however unsteady, of the social determinants of identity seems to me a decisive contribution to psychoanalysis.

Despite the obvious parallels, then, and whatever its other uses, as it stands Erikson's concept of identity does not offer firm grounding for the psychoanalytic interpretive assumption of the cohesive life. But it does suggest issues with which any such groundings must necessarily come to terms. First, unlike Erikson's concept of identity, it must differentiate sharply between conscious and unconscious phenomena and then concern itself primarily with the latter. With more difficulty, it must acknowledge and account for the social formation of the individual without obliterating his or her particularity. That is, the cohesive life must be seen as emerging amidst a matrix of social factors, and the groundings for the assumption must account for the constitutive role of these factors. In a word, the concept we are searching for must be "relational," transpersonal.

2

A series of often long, occasionally obscure, essays by Heinz Lichtenstein provides a beginning. Lichtenstein grounds his discussion of identity in the observation of various ethologists that "preformed structural automatisms" provide lower animals a fixed identity in the form of rigid behavior patterns.[22] No such "schema" exist in man; but as one moves up the evolutionary scale an increased discontinuity between sexuality and procreation can be discerned, together with a gradual enlargement of the cerebral cortex. The enlargement of the brain clearly provides man with the capability for adaptation, a function performed in lower animals by their inborn "schema"; but what is one to make of the disjunction between sexuality and procreation? What function might nonprocreative sexuality perform?

Lichtenstein hypothesizes that man's lack of an inborn identity is compensated for and fulfilled by nonprocreative sexuality; in his words, "human identity is established by a specific use of the nonprocreative sexual function" (IS, 185).[23] Man's comparative lack of a behavioral identity frees him from animallike rigidity and opens the possibilities of his being and becoming almost anything. As it opens up his potential to assume various identities, however, man's lack of an inborn schema creates the complementary threat that he will be nothing. "For his adaptability," writes Lichtenstein, man "is forever threatened with loss or breakdown of his identity, a danger unknown to the animal under natural conditions" (IS, 184). Lichtenstein believes that because extinction continually menaces, "maintenance of identity in man has priority over any other principle determining human behavior" (IS, 189). In fact, he posits an "identity principle" (IS, 246), prior even to Freud's pleasure principle, as the first and most important determinant of human action.

Identity, for Lichtenstein, is "change arrested" (IS, 188), "the capacity to remain the same in the midst of change" (IS, 193). He differentiates sharply between identity and the "sense of identity": the former is "change arrested," the latter, a "consciousness of such continuity of sameness" (IS, 193). Identity necessarily precedes conscious awareness of such continuity through time, and it can and does exist independent of the latter. In insisting upon this distinction Lichtenstein only remains consistent with his ethological basis: "The animal's innate 'schema' refers to the innate object representation of a drive; we have in this schema the guarantee for each animal's identity—not a *sense* of identity, or any form of awareness, but a guarantee of "living sameness" within change, of continuity as an individual of a particular species" (IS, 201).[24]

Lichtenstein locates the origins of a person's identity in the earliest period of one's life, in the symbiotic universe that encompasses the mother-infant relationship. Cartesian categories of subject and object are inadequate for the conceptualization of such relatedness; "the organ of an organism has an identity in terms of its function within the organism; thus, the maternal *Umwelt* (which includes the unconscious of the mother) ordains an organ-function to the child, and it is this primary function in which I see the nucleus of the emerging human identity" (IS, 202). Lichtenstein suggests, then, that a mother "imprints" an identity upon the child, an identity that always expresses "an experience of a potential instrumentality for another one" (IS, 203).

This imprinted identity is trebly specific. It is, first of all, species specific, since only humans receive their identities in this manner. In a more restrictive sense, the identity the mother conveys to her infant represents the potential fulfillment of *her* individual, as against other mothers', needs, at *this* particular time in her life. The maternal stimuli to which the infant responds are "specific for the *individual* mother, and once the infant has been stimulated that way, the infant 'recognizes' *his* mother by the specific individual combination of stimulations as well as frustrations long before there is a true perceptive recognition" (IS, 206). And because the stimulation he receives is specific, so too must be the infant's identity.

Actually, what the mother imprints is not an identity, but what Lichtenstein terms an "identity theme." Once imprinted, the theme itself is *irreversible.* It remains, however, capable of variations, much like a musical theme: "A musical theme is developed as it undergoes variations. But the variations may revert to the original undeveloped theme without destroying the structure of the composition. We could refer to the musical theme as a primary configuration and consider its variations as secondary elaborations."[25] The child receives from his mother a specific mode of relatedness, an identity theme. His relations with others throughout life—be they mother, father, wife, child, boss, subordinate, or political figure—represent secondary elaborations of this primal mode of relatedness; they are variations, not deviations.

Lichtenstein demonstrates the workings of an identity theme through the extensive case history of Anna A. The illegitimate daughter of a vaudeville performer whose youth, career, and subsequent marriage make an inconstant mother, "Anna's one aim was to be what her mother wanted her to be. She became her mother's most ardent lover, and tormented her with her rages of jealousy" (IS, 214). When that marriage failed and her stepfather left, Anna, then fourteen, sought to provide for her mother; shortly, however, the mother deserted Anna's sole custody for another man, prompting the daughter to flee home. Thereafter her life took on a cyclical form: "a lesbian love relationship would lead to fear of desertion, fear of desertion would create panic and depression . . . , and depression would lead to excessive drinking and prostitution" (IS, 216). In light of her mother's desertion of her in favor of men, Lichtenstein suggests that "prostitution was for Anna a defense against the danger of involvement with men"; she herself "was aware that she felt threatened in her relationship to such men who could be potential husbands" (IS, 218). "For her, loneliness was a reason for all the contradictory aspects of her behavior. She would, in her opinion, be quite content if a girl she loved would remain forever faithful: then she would not have to feel lonely and she would not need any men at all" (IS, 219).

One day Anna brought to the session a fantasy that accompanied her bouts of loneliness and that she had written out in "a kind of poetic form." She entitled it "Return":

> Ah, he quiets Sanity, for I hear the sounds of my lover's footsteps.—Is that you beloved, is that you returning to Drown in my madness, to baptise me with the Sweetness of our foolishness? Oh, bring back the strange but happy love. —Bless you, and drink with me my blood to quench our starved thirstiness. . . . Embrace me oh madness, let my nakedness and nudity quench thy thirst for madness with love of a longing heart. (IS, 219)

Arguing from such evidence, Lichtenstein "transcribed Anna's identity theme as 'being another's essence' " (IS, 223). Thus to be alone, whether in the absence of her mother or of the lover of "Return," was for Anna an intolerable condition. Lichtenstein convincingly demonstrates how this identity theme emerged within Anna's early relationship with her mother, and further how her subsequent relations —as lesbian, as prostitute, and in fantasies—represent successive versions of her need to be another's essence. Moreover, some time after the successful termination of her analysis, Anna sent a letter to Lichtenstein that supported his contention of the irreversibility of an identity theme. Anna wrote of her new happiness in a heterosexual relationship: "Never before have I felt peace of mind with anyone, warmth and feeling of wanting to do. I feel so much part of him that when he tells me something that was unpleasant to him, no matter what . . . I hate the thing or person for it. . . . If he is tired, fatigue takes hold of me, and I seem to share his feeling, and usually end up relieving him of it. Does real love make one feel a part of another?" (IS, 229). Although this relationship patently gratifies Anna in ways previous ones did not, it nonetheless clearly manifests her persistent identity theme, for she now exists through and for her male friend. We might even speculate that she achieved a similar relationship with Lichtenstein; in any event her case history surely plays an essential role in Lichtenstein's presentation of his work.

In his first papers Lichtenstein always conceptualizes the identity theme as a mode of relatedness, an interpersonal construct. His more recent essays suggest that this interpersonal definition of identity implies an intrapsychic precipitate. In other words, a unique way of relating with others mirrors a unique psychic correlation: "The reconstruction of normal mental development and the establishment of psycho-analytic aetiology calls for a *constant* correlation of the three metapsychological criteria [e.g., forces, energy, and structure] whose combinations and permutations constitute *transformations* of this constant correlation such that in normal mental development each transformation can be understood as a function of the invariant correlation."[26] The initial mother-infant relationship, therefore, lays down a specific mode of relatedness, which in turn precipitates a sustained intrapsychic structure.

In line with this new interest in intrapsychic structure, Lichtenstein suggests a redefinition of self "as the sum total of all the transformations which are *possible* functions of an early-formed correlation of the various elements of the mental apparatus."[27] We may note in passing that such a self is not predicated upon consciousness, nor can it at any moment be said to be totally present; indeed, what seems specific about Lichtenstein's definition is precisely its displacement of such traditional concerns. Two factors determine which of the various transformations or aspects of the self achieve actualization: first, its formal structure; and second, the particular situation of the individual at a given time (or the sum of them over time) and the possibilities thus afforded for translating the identity theme into actuality.

Although we need not adopt Lichtenstein's formulations in their entirety, I have sketched them in some detail for two reasons. First, they represent the most totalizing and self-consistent attempt within psychoanalysis to ground what I have been calling its enabling interpretive assumption. Without doubt a radical cohesion of the individual life as the identity theme forms and reforms itself self-consistently, elaborating now this and now that of its possible transformations, legitimates a posteriori, on the theoretical level, psychoanalysis's initial assumption of such cohesion on the level of specific interpretations. Equally important, however, are the implications of the location and the conditions within which this uniformity comes into being, for they suggest not only the power of Lichtenstein's theories, but also the ways in which they differ from such apparently cognate notions as identity, subjectivity, and the self.

We must notice, first, that whatever genetic and instinctive resources the neophyte brings to the relationship, his or her identity theme is stimulated by and dependent upon another; that is, it arises not intrapsychically, not biologically, but only within the relationship with the mothering person. This insistence upon the crucial formative role of the mothering person provides psychoanalysis its necessary release beyond its equally necessary biological substrate, for whatever biological necessities the identity theme answers to, it does so in a properly psychological realm. (In fact, the terms "psychological" and "interpersonal" have been rendered nearly synonymous, a point to which we shall shortly return.) Moreover, Lichtenstein's insistence that an identity theme is not a conscious phenomenon (IS, 201) reinforces what is already apparent in the interpersonal formulation, namely, that the concept of "identity theme" does not smuggle anew into psychoanalysis some notion that the unity of the life resides in self-consciousness or self-presence to oneself. The continuities of the identity theme exist outside consciousness; in fact, they exist outside the mind as usually conceived, even outside the physical individual insofar as they necessarily involve the others with whom the individual interrelates. The subject, as Lichtenstein defines it, exists only in-relation-to; it cannot therefore be delineated apart from the relationships that constitute it, as if it existed independent of them.[28]

We can see this stress upon the early mothering person-child relationship, which takes many forms in contemporary psychoanalysis, as an advance upon Freud. For Freud the child's acculturation does not properly begin until the waning of the oedipal period with the interiorization (for the male child) of the father in the dual roles of ego ideal and superego. We can now see that admittedly crucial phase of development as following upon an earlier one. Indeed, Lichtenstein implicitly relegates the father to a secondary role, for the relationship the child eventually establishes with the father as the oedipal phase terminates must be modeled upon, and be a variation of, the identity theme that arose in the earlier relationship with the mothering person. Part of the power of Lichtenstein's formulations is that they allow us to glimpse the relationship between these relationships; moreover, they force us to recognize that the socialization of the child begins with birth and does not wait upon some later phase of development.

Thus Lichtenstein's interpersonal construction of the invariant identity theme allows us to understand Freud's assertion, quoted as an epigraph to this chapter, that "from the very first individual psychology . . . is at the same time social psychology." We might go as far as to say that the psychological realm properly begins at the point it becomes social. Lichtenstein himself rarely extends his analysis beyond the dyad, either the narrow society of the mothering person and child or some later version, but his theory seems inherently capable of extension. In particular, it seems to me that we can graft onto it the dialectic Erikson begins to chart between an individual and ideology. The relational nature of Lichtenstein's formulations should retard any tendency to fall back into static (and irreducible) oppositions, such as inner and outer, or self and other. At the same time, Erikson's concept of ideology provides initial access to the full social dimension that remains virtual in Lichtenstein's own writings.

The sole extant substantive appropriation of Lichtenstein's remarkable work, Norman Holland's in *Five Readers Reading* and elsewhere, follows Lichtenstein in neglecting this crucial dimension. We need not go into the substance of the complex analysis of the reading process Holland offers in *Five Readers;*[29] we can here concern ourselves solely with the formulations he offers of Lichtenstein's work. Although Holland locates the origins of an identity theme in the early relationship with the mothering person, he subsequently shears the notion from its interpersonal bases and thereby returns it to an exclusively intrapsychic concept, a version of the familiar fantasy-defense model he had earlier used so effectively in *The Dynamics of Literary Response.* That is, for Holland identity theme is a truly relational concept only at the moment of its origin; the moment after he rapidly internalizes the notion within the individual subject, making it appear impervious to time and place. Henceforth, the theme alone, the solitary individual, adequately accounts for the terms of his or her interactions with, and constructions of, what Edmund Husserl calls a "life-world." Obviously Holland's construction conflicts with Lichtenstein's insistence that the exigencies of any situation, the resources and demands it presents, play a role in determining which variation of an identity theme will manifest itself at any particular time. I suspect that Holland makes this move to preserve a single datum, an individual's identity theme, from the fate of mediation; in any event, the effect of his construal is that it alone remains real and immediate, all else is mediated by it. By this point it should be obvious that I think Holland has misconstrued the nature of Lichtenstein's notion. The theme and the continuity it produces in the life only emerge amidst the succession of relations with others in which a subject engages. These relations are constitutive of the subject, its theme, its continuity; an adequate accounting of any of the latter can only be achieved if we consider the formative role of the Other.

Alone, therefore, the relational thrust of Lichtenstein's argument cannot provide a warrant against the profound temptation of any psychological theory to develop asocially. Nonetheless, his theory enforces a minimal acknowledgment of the social formation of the individual and of the individual's constitution, through some transformation of his or her identity theme, of the social milieu: mediation is universal. Thus as we ground the interpretive assumption of the cohesive life in the concept of identity themes, we are not simply rearticulating the sanctity of the autonomous individual. The theory of the cohesive life is not a denial of the social formation of the individual, not a covert piece of bourgeois ideology. As we have seen, Lichtenstein demands that we understand the individual as social through and through. The individual lives at the intersection of social vectors, is both constituted by them and constitutes them; the psychological is always (already) social, and the social can only be constituted psychologically. Any attempt to grasp this interpenetration solely from one side or the other must reify the relationship, and thereby hopelessly mystify understanding.

I have consistently stressed the social formation of the individual because that dimension remains virtual in most psychoanalytic theory, causing it to fall back into notions of static oppositions, asocial or even biological unfoldings. A contrary danger, one no less pernicious to the understanding of human processes, exists. The social factors may appear to provide us with some firm, unmediated ground upon which to base understanding; in resisting the fall into biology on the one hand we may unthinkingly collapse psychoanalysis into positivistic sociology on the other, as was done by many of the neo-Freudians. (Obviously, this is the same danger that we examined in the previous chapter, namely, the appeal to the facticity of the life, now manifest at another theoretical level.) Class, age, sex, race, and the like may all seem to exert an irresistible force, each, monolithic in its own way, compelling a necessary reaction. For better or worse such is not the case. We cannot simply reduce the individual to the sum of univocal social influences that impinge upon his or her life; some become querulous or morose with age, others serene; some take the advantages of class with complacent self-righteousness, others with doubt and self-denigration. These factors constitute the individual in three ways. First, a constellation of such factors influences the needs of the mothering person; they are thus inscribed into the child's initial mode of relatedness. The concrete situation, second, facilitates certain transformations of an identity theme and inhibits others. Finally, the stringencies of an identity theme mediate these constitutive factors, defining them and the individual vis-à-vis one another. Thus individuals are not quite epiphenomenal, not simply effusions thrown up by the matrix of social factors; rather, they possess some autonomy within the exigencies of social formation, just as, in Marxian terms, the cultural superstructure possesses some autonomy over against the economic base.[30] With any suppression of this necessary mediation, psychoanalysis lapses out of a properly psychological realm and becomes merely another variant of positivistic sociology. In sum, not only are individuals constituted, they are also constitutive—if not directly of the social and natural forces that impinge upon them, at least of the consequences of that impingement.

It would seem, therefore, that retrospectively Lichtenstein's work adequately legitimates the psychoanalytic interpretive assumption of the cohesive life. Before passing on to Freud, let me reiterate the nature of this legitimation. First, Lichtenstein postulates that at a highly abstract level, one far removed from the contingencies of day-to-day life, the entire life of a subject coheres—that his or her relations with varying people, attitudes toward work and play, politics, aesthetic preferences, even gait and clothing, can all be seen to articulate transformations of a basic way of being in the world. Second, he postulates that this profound continuity cannot be glimpsed if we consider the subject as irreducible, as though he or she could live apart from a human context; rather, it exists precisely in the specific mode of relatedness, flexible yet invariant, established within that context. Thus psychology must always include a social dimension: the relations a subject forms form him or her. Further, since this continuity is at once interpersonal and, by definition, it is located outside of consciousness, outside even the somatic individual, it exists, as it were, in-between, across the space between subject and object, across that space in which a relationship is established defining the one for the other, in terms of the other, in the only way anything can be defined—relationally.[31]

3

It is one thing to find groundings for the interpretive assumption of the cohesive life among certain recent developments in psychoanalysis and quite another to locate them in Freud himself. If I maintain that the cohesive life is the enabling assumption of the magisterial case histories—even of psychoanalysis itself—I must confess that Freud never explicitly addresses himself to it. We can see its sure traces, however, if we turn primarily to his writings on the dynamics of therapy. These texts not only betray the presence and provide the theoretical legitimation for this assumption, but they also generally sustain the apparently contradictory recognition that individual psychology has from the very first been social psychology. We shall focus upon two separate aspects of psychoanalytic therapy—free association, the famous fundamental rule, and the phenomenon of transference. At first they may appear altogether distinct, the one intrapsychic, the other interpersonal, but our analysis will demonstrate that a common dynamic animates them, a dynamic that both accounts for and grounds within Freud's texts our assumption of the radical cohesion of the individual life.

By 1913 it was a matter of indifference to Freud as to what sort of material the patient chose to inaugurate the analytic dialogue. The "patient's life-history or the history of his illness or his recollections of childhood" (SE, 12:134) were equally appropriate beginnings. However, he strictly prescribed the manner in which the patient presented the material. The patient must free associate. Earlier, in *The Interpretation of Dreams,* Freud had described the dual change the fundamental rule sought to impose upon the consciousness of the patient. "We must aim at bringing about two changes in him: an increase in the attention he pays to his own psychical perceptions and the elimination of the criticism by which he normally sifts the thoughts that occur to him" (SE, 4:101). As the patient attends more rigorously to the flow of thought so as to articulate it for the analyst, he or she must concurrently suppress the "critical faculty" and not be misled into suppressing any thought or image because it seems irrelevant, unimportant, offensive, or meaningless. "He must adopt a completely impartial attitude to what occurs to him, since it is precisely his critical attitude which is responsible for his being unable, in the ordinary course of things, to achieve the desired unravelling of his dream or obsessional ideal or whatever it may be" (SE, 4:101). In this way, and to this limited extent, the *" 'involuntary' ideas are transformed into 'voluntary' ones"* (SE, 4:102), as the patient attempts, consciously and conscientiously, to report the meshwork of thoughts seemingly thought beyond him: this is the first, most tentative step in the process of self-appropriation psychoanalytic therapy represents.

When in this calculated drift from association to association the patient reports a dream, the analyst might invoke a more purposive form of the fundamental rule. For whenever they collaborate on the interpretation of a dream, the analyst breaks the dream report down into its constitutive elements, and asks that the patient associate to each element separately. In this phase, then, the analyst initially focuses the patient's attention to each discrete element and asks that the associations to it be articulated. They move through the dream report piece-by-piece, extensively associating to one element before moving on to the next, "confident . . . that in the end, without any active intervention on [their] part, [they] shall arrive at the dream-thoughts from which the dream originated" (SE, 5:527). Freud grants these associations a privileged status precisely to the extent that they arise without the patient's conscious intervention, as if a report from beyond, like the dream itself.

But how is it that these apparently random thoughts prove efficacious in interpreting the dream? Freud's reasoning here is twofold. First, these associations only *seem* free:

> For it is demonstrably untrue that we are being carried along a purposeless stream of ideas when, in the process of interpreting a dream, we abandon reflection and allow involuntary ideas to emerge. It can be shown that all we can ever get rid of are purposive ideas that are *known* to us; as soon as we have done this, *unknown*—or, as we inaccurately say, "unconscious"—purposive ideas take charge and thereafter determine the course of the involuntary ideas. (SE, 5:528).

Moreover, the previously unknown purposive ideas evoked as the patient associates to this and that element of the dream represent an elongation of the very ideas initially constitutive of the dream; they are further links in the psychical chain in which the dream itself is but another link. In one sense, therefore, the associations to the elements of the dream report necessarily lead past the dream itself to the "dream-thoughts" it articulates, however disguised and deformed that articulation. Thus Freud can even argue in the *Introductory Lectures* that the accuracy of the initial dream report is a matter of indifference:

> Now, too, we can understand to what extent it is a matter of indifference how much or how little the dream is remembered and, above all, how accurately or how certainly. For the remembered dream is not the genuine material but a distorted substitute for it, which should assist us, by calling up other substitute images, to come nearer to the genuine material, to make what is uncon-

scious in the dream conscious. If our memory has become inaccurate, therefore, it has merely made a further distortion of this substitute—a distortion, moreover, which cannot have been without reason. (SE, 15:114)[32]

Thus the gaps and distortions of the dream report represent nothing other than a continuation of the original dream-work; this renders the report, however much it deviates from the dream itself, a replica of the original struggle to speech.

What we have here is a series: first the dream-thoughts, the wishes and ideas vigorously repressed in waking life; second, the dream itself, for during the relaxation of sleep these dream-thoughts achieve articulation, although only at the price of undergoing deformation by the dream-work; third, the dream report, itself likely deformed, and by the very agency that distorted the dream and keeps the dream-thoughts unconscious; finally, the clusters of associations to each element of the dream report, all of which represent further elongations of the generative dream-thoughts.[33] Put another way, we could say that the dream, the dream report, and the associations are all derivations of the repressed dream-thoughts. Says Freud in his 1915 essay, "Repression": "If these derivatives have been sufficiently far removed from the repressed representative [i.e., the dream-thoughts], whether owing to the adoption of distortions or by reason of the number of intermediate links inserted, they have free access to the conscious. It is as though the resistance of the conscious against them was a function of their distance from what was originally repressed" (SE, 14:149). But that is only part of their derivation. Although the dream itself, the report, and the various associations derive one aspect of their nature from the repressed idea, I think it would be more accurate to say that each of these links in the psychical chain derives from, and in fact replicates, the structuring conflict that renders the dream-thoughts unconscious and maintains them in that state. We thus have a series of homologous structures, of similarly deformed articulations; and I would argue that it is by moving back and forth along this series, by noting the points of linkage, that the analyst interprets the dream.

Because the psychical chain Freud invokes implicitly reduces the dream to the status of but one among its numerous intermediate links, the figure of the chain takes us past the interpretation of any single dream. Moreover, I believe it enables us to penetrate the so-called navel of the dream, that "spot in any dream at which it is unplumbable—a navel, as it were, that is its point of contact with the unknown" (SE, 4:111 n). Freud returns to elaborate this idea later in *Interpretation:*

> There is often a passage in even the most thoroughly interpreted dream which has to be left obscure; this is because we become aware during the work of interpretation that at that point there is a tangle of dream-thoughts which cannot be unravelled and which moreover adds nothing to our knowledge of the content of the dream. This is the dream's navel, the spot where it reaches down into the unknown. The dream-thoughts to which we are led by interpretation cannot, by the nature of things, have any definite endings; they are bound to branch out in every direction into the intricate network of our world of thought. It is at some point where this meshwork is particularly close that the dream-wish grows up, like a mushroom of its mycelium. (SE, 5:515)[34]

In one sense this passage makes itself available to an internal critique of psychoanalysis: the dream resists interpretation, the tangle of dream-thoughts cannot be unraveled, indeed they apparently extend infinitely. In another sense, however, we can discern in this admission of limitation the means for sublating it. For whatever reason, perhaps because he was so concerned to show precisely that dreams were interpretable, Freud stays at the level of the individual dream; thus in this passage he talks about the "content of the dream." But as we have seen his metapsychology subverts the privileged status of the dream; on the one hand reducing it to merely another intermediate link in a derivative series, on the other connecting it to the dream-thoughts or "repressed representative" out of which it grows. We now see that these dream-thoughts are themselves indefinite, that they "branch out in every direction into the intricate network of our world of thought." In other words, we see that the psychical chains from repressed representatives overlap and connect, that they communicate with one another at nodal points through "switch-words" and "verbal bridges," that starting at any one point we can through a chain long or short arrive at any other point. In a word, the entire meshwork or latticework is of a piece; thus there is some justice in the arguments of skeptics to the effect that the ending of any associative chain in the process of dream interpretation is arbitrary, for in principle the chain is endless (short of death). Thus the series constituted by the dream-thoughts, dream, dream report and associations opens upon and finds its legitimation in this longer all-inclusive chain, each link of which likewise articulates a structuring conflict. I suggest that this chain represents nothing other than the intrapsychical precipitate of an individual's identity theme.

We have, of course, arrived at a theoretical level far removed from that of the metapsychology of dreams we took as our point of departure. Instead of being concerned with the interpretation of a single dream, or even of all the dreams of a single night, the present level must see all an individual's dreams as similarly deformed manifestations of some overarching structuring conflict. Nevertheless I believe Freud's theory legitimizes, even mandates, such an extension, for shearing the associative chain at any point would corrode it everywhere and result finally in making arbitrary any linkages that remained. Indeed, we might turn it around: Freud's discovery of the cohesiveness of the psychical chains alone legitimates and makes possible his interpretations of individual dreams; were he not so intent upon his monumental discovery of the latter, he might have explicitly recognized the full power of the discoveries that alone made it possible.

That power does not remain otherwise untapped, however. If in principle the chains of free associations lack "definite endings," this theoretical fluency rarely pertains within the consulting room. Patients stammer and hesitate; their associations end all too soon. At such moments Freud repeatedly invokes an interpretive rule:

> [Our] experience has shown us—and the fact can be confirmed as often as we please—that if a patient's free associations fail the stoppage can invariably be removed by an assurance that he is being dominated at the moment by an association which is concerned with the doctor himself or with something connected with him. As soon as this explanation is given, the stoppage is removed, or the situation is changed from one in which the associations fail into one in which they are being kept back. (SE, 12:101)[35]

In other words, the associations invariably fail during the moment the figure of the analyst himself is being assimilated into the meshwork. Freud comes to call this phenomenon "transference" and it eventually plays the crucial role in his understanding of the therapeutic process in psychoanalysis.

However, before turning to Freud's eventual usage of the term, I want to look back to its early history in his writings, for that history suggests an internal link, unlike that manifested in the above passage, between free association and transference. In chapter seven of *Interpretation* Freud uses the term while discussing how the day's residues come to play a role in the formation of dreams:

> We have not hitherto been able to explain the necessity for this addition to the mixture that constitutes a dream. . . . And it is only possible to do so if we bear firmly in mind the part played by the unconscious wish and then seek for information from the psychology of the neuroses. We learn from the latter that an unconscious idea is as such quite incapable of entering the preconscious and that it can only exercise any effect there by establishing a connection with an idea which already belongs to the preconscious, by transferring its intensity on to it and by getting itself "covered" by it. Here we have the fact of "transference," which provides an explanation of so many striking phenomena in the mental life of neurotics. . . . If we assume that the same need for transference on the part of repressed ideas which we have discovered in analyzing the neuroses is also at work in dreams, two of the riddles of the dream are solved at a blow: the fact, namely, that every analysis of a dream shows some recent impression woven into its texture and that this recent element is often of the most trivial kind. (SE, 5:562–63)

Here, then, Freud uses the word to describe the process through which the day's residues are assimilated into the associative chain, or alternatively, the process in which the "intensity" of the unconscious idea is displaced—the term Freud would subsequently use—onto the day's residues, their very triviality making them appropriate hosts. This aberrant usage of "transference" allows us to glimpse not only a similarity between it and displacement, but also between the day's residues and the figure of the analyst: as they are assimilated into the meshwork of the patient's associative chains, they become repositories of unconscious ideas, the passive instigators of the dream and transference respectively; only then do they fully attain meaning for the individual. If the assimilation of the analyst causes a blockage of the patient's associations, therefore, it does so only because in another way it represents the elongation of those very chains in another, now interpersonal form.

Four years earlier, in his portion of *Studies in Hysteria,* Freud had already used "transference" in a way that approaches what was in a few years to become the standard definition. Again, however, the differences are instructive. While discussing possible obstructions to the success of "cathartic analyses," Freud mentions an "external obstacle, and one not inherent in the material. This happens," he goes on, "when the patient's relation to the physician is disturbed, and it is the worst obstacle that we can come across" (SE, 2:301). Such disturbances have three causes: a form of personal estrangement, which can "easily be overcome by discussion and explanation" (SE, 2:302); a patient's fear that he or she is becoming excessively dependent upon the physician; and finally what he here calls "transference": this obstacle can arise if

> the patient is frightened at finding that she is transfering on to the figure of the physician the distressing ideas which arise from the content of the analysis. This is a frequent, and indeed in some analyses a regular occurrence. Transference on to the physician takes place through a *false connection*. . . . To begin with I was greatly annoyed at this increase in my psychological work, till I came to see that the whole process followed a law; and I then noticed, too, that transference of this kind brought about no great addition in what I had to do. . . . The patients, too, gradually learnt to realize that in these transferences on to the figure of the physician it was a question of a compulsion and an illusion which melted away with the conclusion of the analysis. (SE, 2:302, 304)

In light of Freud's subsequent usage, several comments seem in order. First, here transference is perceived as an occasional phenomenon and not, as later, one inherent to the therapeutic process. Second, we may note that when it first thrusts itself upon his attention, transference seemed the "worst obstacle" to therapeutic success, and that he greeted it with annoyance. Finally, Freud seems to assume at the time that the first two causes of a disturbed therapeutic relationship (personal estrangement, a fear of excessive dependence) have a "real" basis, one essentially unrelated to the "distressing ideas" developed in the analysis, whereas he would later of course see them as varieties of transference. This lingering emphasis upon the "real" appears again when he declares transference proper the result of a *"false connection,"* as if in the psychological realm he pioneers there are true connections. Nonetheless, to the extent *"false connection"* evokes the associative chain he was to investigate more thoroughly in chapter seven of *Interpretation,* the phrase usefully suggests that transference is an alternative figure for much the same phenomenon.

By the time of his next major discussion of this puzzling phenomenon, in the postscript to the Dora case, presumably written sometime between 1902 and 1905, Freud already recognized that transference was both an "inevitable necessity" (SE, 7:116) of therapy, not happenstance, and also, "if its presence can be detected in time," the "most powerful ally" (SE, 7:117) of psychoanalysis, not its worst obstacle. With these changes, which we must acknowledge come too late for a successful resolution of Dora's analysis, which in all likelihood emerged precisely from his attempt to understand that failure, comes what will henceforth be the classic definition of transference:

> What are transferences? They are new editions or facsimiles of the impulses and fantasies which are aroused and made conscious during the progress of the analysis; but they have this peculiarity, which is characteristic for their species, that they replace some earlier person by the person of the physician. To put it another way: a whole series of psychological experiences are revived, not as belonging to the past, but as applying to the person of the physician at the present moment. (SE, 7:116)[36]

In "The Dynamics of Transference" (1912) Freud further specifies the process. Through some interplay between constitutional factors and environmental influences, every person acquires "a specific method of his own in his conduct of his erotic life—that is, in the preconditions to falling in love which he lays down, in the instincts he satisfies and the aims he sets himself in the course of it. This produces what might be described as a stereotype plate (or several such), which is constantly repeated—constantly reprinted afresh—in the course of the person's life" (SE, 12:99–100). In the normal course of therapy the patient, who anticipates relief from this intercourse with the doctor and who has every reason to anticipate being grateful to the analyst, introduces the physician into the series already laid down according to the contours of his or her stereotype plate. The analyst does not hinder this development; in fact, Freud suggests that the analytic setting—patient on couch, analyst sitting, relatively silently, out of sight behind him—assists the development and isolation of the transference (SE, 12:134).

We need not concern ourselves here with the intricacies of the role that transference assumes in Freud's understanding of the therapeutic process. Suffice it to say that transference emerges as the very ground of psychoanalytic therapy.[37] Since the vagaries of the transference, as it oscillates between positive and negative phases, brings the past forward into the present and actualizes it in the terms of the relationship the patient seeks with the analyst, the "transference-neurosis" supersedes the patient's presenting problems. Working now with this new edition or reprinting of the illness that involves himself, the analyst utilizes the intensity of the transference "for the overcoming of resistances" (SE, 12:143), for continuing the rising to consciousness of the associative chain, in which the analyst is now embedded, and for evidencing for the patient the nature and persistence of his or her demands. Thus transference becomes the vehicle by which the analyst makes the unconscious conscious and thereby "transform[s] the pathogenic conflict into a normal one for which it must be possible somehow to find a solution" (SE, 16:435).

Without question, therefore, transference is a phenomenon engendered by the therapeutic project in psychoanalysis. However, Freud repeatedly insisted that transference was neither unique to psychoanalytic therapy nor even confined to a clinical context. Freud explicates the power of suggestion (SE, 12:106) and susceptibility to hypnosis (SE, 18:126) as unrecognized transference phenomena.[38] More crucially, as should already be apparent from the image of stereotype plates, over and over Freud declares that it "is a universal phenomenon of the human mind, it decides the success of all medical influence, and in fact *dominates the whole of each person's relations to his human environment*" (SE, 20:42, my emphasis). Thus in his "Observations on Transference-Love" (1915), Freud concedes that such affection "consists of new editions of old traits and that it repeats infantile reactions," but goes on to argue that it is no less genuine than "real" love for that, for such "is the essential character of every state of being in love. There is no such state which does not reproduce infantile prototypes" (SE, 12:168).[39] Thus transference in the clinical setting represents nothing other than the patient's assimilation of the figure of the analyst to the now long series of stereotypical relations he or she has established with significant other people.

If we accept this more inclusive understanding of transference's domain, we can no longer think that it "melts away" or "dissolves," figures Freud himself employs,[40] as therapy enters its terminal phases. Doing so would imply that analysis altogether liberates a patient from his or her past, shears the associative chain or splinters the stereotype plate, whereas we have seen Freud assert that all relationships are figured by earlier prototypes. Rather, what must happen during the course of an analysis is that the transference, as the patient consciously appropriates his or her previously unknown reasoning, becomes more flexible; now mediated by consciousness, the transference depends less directly upon infantile patterns, although it remains nonetheless bound by them.[41]

Freud's discussions of transference in this larger sense constitute for me nothing less than his anticipation of Lichtenstein's positions. Not only do they implicitly postulate the coherences of any individual's life, but they do so, as Lichtenstein will do, in interpersonal terms; the coherence resides not so much within individuals as within the ways they situate themselves vis-à-vis their worlds. Thus we cannot attribute the cohesion to consciousness, nor even locate it solipsistically within the somatic individual; it is an irreducibly relational phenomenon. What appears to be inherently individualistic—phenomena such as the associative chain that characterizes any person's mental processes—must be seen as precipitates of this interpersonal process.[42] Moreover, Freud too, although less systematically, derives this lifelong consistency ultimately from patterns laid down very early. We glimpse this when he discusses each individual's "specific method of his own in his conduct of his erotic life" which he images as a "stereotype plate," and again where he insists that all love relationships "reproduce infantile prototypes," but it emerges even more clearly in the final pages of *Three Essays on the Theory of Sexuality*, written at about the same time that Freud was coming to grips with transference in the postscript to the Dora case history. "The finding of an object," Freud declares, "is in fact a refinding of it" (SE, 7:222). That is, the vicissitudes of the mothering person-infant relation, which Freud insists has a sexual basis, lay down patterns that the infant will repeat in varying ways in his or her subsequent life. Although the "closer one comes to the deeper disturbances of psychosexual development, the more unmistakably the importance of incestuous object-choice emerges" (SE, 7:227), Freud does not equate them with illness, for "there can be no doubt that every object-choice whatever is based, though less closely, on these prototypes" (SE, 7:228). "There are thus good reasons why a child sucking at its mother's breast has become the prototype of every love relation" (SE, 7:222), for this is more than a piece of folk wisdom: the earliest patterns of relating do indeed persevere. Thus Heinz Lichtenstein's work represents a legitimate extrapolation of Freud's thought, an extension that Freud's corpus anticipates in most respects.

But finally I want to argue a stronger point: not just that Freud anticipates Lichtenstein, but that he must do so. Unless Freud postulates the achieved unity of the individual life—a unity that transcends the discriminations between conscious and unconscious, normal and pathological, subject and object, among ego, id, and superego—the entire psychoanalytic project founders. Thus the discovery of parallels between Freud and Lichtenstein is more than fortuitous, for these similarities exist at the level of the necessary groundings for the psychoanalytic enterprise. The postulation of the cohesive life is only a stronger form of (and logical conclusion to) Freud's discovery of the interrelations in the chain constituted by the dream-thoughts, dream, dream report and clustered associations. This discovery is the enabling moment of psychoanalytic interpretation, for without the systematic interplay along such a chain the meaning of any dream must remain either locked away or arbitrary. And such limited series are themselves enchained and therefore grounded in the longer series that is coextensive with the entire life. We have already seen Freud invoke that series when he connects phenomena from quite disparate spheres and periods of Schreber's life, such as his attitude toward Flechsig and his collapse during his wife's vacation. At that point the assumption may have seemed a heuristic convenience, but we are now in a position to see that it is much more than that: the cohesive life constitutes at once both the enabling ground of psychoanalysis and its most misperceived discovery.

4

We have seen that if pressed to its limits Freud's figure of the associative chain, the meshed ganglion of merged events, characters, and affects, reveals the notion of the cohesive life. Its formulation was the enabling moment of psychoanalysis both as a general psychology and as a therapeutic strategy. The famous fundamental rule of psychoanalytic therapy is designed precisely to permit the analyst and patient better access to this phenomenon. Much of the apparently desultory therapeutic action involves clarification as to the already constituted links along this chain: their content, their structure, their sequence, and crucially the means by which they are enchained. At other times, however, the attention shifts. When analyst and patient focus upon the fate of the day's residues in the formation of dreams, even more when they consider transference reactions, they take as their object the process by which the chains are constituted, by which new events become enmeshed in the associative network. As they do, two aspects of this process become clear. First, if the sequence of the associative chains is not that of mere temporality, not that of the chronicle or log, it is nonetheless true that they formed in time. Second, the associative chain emerges as the intrapsychic deposit or precipitate of the individual's engagement with his or her natural and social environment. We already possess a clinical illustration: if free associations fail, they do so at the juncture in which the figure of the analyst is being insinuated into the latticework. Actually, there is no proper stoppage; it is only that the patient is reluctant to divulge the next and latest link. In this instance the patient's relations with the analyst are the occasion for the elongation of the associative chain, but the example is paradigmatic: the associative chain is the product of relations that occur in time and must be understood in terms of those relations.

Beyond serving as the legitimation in Freud's own work for the interpretive assumption of the cohesive life, the figure of the associative chain suggests as well that the "psychoanalytic narrative" is the necessary interpretive mode of psychoanalysis. In a well-known aside in *Studies in Hysteria* Freud spoke almost apologetically about the similarities between these narratives and fictional stories:

> I have not always been a psychotherapist. Like other neurologists, I was trained to employ local diagnoses and electro-prognosis, and it still strikes me myself as strange that the case histories I write should read like short stories and that, as one might say, they lack the serious stamp of science. I console myself with the reflection that the nature of the subject is evidently responsible for this, rather than any preference of my own. (SE, 2:160)

The nature of the subject does indeed impose this necessity. As we saw in the previous chapter, "the core of the psychoanalytic explanation . . . lies in a general, over-all account of the patient's life history and 'life-style,' the peculiar modes and patterns of behavior which mark that history."[43] These narrative accounts are not spun out additively or ad hoc, extending understanding first to one action or belief and then to another and so on; rather, their logic is economically holistic, that is, they limn the cohesive pattern inscribed within the entire life. We are now in a position to understand the holistic aspirations of this interpretive strategy: they are grounded in nothing other than what Lichtenstein terms an individual's identity theme, or what Freud suggests in the figure of the associative chain. Within the therapeutic setting, the developing narrative attempts to render explicable the apparent anomalies, the gaps and contradictions, of the patient's initial recounting of his or her story by seeing them as more or less ineffectual transformations of a primal mode of relatedness. The cohesive life, therefore, is not so much a denial of the disjunctions with which psychoanalysis so obviously concerns itself as the structure within which they attain significance. The privileged gaps and contradictions exist at or in relation to the level of consciousness, whereas the notion of the cohesive life is proper to a highly abstract theoretical level; in no way does the latter represent a simple denial of the former. In fact, it permits our understanding of the former, for lacking some such notion, interpretation of the anomalies psychoanalysis takes as its subject would become ad hoc, even random (as alas it too frequently does).

Moreover, the very nature of the cohesive life as revealed in Lichtenstein's formulations or in Freud's figure of the associative chain dictates that its proper understanding take a narrative form. Because for both the subject has no existence apart from or prior to the series of relationships in which it is both constituted and constitutive, defined and defining, we can only grasp it through an understanding of these temporal relationships. Erikson acknowledges the importance of this social tissue when he chastizes his analytic colleagues for naively assuming that they can alter an individual's residence, background, and occupation in publishing case histories without substantive loss.[44] All these factors (and of course many more) play their roles in any individual's location of himself vis-à-vis his culture. Thus the explanatory narrative cannot treat the individual as though he or she exists in isolation, independent of time and place—a pure mathematical function; such a procedure would not only ignore the social formation of the individual, but would also necessarily misconstrue the profoundly relational nature of human existence.

Given the relational nature of the human subject, narrative is the appropriate interpretive mode in psychoanalysis. The interpretive narrative assumes the cohesion of the individual life; its task is the rendering of the terms and particular nature of that cohesion. The story it tells is the story of the subject's life as it develops through the relationships that constitute it. However we must not mistake the nature of this story. Like the associative chain, it is a story formed in time but not one necessarily dominated by pure seriality, one event after another. Nor is it the "true" or "real" story as we usually understand these terms, some diligent reconstruction of the actual events of the life. As we saw in chapter three, attributes drift forward and slip backward along the associative chain. This movement accounts for the coherence of the life, the linkages of the associative chain, but it also means that the original events are revised beyond recovery. Scenes are constructed along the lines of previous scenes; attributes and figures of subsequent events slip backward to cover original constructions; each link becomes a veritable palimpsest, rewritten time and again, so that no single inscription can be cleanly disengaged. We might say that psychoanalytic interpretations not only resemble literary stories in their narrative form, but as well in their concern with essentially fictive events. Since these transpositions are systematic, we need not despair. Each event in the associative chain initially represents the deposit of a relationship; subsequent revisions are the markings of other relationships perceived to be analogous in some ways. By attending to the series of relationships mentioned—to his posture within them, his characteristic expectations and fears, his choice of objects—relationships that are in fact constitutive of the subject, one can begin unpacking an individual's crabbed, fictive history. Such is the truth of Freud's monumental discovery of transference. And that is the case even, as with Schreber, when these relationships are clearly delusional.

5 : The Unsure Prophet Remembers

It is the explanation of things that we make to ourselves that discloses our character: the subjects of one's poems are the symbols of one's self or one of one's selves.[1]

. . . The unsure // egotist is not / good for himself.[2]

Freud himself sanctions our reinterpretation of Schreber's *Memoirs of My Nervous Illness.* The brief postscript, added the year after the initial publication, begins this way:

> In dealing with the case history of Senatspräsident Schreber I purposely restricted myself to a minimum of interpretation; and I feel confident that every reader with a knowledge of psychoanalysis will have learned from the material which I presented more than was explicitly stated by me, and that he will have found no difficulty in drawing the threads closer and in reaching conclusions at which I no more than hinted. (SE, 12:80)

Immediately thereafter Freud initiates this interpretive accretion, for he adds to the original essay a brief discussion of the possible symbolic significance of Schreber's favored relationship with the sun, drawing upon mythological parallels that had recently come to his attention. In fact, I would argue that in a real sense "Psychoanalytic Notes on an Autobiographical Account of a Case of Paranoia (Dementia Paranoides)" does not offer an interpretation of Schreber's *Memoirs* at all. We must take Freud's title seriously; these are notes toward an interpretation he did not write. I sense that Freud's enthusiasm for *Memoirs* resides chiefly in the opportunity the volume affords him to present a segment of his evolving psychology—the theory of paranoia—to the psychoanalytic community. However exactly insofar as theory concerns Freud, the case history recedes in importance and completeness, for as we saw in chapter three, asymmetry characterizes their relationship. Thus in the most confidently titled section of the essay, "The Mechanisms of Paranoia," Schreber is mentioned only incidentally; he becomes the interchangeable illustration of a theoretical argument. His very expendability here signals his true role in Freud's essay, a role inconsistent with the subject of a case history, who must hold the center of attention, not the periphery. In what follows, then, I reverse the proportions of Freud's seminal essay; that is, I shall place Schreber's *Memoirs* at the center of attention and shall turn to some theoretical issues that the interpretation raises only in my Epilogue.

1

We live in a time when the term "paranoia" has become nigh inescapable. It has been used to characterize those entrenched in power, those who consciously oppose them, those others, huddled at the corner tavern, who find themselves estranged from both the powers-that-be and those that would-be. Following the "triumph of the therapeutic," which transforms all issues into a resolutely psychological dimension, paranoia has become the ultimate put-down, or alternatively, a badge of honor, a sign of special grace. Thus when I first read *Memoirs of My Nervous Illness* in the early years of the seventies the expectations I brought were shaped by much more than my reading of Freud; in particular, I braced myself for long, hateful harangues, because a freely floating rage seemed the common denominator of the various conceptions of paranoia. Whether we turn to Freud or to Pynchon and Hunter Thompson, a psychiatric textbook like *The Paranoid* or a novel like *A Fan's Notes*, we find rabidness given a definitive place. *Memoirs* did not altogether disappoint this expectation, but as we shall see, Schreber's anger characteristically takes a curious form.

Schreber does tell us about several fights that erupted between him and other inmates or attendants. He felt that the senior attendant at Pierson's asylum, whom he calls von W., submitted him to innumerable indignities. In revenge Schreber once addressed him simply as W., "thereby insulting him by omitting his title"; later he took physical retribution, although disavowing any eagerness to do so: "On a later occasion I even boxed his ears; I cannot remember my immediate incentive, but I do know that, as he had made some unfair demand on me, the voices challenged and mocked me for my apparent lack of manly courage until at last I struck him" (M, 108). When he feared being forsaken, abused sexually and then left to rot, the inner voices whispered that "it was [his] duty to fight now and then to prove [his] manly courage" (M, 76).

In all Schreber recalls ten or twelve such incidents (M, 161), which, if we can trust his account, does not reflect any extraordinary combativeness. He gives each physical expression of violence similar characteristics. First, he initially finds himself an innocent victim. "In all instances concerning other *patients,*" Schreber assures his readers, "I was always the attacked party" (M, 161). As for the staff, they constantly provoked him, submitting him to harassments no man could simply ignore. Thus Schreber's violence is always secondary, a form of justified retribution. Even so, second, he rarely claims responsibility for these justified reactions; his constant companions, the voices, generally suggest such defenses of his manly honor. This yet again distances Schreber from his own hostility: not only do others always provoke and earn his rage, but also it only appears at the goading of the voices. The voices thus occupy a curious position in that they join Schreber's attendants in determining his actions, yet urge his defense of the very manly honor they constantly violate. Finally, according to Schreber, these scenes of violence occurred only in the past. Writing sometime in 1900 he tells us that the last of these physical confrontations "took place on the 5th of March 1898" (M, 161), thereby distancing himself in a third way from his own rage.

Judging from *Memoirs* and the appended legal documents by Dr. Weber, the director of Sonnenstein sanatorium, by 1900 Schreber only acted belligerently toward nonhuman agents, and then only verbally. Weber described Schreber's "bellowing very loudly at the sun . . . threats and imprecations . . . that she [i.e., the sun] was afraid of him, and that she had to hide from him the *Senatspräsident* Schreber. . . . Or he raved in his room . . . , harangued for some time the 'soul murderer' Flechsig, repeated endlessly 'little Flechsig,' putting heavy accent on the first word" (M, 269). Surely *Memoirs* documents Schreber's rage at the God whose emblem is the sun, but again this is not simple malignancy. *Memoirs* presents a Job-like Schreber whose God has used him harshly. And although the miracles that plague his every minute have of late become less terrifying, Schreber reports that he is "often forced in self-defense to *mock* God with a loud voice; [he] simply [has] to do this at times to convince that distant place which tortures [him] . . . that one is not dealing with a dement, but with a human being in full command of the situation" (M, 238). Again the language diminishes Schreber's responsibility for these tirades, suggests he has no recourse—he is "forced." Moreover, while unraveling the "symbolic meaning" of the miracles that hinder his every attempt to defecate, Schreber concludes that anyone "who entered into a special relationship to divine rays as [he has] is to a certain extent entitled to sh—— *[sic]* on all the world" (M, 177). The souls of Flechsig and von W. and God now absorb the full impact of Schreber's hostility, but it is only verbal, and fully justified. Thus again Schreber muffles his rage, for as he lifts it into an extraterritorial dimension, he largely spares those about him from his scornful reproaches.

However this shift is more apparent than real. Schreber still rants against significant persons, but his deprecations take a persistent form. He no sooner criticizes someone than he takes it away, repetitively denying that he intends any reproach, that he harbors any spite. In the course of *Memoirs of My Nervous Illness* the figure of disavowed criticism swells to a virtual litany: "Naturally nothing is further from my mind than to wish to denounce the attendant M. or any other attendant to his superiors by relating the indignities I had to suffer" (M, 131); "In writing these lines I do not mean to recriminate about the past" (M, 147); "I repeat that I do not wish to raise any complaints about the past" (M, 161); "It will be appreciated that I do not wish in any way to attack the honor of the living Professor Flechsig" (M, 243); "As I write this sentence *I do not want to offend the medical specialist in the least; I do not doubt at all that his report was given in good faith*" (M, 286); "Nothing in these words is meant as a reproach for the treatment I received earlier on in the Asylum" (M, 297); "I close by repeating the hope that the medical expert will not take any of my statements amiss, as I have no intention whatever of offending him or denying him the high respect which is his due" (M, 313).

The very repetition of such negations suggests powerful necessities. Not only must rageful recriminations be constantly with Schreber as he re-creates his experiences while writing *Memoirs,* but he also seemingly writes under a prohibition against such feelings. He simply refuses to own any bad will toward his fellow humans, no matter how justified, as if aggression were somehow taboo. His apparent tolerance and forgiveness are saintly. But the denials rarely convince me, and not only because their very repetition makes me suspect that like the Player Queen he protests too much. The erasures are never quite complete, and resentment leaks through the surrounding sentences. Thus they only succeed in transforming Schreber's earlier pugnacity into a covert resentment that requires our elaboration precisely because of his strenuous denials of its very existence. To demonstrate this persistent "return of the repressed," let us look carefully at "The Open Letter to Professor Flechsig" that prefaces *Memoirs.*

Schreber originally wrote Flechsig privately asking for whatever confirmation his former physician could provide for the theories and happenings in *Memoirs,* but the final paragraph shows that even then Schreber planned to publish the letter as a preface to the book. Schreber recognizes that parts of the book may pain or embarrass Flechsig; he regrets the necessity of such inclusions and quickly disavows any harmful intent: "In any case it is far from me to attack your honor, as indeed *I do not harbor any personal grievance against any person*" (M, 33), much less against Flechsig himself. Besides, *Memoirs* contains revelations Schreber believes of some moment for mankind; he trusts, accordingly, that Flechsig possesses the "courage of truth" (M, 35) to nudge him beyond personal considerations and to extend the scientist's validation to his former patient's discoveries.

The letter presents Schreber with a delicate rhetorical exercise. He must harmonize his respect for Flechsig the scientist, from whom he now seeks support, with his knowledge of the role Flechsig indisputably played in the calamities he yet suffers. "For years," he writes, "I have pondered how to reconcile these facts with my respect for your person, *whose integrity and moral worth I have not the least right to doubt*" (M, 34). The wording suggests that, rightly or not, Schreber is not altogether sure of Flechsig's integrity and moral worth, but he does refrain from outright denunciation of his former physician. He solves this predicament through a remarkable dissociation. In the first place, Schreber's communication with supernatural powers undoubtedly began due to *"influences on* [his] *nervous system emanating from* [Flechsig's] *nervous system"* (M, 34). How? Schreber hypothesizes at some length:

> I think it is possible that you—at first I am quite prepared to believe [but do not quite?] only for therapeutic purposes—carried on some hypnotic, suggestive, or whatever else one could call it, contact with my nerves, *even while we were separated in space.* During this contact you might suddenly have realized that other voices were speaking to me as well, pointing to a supernatural origin. Following this surprising realization you might have continued this contact with me for a time out of scientific interest, until you yourself felt as it were uneasy about it, and therefore decided to break it off. But it is possible that in this process a part of your own nerves—probably unknown to yourself—was removed from your body, a process explicable only in a supernatural manner, and ascended to heaven as a "tested soul" and there achieved some

> supernatural power. This "tested soul" . . . then simply allowed itself to be driven by the impulse of ruthless self-determination and lust for power, without any restraint by something comparable to the moral will power of man. . . . (M, 34)

This extraordinary chain of suppositions almost absolves Flechsig himself of responsibility for Schreber's suffering. He now sees the disembodied tested soul, not the good doctor whose moral worth he has no right to doubt, as the agent of his suffering. If all this somehow proves true, Schreber writes to Flechsig, "there would then be no need to cast any shadow upon your person. . . ." But the absolution is not complete, for this sentence continues by negating its initial negation: "the only mild reproach would perhaps remain that you, like so many doctors, could not completely resist the temptation of using a patient in your care *as an object for scientific experiments* apart from the real purpose of cure" (M, 34). Moreover, it is only probable that some nerves severed themselves from his nervous system without Flechsig's knowledge. The very elaborateness of the above quotation testifies to Schreber's present need to absolve Flechsig of responsibility, but despite such baroque reasoning, and notwithstanding his alleged respect, ambivalence yet riddles the "Open Letter." Open animosity now considerably discomforts Schreber; we do not find here any of the open ridicule and rancor that Weber reported to the court in 1899 (M, 269) and that characterizes much of the text itself, written more than two years earlier. Nonetheless his harsh fate still rankles Schreber, and he cannot altogether put aside his resentment, however much it unsettles him.

Much earlier, in writing *Memoirs*, Schreber partially attenuates Flechsig's responsibility through another maneuver. In chapter two Schreber conjectures that the Order of the World's miraculous structure was rent by some conflict, perhaps initiated more than a hundred years previously, between the Schreber and Flechsig families. Presumably

> a bearer of the name Flechsig—a human being carrying that name—succeeded in *abusing* nerve-contact granted him for the purpose of divine inspiration or some other reasons, in order *to retain his hold on the divine rays*. . . . It seems very probable that contact with divine nerves was granted to a person who specialized in nervous illnesses, partly because he would be expected to be a highly intellectual person, partly because everything concerning human nerves must be of particular interest to God, starting with His

instinctive knowledge that an increase of *nervousness* among men could endanger his realms. (M, 56)

Again the conjectures pile up dizzily, but their general direction should now be clear. In this version, written perhaps two full years before the Open Letter, Schreber attenuates the guilt of his physician in other ways. The initial villain here remains a human agent, not a disembodied soul, but he remains nameless, anonymous except for his patronym. More crucially, Schreber effects this absolution by removing the instigating events into some misty past, long before the births of him and his physician. Thus Professor Paul Flechsig could not have initiated the conditions contrary to the Order of the World. That safely established, Schreber replicates for the distant past conditions that probably existed for the present Flechsig—indeed, that parallel the constructions of the Open Letter. Again however Schreber spares the physician, now not through the creation of an autonomous soul but rather by displacing these events into an immunizing past.

I could pile up examples as dizzily as Schreber offers conjectures—his attitude toward his God in particular is richly ambivalent—but my central point should now be clear. Yes, Schreber's *Memoirs* display the enmity we expect of those called paranoid. However, Schreber's rancor takes a characteristic, perhaps unexpected form. Freud's brilliant transformations of the paranoid's needs, deriving "I do not *love* him—I *hate* him, because *he persecutes me*" from an initial "*I* (a man) *love him* (a man)" (SE, 12:63), suggest an open, unqualified animosity. Indeed, the very derivative status of the hostility, the fact that it must decisively negate an unexpressible longing, should guarantee a propulsive expression. Yet precisely here, Schreber, whom Freud's essay transforms into the exemplary case, swerves significantly from the paradigm. Schreber cringes before his own anger, denying its existence with a force equaled only by its demand for expression. Thus Schreber articulates hostility only covertly, although he can never mask its presence by more than periodic denials whose very contexts easily subvert them. Whatever his precautions, he cannot clot its seeping into *Memoirs*.

We have evidence from Dr. Weber and Schreber himself that this reticence has not always been the case. He had previously resisted the attendants with brute force and contemptuously jeered at his God and "little" Flechsig. He writes: "Later on I desisted from all opposition because it led to senseless scenes of violence; I kept silent and suffered" (M, 131). That is, his open rancor undergoes a fate comparable to that theoretically reserved for a paranoid's homosexual longings. Why has Schreber's hostility become relatively mute? Why can it now only insert itself into the text sideways, as it were? After all, although most of us shy away from the full force of our possible aggressiveness, we can own it partially, intermittently. But Schreber rarely can. What personal strictures prohibit this moderate course, what seemingly necessitates this complete disavowal? Such questions are crucial to any understanding of Schreber's *Memoirs of My Nervous Illness.* Before we can tender possible answers, however, we must investigate the reasons Schreber offers for his anger, the nature of the presumed indignities he has suffered.

2

I suspect we should begin with Schreber's most famous complaint, namely, that he has been the victim of an attempted soul murder. This notion has achieved something of an autonomous existence. It figures prominently as the title of Schatzman's book, as a literary metaphor in Mark Smith's *The Death of the Detective,* as a psychological concept offered by Leonard Shengold for general usage.[3] For all its notoriety, however, the specifics of soul murder remain troublesomely vague, not the least because the two censored passages in *Memoirs of My Nervous Illness* promised revelatory material. At one point, for instance, just when Schreber seems set to offer the full extent of his own ruminations, we read: "Apart from these hints I cannot enlarge on the essential nature of soul murder or, so to speak, its technique. One might only add (the passage which follows is unfit for publication)" (M, 58). This indeterminacy warrants caution, for I doubt we can reconstruct in any detail this, Schreber's most famous, grievance. Nonetheless, *Memoirs* offers enough suggestions for us to apprehend its "essential nature," as Schreber puts it.

In chapter two, written in early 1900, Schreber makes attempted soul murder causally significant to the upsetting of his personal fate. He initially elaborates the idea of soul murder by making recourse to various folkways and literature, in much the way Freud seeks validation for symbolism: "To start with [soul murder]: the idea is widespread in the folklore and poetry of all peoples that it is somehow possible to take possession of another person's soul in order to prolong one's life at another soul's expense, or to secure some other advantages which outlast death" (M, 55). Because such legends are so widespread, Schreber reasons "it is hardly likely that such ideas could have been formed by so many peoples without any basis in fact" (M, 55). Moreover, the voices that incessantly talk to Schreber stress "the fact that the crisis that broke upon the realms of God was caused by somebody having *committed soul murder*" (M, 55); this is an unimpeachable authority—the testimony of the voices alone puts the existence of the act beyond reasonable doubt.

The situation immediately becomes more confusing, however. Schreber cannot isolate the original instigator; perhaps it was Flechsig, but the voices have recently whispered Schreber's own name; perhaps something happened between earlier generations of these families that "amounted to [but was not?] soul murder"; perhaps it occurred in "a battle arising out of jealousy between souls already departed from life" (M, 55). Indeterminacy reigns; we have now returned a second time to what I can only take as Schreber's half-hearted exculpation of his physician: some other Flechsig, at some much earlier time, must have originated the concatenated events that now embroil Schreber. Having glimpsed the supernatural, Flechsig's ancestor, perhaps out of "keen scientific interest, . . . may then have tried to influence the nerves of his contemporaries by exerting his will power after the fashion of thought readers . . . and he may thus have found that this was possible to a certain extent" (M, 57). A conspiracy may then have arisen years before between this Flechsig and some dissolute souls posed against the Schreber family. Perhaps all this occurred unknown to god, or maybe he underestimated the potential threat it harbored to the very existence of his realms. Thus "it may have come about that one did not immediately and resolutely oppose efforts inspired by ambition and lust for power, which could possibly lead to soul murder—if such a thing exist—that is to say to the surrender of a soul to another person perhaps for prolonging earthly life, for appropriating his mental powers, for attaining a kind of personal immunity or some other advantage" (M, 58).[4] This passage doubly attenuates the actual occurrence of soul murder. The conspiracy could only "possibly lead" to soul murder; more crucially, he parenthetically opens to doubt the very existence of such a phenomenon. At this point the perpetrator, victim, time, and place, even the very crime itself, are all in doubt.

In the "Open Letter," written in March 1903, approximately

three years after the second chapter, Schreber deepens the uncertainty. As we have seen, at first Professor Flechsig seems the perpetrator, thus dissolving the historical maze in which the crime becomes lost in *Memoirs.* In fact, Schreber's scenario here repeats that offered in the second chapter, but this time it involves his physician. As we have seen, however, the onus quickly shifts to a mysteriously created tested soul: "It is possible therefore," writes Schreber, "that all those things which in earlier years I erroneously thought I had to blame you for—particularly the definite damaging effects on my body—are to be blamed only on that 'tested soul' " (M, 34). But Schreber again goes on to call the status of soul murder into question; it may be pure hyperbole:

> One might even raise the question whether perhaps all the talk of voices about somebody having committed soul murder can be explained by the souls (rays) deeming it impermissible that a person's nervous system should be influenced by another's to the extent of imprisoning his will power, such as occurs during hypnosis; in order to stress forcefully that this was a malpractice it was called "soul murder," the souls for lack of a better term, using a term already in current usage, and because of their innate tendency to express themselves hyperbolically. (M, 34—35)

Perhaps the entire episode reduces to a verbal misunderstanding, a poverty of language.

Or does it? Of course painfully little is stable in all this; as version replaces version their very succession can seem our only constant. The persons involved, the timing, the scene are all clothed in doubt. If we look again, however, we can discern another constant, the exclusivity of which lends it authority. Whenever Schreber approaches the "essential nature" of soul murder we find phrases such as "imprisoning his [the victim's] will power," "take possession of another person's soul," "the surrender of a soul to another person," or "he . . . tried to influence the nerves of his contemporaries by exerting his will power after the fashion of thought readers." Simply, the issue seems to be one of self-determination. That is, the crime involves the usurpation of another's autonomy, the malevolent, self-serving appropriation of another's rights. This converts the victim into a mere pawn, just as in Schreber's muted accusation against Flechsig that he, "like so many doctors, could not completely resist the temptation of using a patient in [his] care *as an object for scientific experiments* apart from the real purpose of cure" (M, 34). So if in 1903 Flechsig no longer stands explicitly condemned as the perpetrator of soul murder upon Schreber, he still has hypnotized him, stiill treated him as an object for scientific experiments. But the accusations are not erased, for soul murder and hypnotism are identical: they equally deprive the subject of the possibility of self-determination, place him in helpless thrall to the will of another. Whatever else it may be, then, whatever specific form it takes, for Schreber soul murder encompasses an irreducible relationship—the violation of one individual's autonomy by another.[5] Interpreted in this way, soul murder becomes a paradigm for the long litany of grievances Schreber forcefully presents. Again and again his sufferings reveal themselves as various transformations of this radical complaint: another's usurpation of his will.

The miracles enacted upon Schreber's body demonstrate this infringement of autonomy most clearly. Although he confesses that his limited knowledge of anatomy may introduce incidental errors into his descriptions (M, 132 n), Schreber cannot doubt that the miracles have compromised the integrity of his body. At one time or another he has had a different heart; felt the lobes of his lungs absorbed, perhaps by lung worms; occasionally had his ribs smashed; lived without a stomach, or with "a very inferior so-called 'Jew's stomach' " (M, 133); had putrid matter ruthlessly thrown into his stomach; even had his skull temporarily thinned, a miracle effected "through the bony material of [his] skull being partly pulverized by the destructive action of the rays" (M, 136). Besides these more serious threats, the miracles also compromise Schreber's autonomy in lesser, but still annoying ways. Whenever he plays the piano or writes, for instance, "attempts are made to paralyze [his] fingers" (M, 136). Even his eyelids are constantly assailed by miracles:

> [Attempts] were made early on and kept up throughout the past years, to close my eyes against my will, so as to rob me of visual impressions and thus preserve the rays' destructive power. This phenomenon can be observed on me at almost every moment; whoever watches carefully will observe that my eyelids suddenly droop or close even while I am talking to other people; this never occurs in human beings under natural conditions. In order to keep my eyes open nevertheless, a great effort of will is needed. . . . (M, 137)

From the critical to the mundane, therefore, these bodily miracles compromise the integrity of Schreber's physical being. Every moment of every day he feels his physical autonomy usurped and himself threatened by being transformed from a purposeful individual to the hapless plaything of inimical supernatural forces. Only extraordinary efforts of will preserve whatever shreds of dignity and autonomy he retains.

Of course the most justly famous bodily miracle Schreber must endure is his unmanning or gradual transformation into a woman. As discussed in the second chapter, Schreber construes unmanning as a process consonant with the Order of the World. In that miraculous structure it exists as a possibility in case "moral decay" (M, 72), nervousness, or some other catastrophe necessitates the destruction of the human race. "In such an event," Schreber writes, "in order to maintain the species, one single human being was spared—perhaps the relatively most moral—called by the voices that talk to me the *'Eternal Jew.'*... The Eternal Jew... had to be *unmanned*... to be able to bear children" (M, 73). A prodigious sleep would effect this transformation during which "fleeting-improvised-men" would attend the body of the expectant mother.

However, just as the supposedly attentive fleeting-improvised-men have degenerated into Schreber's tormentors, in the conditions contrary to the Order of the World that exist, the regenerative purposes of unmanning may have been perverted in Schreber's case. His nerves attract divine rays and as they are absorbed into his body its soul-voluptuousness and unmanning proceed apace. Thus began a "*policy of vacillation* in which attempts to cure [Schreber's] nervous illness alternated with efforts to annihilate [him] as a human being who, because of his ever-increasing nervousness, had become a danger to God Himself" (M, 75). Schreber conjectures that one countermeasure involved a plot, perhaps initiated in March or April 1894 (that is, five or six months after his commitment). Here is Schreber's reading of the supposed conspirators' intentions:

> [The] purpose... was to hand me over to another human being after my nervous illness had been recognized as, or assumed to be, incurable, in such a way that my soul was handed to him, but my body—transformed into a female body and, misconstruing the above-described fundamental tendency of the Order of the World—was then left to that human being for sexual misuse and simply "forsaken," in other words left to rot. (M, 75)

Flechsig's soul, some dissolute rays, and perhaps his very god thus conspire a multiple invasion of Schreber's autonomy. Not only will his unmanning shatter his bodily integrity but, emasculated, his body will be forcefully "prostituted like that of a female harlot" (M, 99), and eventually killed. When Schreber first recognized this "abominable intention," his "whole sense of manliness and manly honor, [his] entire moral being, rose up against it" (M, 76), just as more mundanely he resolutely forced open his miraculously closed eyes. At every level, therefore, from the most commonplace to the most important, Schreber feels that his own nerves are influenced externally, often against his own will, by Flechsig, some divine rays, even his God. "This influence," he reports, "has in the course of years assumed forms more and more contrary to the Order of the World and to man's natural right to be master of his own nerves" (M, 69–70). These influences manifest a constant, insidious assault upon his "natural rights." In that sense, at least, they replicate the central issue of soul murder, for they provide an image of an embattled Schreber courageously and rightfully resisting the purportedly hostile forces arrayed against him, all of which represent grave threats to his integrity, physical and moral alike.

Despite his lively appreciation of the gravity of these dangers, especially of the conspiracy to forsake him, Schreber reserves a special intensity for his accounts of compulsive thinking. Understanding this miracle requires that we recall from the second chapter two facts about Schreber's God. First, normally contact exists between souls and Schreber's God only after death, for no danger then exists that their nervousness will endanger Him. Second, "God cannot learn by experience"; consequently, *"Every attempt at an educative influence directed outwards must be given up as hopeless"* (M, 155). Because God generally deals only with dead souls, and because, further, He is mysteriously uneducable, it follows, reasons Schreber, that He cannot comprehend the human condition.

A variation on the conspiracy to forsake Schreber is God's subsequent intention to destroy his reason. This in itself holds dangers for Schreber, but when combined with God's ignorance of the human condition unexpected complications arise. In His ignorance Schreber's God apparently believes that Schreber is demented whenever His nervous victim relaxes mentally, whenever he gives himself "up to thinking nothing"; then all matter of nonsense immediately starts so that God can safely withdraw from His reluctant host. Says Schreber: "Every time my thinking activity ceases God instantly regards my mental powers as extinct, the desired destruction of my reason (the 'dementia') achieved and the possibility of a withdrawal thus brought about" (M, 166). To avoid the miraculous interferences, which divert Schreber's attention and so ease God's withdrawal (M,

128), Schreber is compelled to keep his mind as active as possible.

Several miracles conspire to deprive Schreber of the necessary relaxation; we need mention only a representative sample. One is the famous talking birds Freud analyzes in his essay; another Schreber calls the *"system of not-finishing-a-sentence."* Since the nature of nerves demands that fragmentary utterances be lifted to meaning, when the rays vibrate his nerves to produce unfinished ideas, his mind has "to supplement to make up sense" (M, 172). This system had a double aim; not only did it constantly test Schreber's mind but it also slowed the rays' dissolution in his body, for it appears that, like soul-voluptuousness, " 'intellectual deliberation' " (M, 173)—even the uttering of a grammatically complete sentence—would cause the rays to be led straight to Schreber's body.

The nigh inhuman demand that he think constantly deprives Schreber of even the possibility of mental relaxation. Perhaps drawing on his experience with the law, he repeatedly denounces compulsive thinking as a violation of his basic human rights: "The nature of compulsive thinking lies in a human being having to think incessantly; in other words, man's natural right to give the nerves of his mind their necessary rest from time to time by thinking nothing (as occurs most markedly during sleep) was from the beginning denied me" (M, 70);[6] it "contravenes man's natural right to mental relaxation, of temporary rest from mental activity through thinking nothing, or as the expression goes in the basic language, it disturbs the 'basis' of a human being" (M, 171–72). To give us a better idea of this pernicious condition Schreber resorts to a graphic metaphor:

> One can only get an idea of the *enormous infringement of man's most primitive rights* which compulsive thinking constitutes and of how my patience was tested beyond all human conception, when one pictures a human being behaving to another human being in human language in the way that rays behave to me to this day in the nerve language. Imagine a human being planting himself before another and molesting him all day with unconnected phrases such as the rays use towards me. . . . Can one expect anything else of a person spoken to in this manner but that he would throw the other out of the house with a few fitting abuses? I also ought to have the right of being master in my own head against the intrusion of strangers. (M, 175 n)

This passage admirably sums up the concerns we have thus far traced. Most obviously, it demonstrates Schreber's anger and resentment, but it articulates them abstractly, as a general proposition, thereby characteristically rendering them covert. Moreover, the passage locates the source of Schreber's anger in a perceived infringement of his autonomy, his basic rights, in his frustration at not being master of his own head.

3

As we have seen, then, compulsive thinking deprives Schreber of easement. He desperately needs to relax, but compulsive thinking and like miracles deny him the necessary opportunities. In this way compulsive thinking provides linkage between infringed autonomy and another complex of issues that pervade *Memoirs of My Nervous Illness,* the anomalous stance toward passivity. We shall concentrate on three more or less parallel issues: his catatonic period, his perceptions of sleep's role in his illness and his increasing soul-voluptuousness.

Schreber dates his catatonic period in the summer or autumn of 1894 (M, 145), shortly after his transfer to Sonnenstein, more than six months after he was institutionalized. He describes his outward condition this way: "Apart from daily morning and afternoon walks in the garden, I mainly sat *motionless* the whole day on a chair at my table, did not even move towards the window, where by the way nothing was to be seen except green trees . . . ; even in the garden I preferred to remain seated always in the same spot, and was only occasionally urged by the attendants to walk about, really against my will" (M, 127). Although conditions then offered him scant opportunity for usefully occupying his time—most possessions were scrupulously locked away, so he had no writing materials and few books—this poverty did not account for his immobility. Schreber says he willed such behavior; he writes, "I considered absolute passivity almost a religious duty" (M, 127).

The reasons quickly lead back to God's ignorance of living humans: "That rays could ever expect me to remain totally immobile ("not the slightest movement" was an often-repeated slogan), must again be connected I am convinced, with God not knowing how to treat a living human being. . . . Thus arose the almost monstrous demand that I should behave continually as if I myself were a corpse . . ." (M, 127). Thus far the catatonia seems another of the cruel chain of necessities imposed upon Schreber, another "monstrous demand" that violates his autonomy. When Schreber returns to the subject after a brief excursus, however, the situation considerably alters. "I considered the immobility demanded from me," writes Schreber, "a duty incumbent on me both in the interests of self-preservation and of God, so as to liberate Him from the embarrassment in which He found Himself owing to the 'tested souls' " (M, 128–29). Thus, although Schreber still feels immobility a duty incumbent upon him, he consciously fulfills this obligation rather than finding it an altogether alien invasion of his autonomy. He explains that he had come to think that rays would be destroyed if he moved, and since he then had no certainty about eternity, he "considered it [his] task to prevent any squandering of rays as far as was in [his] power" (M, 129). Moreover, he then thought that immobility would facilitate his absorption into his body of the "tested souls," thereby restoring God's heavenly supremacy: "I therefore made the almost incredible sacrifice of desisting from every movement and of course from every occupation for several weeks and months, the conversation of voices excepted; this went so far that not even at night did I dare change my position in bed, because the spending of tested souls was to be expected mostly during sleep" (M, 129).

From other passages in *Memoirs* we can glean the means by which Schreber's catatonia was calculated to draw down the tested souls: soul-voluptuousness. The above passage tells us that sleep aided his absorption of the tested souls; we learn elsewhere that soul-voluptuousness was especially strong when he was in bed, for then "it requires only a little exertion of my imagination to attain such sensuous pleasure as gives a pretty definite foretaste of female sexual enjoyment" (M, 201). Of course in 1894 he did not consciously await such pleasures avidly, indeed he says he found them repugnant; rather he was then hoping to reestablish the Order of the World, initially violated by these same tested souls, and obtain through sleep a complete cure of his nervousness. One night—he dates it in July 1894, during his catatonic period—he almost succeeded: through "immense mental effort" (M, 118) he drew down all tested souls, but God, already vacillating in his attitude toward Schreber, failed to provide a " 'covering with ray' " necessary to complete the restitution. Thereafter Flechsig's soul, which, unlike God, could learn from experience, instituted *"mechanical fastening"* and finally "tying-to-celestial-bodies" (M, 118) to counteract the increasing attractiveness of Schreber's feminized body.

These elaborations reverse Schreber's original statement (a common enough occurrence in *Memoirs,* and a potent block to our task). What initially appears to be yet another imposition upon Schreber, yet another cruel violation of his will, soon stands revealed as a possibly willed, motivated action. Rather than being the plaything of an idle and rather dissolute divinity, Schreber now asks that we view him as an agent attempting nothing less than that very God's release from the bondage of their common enemy. The altered perception of Schreber likewise transforms our perception of the act itself. What his physicians and attendants might have justly perceived as the inactivity of a "stuporose dullard" (M, 130), he asserts is more a reasoned immobility achieved by an "almost incredible sacrifice" (M, 129).

To discuss Schreber's catatonic period I have found it necessary to make references to his equally complicated attitudes toward both sleep and soul-voluptuousness. Long familiarity with *Memoirs of My Nervous Illness* leads me to suspect that catatonia, sleep, and soul-voluptuousness form an interconnected series. Thus we must turn to these latter phenomena for insight into the contradictions apparently inherent in Schreber's description of his brief catatonic phase.

From the very beginning sleep plays a critical role for Schreber. We recall that the earliest manifestations he recalls of his approaching illness were several dreams. Some prophesied the return of his earlier illness; another, even more repellent, insinuated "the idea that it really must be rather pleasant to be a woman succumbing to intercourse" (M, 63). When he takes up his new duties as *Senatspräsident* he "overtaxed [himself] mentally," which resulted in insomnia just "at the very moment when [he] was able to feel that [he] had largely mastered the difficulties of settling down in [his] new office and in [his] new residence" (M, 64). When nothing seemed to help he sought Professor Flechsig, whom his wife credited with the cure of his first breakdown. Flechsig reassured his badly rattled patient; among other things, he "gave [Schreber] hope of delivering [himself] of the whole illness through one prolific sleep" (M, 65). Although this immediate cure proves elusive, in the midst of his delusions Schreber long clings to the hope that a prodigious sleep could deliver him of his illness. However, miracles continually frustrated such a "cure by a complete calming of my nerves through sleep" (M, 117), for the tested souls resisted his return to health as a threat to their very existence. *"In other words,"* Schreber at one point summarizes, *"right from the beginning the more or less definite intention existed to pre-*

vent my sleep and later my recovery from the illness resulting from the insomnia . . ." (M, 64).

At some point Schreber relinquishes belief in such purgative sleep; he does not date the change but complementary alterations suggest late 1895. Rather than entirely losing its efficacy, sleep now becomes a prerequisite for Schreber's unmanning. That is, just as the Eternal Jew's transformation into a woman "might have been completed in a sleep lasting hundreds of years" (M, 73–74), a prolific sleep would speed Schreber's. Of course the tested souls (and in one version, God Himself) resist this transformation for which Schreber later longs, for the increased attractiveness it portends gravely threatens their absorption into his body. Thus they continually plague Schreber's efforts to sleep with a barrage of miracles that allow them to maintain their continued, unnatural existence.

Such reasoning implies that sleep enhances Schreber's soul-voluptuousness. In other passages, however, *Memoirs* suggests a contrary causality, or at least that the two are mutually reinforcing. An incorporated letter to Dr. Weber, written on 30 March 1900, argues, in the face of his physician's skepticism, that nerves of voluptuousness now pervade his anatomy, much as he thinks they do in a woman. He offers the following experiment in proof: "Through pressure on one such structure [nodes of voluptuous nerves] I can produce a feeling of female sensuous pleasure, particularly if I think of something feminine. I do this, by the way, not for sensual lust, but I am absolutely compelled to do so if I want to achieve sleep or protect myself against otherwise almost unbearable pain" (M, 205). Here sensuality eases Schreber into sleep, not, as he usually argues, the other way around. The tight nexus between the two we see again in the following, written in the late summer of 1900: "My sleep is on the whole very much better than before; I have already mentioned that sometimes I cannot remain in bed because of persistent states of bellowing [another noxious miracle that prevents sleep] (which alternate with high-grade sensuous pleasure)" (M, 202). As I read it, this passage all but equates sleep and soul-voluptuousness. Schreber's enemies surely treat them indiscriminately; they strenuously resist both for the dangers they commonly hold for the continued autonomous existence of the tested souls, of even God Himself, who finds Himself hopelessly attracted by Schreber's nervousness.

In discussing Schreber's comments on sleep I have necessarily broadened my horizon to include some more well-known attitudes toward soul-voluptuousness. To elucidate these latter ideas more fully, however, we should initially return to Schreber's cosmology, for it contains concepts that can guide our progress. Recall that purified souls ascend to heaven and attain the "*state of Blessedness.* This consisted of uninterrupted enjoyment with the contemplation of God" (M, 51). Although the idea of "perpetual idleness" (M, 51) may be unbearable for man, Schreber cautions us against measuring the souls' state by earthly standards. "Souls' greatest happiness lies in continual revelling in pleasure combined with recollection of their human past" (M, 52). The state of Blessedness the souls attain as they again near God consists chiefly of voluptuousness (hence the term, "soul-voluptuousness"), which God grants the souls in perpetuity (M, 208). Thus, although by human standards souls may appear vain (M, 55) and not a little dissolute, we must withhold any criticism and recognize these qualities as simply part of their essential nature. Finally, in his cosmology Schreber differentiates between male and female states of Blessedness. The latter consist largely of an "uninterrupted feeling of voluptuousness," and although he holds the former superior, he nowhere describes the nature of its superiority (M, 52).

The first symptoms of his impending deteriorization Schreber finds in several dreams, one of which has occupied all his commentators: "It was the idea that it really must be rather pleasant to be a woman succumbing to intercourse. This idea was so foreign to my whole nature that I may say I would have rejected it with indignation if fully awake" (M, 63). Of course this is not yet soul-voluptuousness, only its sure precursor, but Schreber's waking repugnance anticipates his initial reactions to the subsequent recognition that his body was becoming a seat of voluptuousness. When he feels himself the victim of a plot to forsake him after being sexually abused, his "whole sense of manliness and manly honor" (M, 76) energetically opposes the conspirators, to the point of actively considering suicide as the sole honorable alternative "to so degrading an end" (M, 76). His strenuous resistance proves futile: "[My] will power could not prevent the occurrence, particularly when lying in bed, of a sensation of voluptuousness which as so-called 'soul-voluptuousness' exerted an increased power of attraction on the rays" (M, 120). After five long tortured years, only an untiring exercise of his will even slowed his unmanning. He writes of November 1895, a critical time:

In the immediately preceding nights my male sex organ might actually have been retracted had I not resolutely set my will against it, still following the stirring of my sense of manly honor; so near completion was the miracle. Soul-voluptuousness had become so strong that I myself received the impression of a female body, first on my arms and hands, later on my legs, bosom, buttocks and other parts of my body. (M, 148)

I can only read this passage as an equation of unmanning and soul-voluptuousness, a covert denial of the possibility of some male voluptuousness. Thus, insofar as Schreber resists his unwilled feminization, he likewise suppresses an undesired (or unowned) increase of his own sensuality, now defined exclusively in female terms.

In November 1895, Schreber comes to several fateful recognitions. His unmanning simply seemed irreversible and resistance a vain flailing against the inevitable:

Several days' observation of these events sufficed to change the direction of my will completely. . . . [Now] I could see beyond doubt that the Order of the World imperiously demanded my unmanning, whether I personally like it or not, and that therefore it was *common sense* that nothing was left to me but reconcile myself to the thought of being transformed into a woman. . . . Since then I have wholeheartedly inscribed the cultivation of femininity on my banner, and I will continue to do so as far as consideration of my environment allows, whatever other people who are ignorant of the supernatural reasons may think of me. (M, 148–49)

If until now Schreber has steadfastly resisted his unmanning, he now aligns himself with its relentless aims, which is not to say that he himself unequivocally embraces the transformation. Rather he more accedes to its inevitability, "whether [he] likes it or not." In fact, in a postscript written a year later, he continues his denigration of soul-voluptuousness, whose champion he now is: "This state of Blessedness is mainly a state of voluptuous enjoyment, which for its full development needs the fantasy of either being or wishing to be a female being, which naturally is not to my taste. I must however submit to the necessity of the Order of the World which forces me to accept these ideas . . ." (M, 240). So Schreber's new course is not altogether voluntary; circumstances force Schreber to this altered view, not his own unfettered sensuosity. He thinks the issue quite simple: "I would like to meet the man who, faced with the choice of either becoming a demented human being in male habitus or a spirited woman, would not prefer the latter. Such and *only such* is the issue for me" (M, 149). Given this limited choice, reason compels Schreber's course, just as circumstances dictate the necessity of the choice.

However we must not think that Schreber becomes merely a

passive partner to his unmanning. He actively cultivates femininity; he works to bring the inevitable closer to hand. He describes to the court that is deciding his tutelage occasions when to passers-by he "was seen standing in front of a mirror or elsewhere with some female adornments (ribbons, trumpery necklaces, and suchlike), with the upper half of [his] body exposed" (M, 300). These acts form part of his conscious program to hurry his unmanning along and simultaneously avoid the noxious miracles that occur whenever converging rays are not met by soul-voluptuousness in his body. Indeed, Schreber even argues that his cultivation of soul-voluptuousness, far from being profligate, is " 'God-fearing' " (M, 210), his positive "duty" to a divinity who demands "*constant enjoyment,* as the normal mode of existence for souls within the Order of the World" (M, 209). And if Schreber derives some "little sensuous pleasure in this process," he feels "entitled to it as a small compensation for the excess of suffering and privation that has been [his] for many years past" (M, 209).

Even in this seeming accommodation to the inevitable Schreber meets continued resistance. However much it is Schreber's divine duty, his God openly aligns Himself with the tested souls against this new-found purpose. Ever since Flechsig or his tested soul established nerve-contact with Schreber and rent the "miraculous structure" of the Order of the World, God has been at odds with His earthly creation. He fears Schreber's increasing voluptuousness as a threat to His continued existence; even as Schreber writes the forecourts of heaven are depleted, having been absorbed into his attractive body. When God conspires to deprive His victim of his reason to sunder that attractiveness, He joins the tested souls in acting contrary to the Order of the World. Schreber's presumed moral authority, therefore, derives not from an alliance with God, but rather from his solitary adherence to the superior strictures of the Order of the World, an alliance he feels guarantees his inevitable triumph, vindicates his long suffering, and insures some appropriately extraordinary recompense.

Thus, although Schreber initially resists his increasing soul-voluptuousness and unmanning (they come to the same thing), after late 1895 he becomes their fervent cultivator. Neither course of action proves easy; supernatural forces work against both. Once the tested souls—perhaps acting alone, perhaps acting as agents of God's craven desires—established nerve-contact with Schreber, the Order of the World demanded his unmanning, whether or not the conspirators also planned to forsake him. Beyond the tested souls, then, Schreber's first opposition comes from fate itself, dooming his protection of "manly honor" to futility. After the momentous reversal of November 1895, Schreber aligns his purposes with his perceived fate. But even that generous accommodation was opposed by the tested souls, and God Himself. There are no easing solutions. Schreber inhabits a world deeply at odds with itself, one that places mutually excluding demands upon him; whichever way he turns a combative stance seems his constant necessity.

Schreber's efforts to remain immobile and to achieve sleep are parts of this necessity, as indeed is his entire life since the onset of his "nervous illness." I have singled them out for special consideration because of other features they share with his evolving attitude toward his unmanning. As we have seen, he finally recognizes all three as willed, intentional actions, no matter how irrational or mad they may seem to others. He tells the court he has "*very good and important reasons* for this behavior" (M, 300), and although he writes there only about his transvestite actions, he offers elsewhere explanations for his catatonia. In each instance Schreber intends to draw down the tested souls or divine rays into his body, thus each in its way is perceived as a curative action. If his immobility facilitates his absorption of the tested souls, he would effect "the restoration of God's sole power in the sky" (M, 129); a prolific sleep will either permit the restitution of his health, as Flechsig initially promised, or later hurry his unmanning and the salvation of the Order of the World. Thus we can consider Schreber's catatonic phase as a first intimation of the course he would subsequently elect.

The catatonia also anticipates the cultivation of femininity in a more crucial way: the rigid immobility of the catatonic Schreber graphs the paradoxical quality of Schreber's fight for sleep, and of a "God-fearing" voluptuousness. Put differently, Schreber's world apparently denies him the possibility of simple rest. He cannot let up; he cannot permit himself the luxury of relaxation or passivity; he must manipulate himself as relentlessly as do supernatural forces. If I read *Memoirs of My Nervous Illness* at all correctly, it is precisely this inability to achieve easement that constitutes what Schreber perceives as the grossest invalidation of his autonomy. We see this most clearly in the shrill intensity of his complaints against the "*enormous infringement of man's most primitive rights*" (M, 175 n) which prohibits him from thinking nothing, from mental relaxation or passivity.

But the miraculous interferences that block his efforts to sleep and the cruel mockery of the voices (" 'Are you not ashamed in front of your wife?', or still more vulgarly: 'Fancy a person who was a *Senatspräsident* allowing himself to be f——d' " [M, 148, deletion in original]) also block any uncomplicated relinquishment of vigilance, any simple easement. In such frustrating circumstances what rest Schreber achieves is always compromised, hedged by rigid necessities. Hence we can see the stiff immobility of the relatively brief catatonic phase as an anticipation of Schreber's eventual solution. The immobility is strained, not restful, maintained only by "almost incredible sacrifice" (M, 129) because he "considered absolute passivity almost a religious duty" (M, 127). Likewise, Schreber can only permit himself to cultivate sensuality after he sees it as his service to god. Until that time, for two tortured years, Schreber's "manly honor" suppresses all traces of voluptuousness, as though pleasure or relaxation were somehow essentially tainted, in need of sanction from higher authorities to rescue them for respectability. However, as Schreber defines pleasure and relaxation in terms of duty, he creates oxymorons. He can only appropriate a rigid immobility, an active passivity, a dutiful sensuality, which remove them surely from the realm of utter easement. Such compromises negate the very possibility of total relaxation, the rest of a sleep free from the world's demands; despite the limited easement they may offer, the necessity for them constitutes perhaps the cruelest and most durable limitation of Schreber's autonomy.

4

Thus far our reading of *Memoirs of My Nervous Illness* has stayed close to the fate of Schreber himself. And rightly, for he is, after all, our subject. However we must guard against unwittingly following too closely Schreber's assertion that "*everything that happens is in reference to* [him]" (M, 197). Despite his claim to a unique fate, *Memoirs* evidences the contrary view that the infringements upon self-determination that threaten Schreber in fact pervade his environment, affecting the tested souls, even God. Thus before venturing some comprehensive interpretive commentary on Schreber's *Memoirs,* we should briefly investigate the pervasiveness in this world of the issues that so concern Schreber.

Clearly Schreber presents himself in *Memoirs* as a victim. Miracles constantly assault the integrity of his body, removing some organs and deforming others; they deny him sleep, even the modest easement of "thinking nothing"; they break the strings of his piano, cause him to bellow, perversely send others to the lavatory exactly when he must relieve himself. And if these miracles have of late been largely reduced to mere nuisances, if they progressively "take on a more and more harmless character" (M, 246), the more pernicious still occasionally appear. But Schreber's powerlessness is at once illusory and shared. That is, if we briefly consider the plights of the tested souls and of God we discover they too are victimized in their ways, and the agent of their helplessness is Schreber himself.

While immunizing the person of Professor Flechsig from his charges in the "Open Letter," Schreber describes the disengaged soul: "This 'tested soul' still endowed with human faults like all impure souls—in accordance with the character of souls which I have come to know with certainty—then simply allowed itself to be driven by the impulse of ruthless self-determination and lust for power, without any restraint by something comparable to the moral will power of man . . ." (M, 34). This ruthless, willful tested soul, together with the von W. soul that appears during this brief stay in Pierson's asylum (June 1894), is the chief architect of Schreber's plight. On the motivations of these tested souls Schreber remains characteristically ambiguous; perhaps they desire revenge upon the Schreber family for some ascendency, perhaps they only want the cheap thrills of his soul murder and forsaking, perhaps they are now jealously guarding their unique contact with divine rays. (At one point Schreber says: "I was for them only a means to an end to capture the divine rays brought nearer by the power of attraction with which they then adorned themselves, like a peacock with strange feathers, so attaining the gift of miracles" [M, 110].) Whatever their intentions, they ruthlessly victimize an innocent Schreber. In fact, in one version of these events offered in *Memoirs* even God finds Himself in "dependence on Professor Flechsig, or on his tested soul" (M, 75), thus making the ascendency of the tested souls almost total.

Such is not long the case, however. An ironic twist soon reverses the situation, placing the tested souls in helpless thrall to their intended victim. At some point Schreber's soul-voluptuousness, their bait for capturing the converging divine rays, represented a threat even to them. They responded to this threat by "tying-to-celestial-bodies," but even that unearthly expedient proved futile. Whereas at one time some forty to sixty Flechsig souls and a somewhat lesser number of von W. souls "were strung over the whole heavenly vault" (M, 109), Schreber tells us that by late 1897 von W.'s disappeared completely and Flechsig's were reduced to a "meager remnant" (M, 158). Moreover, Schreber's wily opponent has ironically succumbed to a fate that its victim long feared as his own: "it progressively lost its intelligence so that now hardly a trace of awareness of its own identity remains" (M, 117). Finally, as if emboldened by Schreber's startling successes, God breaks His dependence (or with His fellow conspirators, depending on the version) and "start[s] a raid among [the tested souls] one particular day" (M, 157), completing the decimation Schreber began. Thus the ruthless tested souls suffer a severe poetic justice: their hapless victim eventually turns and overwhelms them.

God's role in Schreber's experience remains more vague, but His divine autonomy is no less compromised. Although Schreber long thought God his ally against his wily enemy, by 1900 his perception shifts: "It occurred to me only much later, in fact only while writing this essay did it become quite clear to me, that God Himself must have known of the plan, if indeed He was not the instigator, to commit soul murder on me, and to hand over my body in the manner of a female harlot" (M, 77). How such an action would profit God is not addressed, but Schreber harbors no doubt that, whether or not God initiated the conspiracy against him, an "unequal battle between one weak human being and God Himself" (M, 79) was joined. The nerve-contact between him and the tested souls represents "a kernel of danger" (M, 59) to God's autonomy, as Schreber explains in the chapter on cosmology: "[The] nerves of *living* human beings particularly when in a state of *high-grade excitation,* have such a power of attraction for the nerves of God that He would not be able to free Himself from them again, and would thus endanger His own existence" (M, 48). Thus God is "forced" (M, 196) to "succumb" (M, 128)[7] to Schreber's ever increasing soul-voluptuousness: "God is inseparably tied to [Schreber's] person through [his] nerves' power of attraction which for some time past has become inescapable; there is no possibility of God freeing Himself . . ." (M, 209).

In His desperation, however, this uneducable divinity, who cannot understand His living creations, nevertheless mightily resists His appointed fate. He too plagues Schreber with miracles intended variously to derange Schreber or more simply to divert his attention, enabling Him to withdraw to a safe distance. His efforts avail Him not. However noxious God's miracles, He cannot disengage Himself from the powerful attractiveness of Schreber's feminized body; Schreber constantly hears "cries of 'help' " (M, 210) from those of God's nerves doomed to absorption in his body. Thus God stands helpless before Schreber; the victim ultimately reigns victorious. Schreber attributes his ascendency over God to the latter's deviation from the Order of the World—that is, from "the lawful relation which, *resting on God's nature and attributes, exists between God and the creation called to life by Him*" (M, 79 n)—and not to any innate supremacy of his own. Nonetheless, the depiction of God's fate in *Memoirs* leaves us no doubt that His beleaguered but staunchly moral victim humbles a wayward divinity, returning Him finally to "lawful" relations with His creations.

These fates suffered by the tested souls and God demonstrate that the loss of self-determination Schreber bemoans is not uniquely his own. A strict poetic justice rules Schreber's world; he ends by capturing the wills of his tormentors as surely as they initially fettered his own. Put another way, if "wherever the Order of the World is broken, power alone counts, and the right of the stronger is decisive" (M, 78), then the intended victim here emerges as the most powerful. All this subtly alters our image of Schreber. Not only are his travails not solitary, but he also ends up at least figuratively as the victor over an irresolute God. In sum, Schreber's *Memoirs* suggest that no one—not even his God—in this world is the iron master of his fate.

5

As should be obvious by now, I lodge the issue of self-determination or autonomy in its many permutations at the thematic center of Schreber's *Memoirs of My Nervous Illness*. Schreber persistently depicts the miracles, his unmanning, his treatment within the institutions, even his earlier hypochondria, which enacts his body's betrayal of him, as infringements of his autonomy, or in his own words, of his will or natural rights. Not only does he find himself manipulated by external forces—from Professor Flechsig, to the various attendants, to the tested souls, to God—but he also manipulates himself to an extraordinary extent. Thus he tells about his remarkable abstinence while remaining immobile for several months, "the immense mental effort" (M, 118) required to absorb temporarily the tested souls, and many other remarkable feats of perseverance. Having, I hope, demonstrated the relevance of this Eriksonian theme, I want now to trace some of its transformations and ramifications in *Memoirs*.

When Schreber calls an assault upon his autonomy an infringement of his "natural rights," he signals a first transformation: his preoccupation with justice, the law. This concern obviously prepares him admirably for his profession as lawyer and judge of the Superior Court in Dresden. Indeed, he must have been extremely competent, for we learn that when he was appointed *Senatspräsident* (or presiding judge) to the Dresden court "almost all" the other judges "were much senior to [him] (up to twenty years)" (M, 63). His vocational skills carry over in many ways into *Memoirs.* The reasoned tone and the calm, apparently considered, presentation of evidence for his delusions proved a discordant aspect of my initial readings of *Memoirs,* for I had expected something altogether outrageous. Undoubtedly, the most persuasive evidence of the persistence of Schreber's legal capacities and concerns in the midst of his delusions, so it seems to me, is his appended essay, "In What Circumstances Can a Person Considered Insane be Detained in an Asylum Against his Declared Will?" and the brief for appeal of his tutelage. Partially on the grounds of this latter document, the court—although conceding that he was "insane" (M, 342)—nonetheless restored to him the legal right to manage his own affairs.

Even some of the more flamboyant aspects of Schreber's illness can be seen as elaborations of these legal issues and training. In a sense Schreber displaces much of his concern from the German law to the more exalted Order of the World. Even then he concerns himself with rights and wrongs, though in the process he becomes both victim seeking redress and judge. Thus in the unequal struggle between himself and God, Schreber feels he must emerge victorious "because the Order of the World [that is, the "lawful" relations of God to His creations] is on [his] side" (M, 79). Moreover, by 1900 Schreber seems confident that "some *great* and *magnificent satisfaction*" will justly reward his perseverance, for "*there must be an equalizing justice and it can never be* that a morally unblemished human being with feet firmly planted in the Order of the World should have to perish as the innocent victim of other people's sins in a struggle carried on against him by hostile powers" (M, 214). Thus despite his personal torment Schreber never relinquishes his faith in the efficacy of the legal system. He now brings his grievances before the bar of the Order of the World, and as *Senatspräsident* finds himself innocent, God wayward, and reparations long overdue.

Schreber's suit for the removal of his tutelage likewise demonstrates the persistence of his vocation through the travails of his illness. Moreover, his attitudes and actions in this case clearly demonstrate the determinative role his concern with autonomy plays in his life. Macalpine and Hunter inform us that tutelage is a "German legal procedure for dealing with cases of insanity: by order of the Court the patient was placed under the care of a guardian or Committee of the person, deprived of the management of his affairs and disposal of his person" (M, 4 n). In sum, placement under tutelage severely restricts the autonomy of those considered insane. Schreber was apparently placed under temporary tutelage as early as 1895, although he did not learn of it until later, perhaps 1899. In that year he asked that the issue be resolved, but "contrary to [his] expectations, a formal order for [his] tutelage was made in March 1900 by the District Court Dresden" (M, 200). Schreber appealed this decision unsuccessfully in 1901; only in a subsequent appeal was he successful, and in September of the following year his tutelage was finally rescinded and his full legal rights restored.

In appending the several legal documents to the published *Memoirs* Schreber has signaled the crucial importance that tutelage has for him. From what I can tell, the question under argument is how far Schreber, who acknowledges that he suffers a "nervous" but not a mental illness (M, 286), is capable of managing his personal affairs. A paragon of reasonableness, Schreber shrewdly argues that *"a person can be placed under tutelage only in his own interest"* (M, 303); that is, tutelage cannot legally be employed to safeguard others against possible attack or annoyance. Thus, because he demonstrates cognizance of the possible consequences of publication of *Memoirs* upon his family, of his unmanning upon his marriage, of his bellowing upon his neighbors, yet seems willing to endure them, the court has no right to withhold his legal freedom.

Notice that Schreber does not demand his immediate release from Sonnenstein. Indeed, after his successful petition he lingers there several months; the court rescinded his tutelage in September 1902, but the preface, dated the following December, indicates that he has not yet left Sonnenstein (M, 32). His appeal moreover suggests that he would consider permanently residing there even after removal of his tutelage if he cannot live comfortably with his wife, or even if a servant could not endure frequent bellowing, or if he cannot sleep without medication. (We know he did return to Sonnenstein in 1907; but I cannot determine whether or not he did so willingly.)[8] The issue is not immediate release; the much more crucial issue for Schreber involves autonomy, his ability to determine his fate. As he writes the court: "After all it is a *point of honor:* which person of my high intellectual standing would not feel it an indignity to be treated in legal matters like a child under the age of seven, to be denied every disposition of his fortune even in written form, and what is more, to be prevented from obtaining information about his financial affairs, etc. etc." (M, 313). What exercises Schreber, then, is not so much his confinement to Sonnenstein—as his tardy removal itself suggests—as the principle that tutelage abridges his right to self-determination. With it restored, he quite leisurely goes about securing his eventual release. Only extreme sensitivity to his autonomy, I suggest, reconciles his rigorous appeal of tutelage on the one hand with his more casual subsequent actions.

In this entire series of episodes, extending from long before his breakdown until after he writes the main body of *Memoirs,* Schreber's concern with autonomy governs his actions. As a lawyer and then a judge Schreber's vocation concerned him with protecting individual rights and finding redress wherever they were abridged. I suggest, then, that his concern with autonomy greatly antedates his breakdown; further, I would argue that precisely this sensitivity to such issues was instrumental in his professional success. After 1893, Schreber for some unknown reason displaces these same interests, so that the Order of the World replaces the German law as the impersonal highest authority. Schreber now enacts a dual role: as claimant he presents grievances against the tested souls and God, as judge he declares his own innocence and finds his opponents in violation of the law. Finally, when tutelage infringes his autonomy, he resists strenuously up to the point it is rescinded, but then remains content to linger several months in Sonnenstein. But he does so now of his own volition—that, for Schreber, is the crucial issue: is he free to resolve his own fate?

Such preoccupation with one's will suggests as a corollary a militant sensitivity to issues of dominance and submission, for the authority of others must always hold a threat to our autonomy, can reduce us—so this logic runs—to the humiliations of dependency. Here we see the reasons for Schreber's hostility to many in his environment. Schreber's initial appeal to Flechsig for assistance makes him dependent upon his physician. In other words, the very respect he professes for Professor Flechsig (without which he would scarcely have become his patient) becomes a grievance in a doctor-patient relationship because it makes Schreber dependent upon him, and thereby endangers his fragile sense of autonomy. We have seen Schreber go to great lengths to reconcile his respect for Flechsig with his accusations, but such baroque reasoning is not necessary. Flechsig's professional ascendency threatens this struggling patient and converts the physician into a ready target for the latter's defensive deprecations.

Simple reflection reveals that all the targets, real and imagined, of Schreber's aggression in *Memoirs* share this dominance over him. Flechsig and his attendant at Pierson's, von W., whose ascendencies are given metaphoric expression when they become tested souls, of course come in for the greatest portion of his vengeance. But others share in it. He also lodges grievances against M. (M, 130–31), his attendant at Sonnenstein, and Dr. Weber, whose reports as director there were instrumental in placing Schreber in tutelage (M, 286). However, he heaps his scorn most vehemently upon his God, almost as if he calibrates the volume of his hostility by the degree of dependence he feels upon his victim. All these agents share a common predominance over Schreber; even the lowly sanatorium attendants are empowered to dictate to this fallen man, which only underscores his present vulnerability.

We have seen, however, that Schreber's hostility takes a perhaps unexpected turn. Although he apparently for sometime expressed his hostility quite openly—fighting attendants and other patients, bitterly shouting abuse at his God—he no longer does so. Now he denies it. He no sooner articulates some complaint than he takes it away; or alternatively, he depersonalizes the object of his hostility. Thus he declares no intention to disparage Professor Flechsig personally; it must have been a tested soul miraculously independent of Flechsig who had earned Schreber's spite. Perhaps the most extreme example of this depersonalization occurs when Schreber hits upon his God as his chief tormentor, for this immunizes the entire human world of complicity in Schreber's plight. Even here Schreber hedges, for if he is "forced" (M, 238) to abuse God, he has "never been an *adversary of God* . . . ; it would be absurd for a human who once acknowledged God to say such a thing of himself" (M, 252). I suggest, therefore, that such depersonalizations serve to blunt Schreber's aggressiveness just as thoroughly as do his repeated denials. Thus although many pages of *Memoirs* are given over to vituperation, Schreber subverts his own anger by intentionally blurring its objects.

I was unprepared for this turn. After all, I had assumed that unbridled hostility characterized paranoia; had not Freud made Schreber the very paragon of this disorder? Obviously something was amiss. Either the theory was fragmentary, perhaps incorrect, or Schreber was not a classic paranoid. If nothing else, this gap articulates the chasm that necessarily exists in most instances between theory and the individual circumstance we wish to understand. I long puzzled over this apparent inconsistency. Only when I recognized another anomaly between the theory and Schreber's *Memoirs* did I begin to understand the covertness of his hostility.

Schreber hungers for our, his readers', respect. I had anticipated that Schreber (as a paranoid) would be either quite indifferent to our reaction to his theories and accusations or, more probably, that he would already view us suspiciously, as potential agents in the conspiracy whirling around him. In neither case would he court our approval, but woo us he does. He strikes me as positively solicitous of our respect and admiration; the courtship takes many forms. In the simplest he merely repeats for us instances of the approbation and favor he has won from others. For example, he relates the circumstances in which he learns of his promotion to *Senatspräsident:* "In June 1893 I was informed (in the first place by the Minister of Justice, Dr. Schurig in person) of my impending appointment as *Senatspräsident* to the Superior Court in Dresden" (M, 63). The sentence reads well without the parenthetical addition; in a sense it is gratuitous. It serves another function, however, for Schreber feels it crucial that we know the Minister of Justice himself notified him, and did so in person, perhaps at some personal inconvenience. (When I read the sentence I cannot help but accentuate those last two parenthetical words.) The literature terms the typical paranoid an "injustice collector," and to an extent of course Schreber complies; however, he also collects and broadly displays signs of his acclaim in an effort to number us too among his admirers.

Another form Schreber's courtship takes I find especially poignant. This delusional man over and over pleads his reasonableness, desperately wants us to think him the very soul of rationality. He does not simply assert the validity of his delusions but marshals such evidence as he can to prove it. At times when matters altogether resist elucidation, with admirable modesty he confesses his limitations; thus we repeatedly find admissions such as the following: "This is in fact *even for me* a riddle which I can only partially solve, and which would be quite unsoluble by purely human notions" (M, 51 n, my emphasis). Schreber obviously values rationality highly, and we recall that among the miracles he most feared were those intended to make him deranged. In the face of those miracles, and more palpably in the face of his daily existence in Sonnenstein—at times abused by lowly attendants, committed to padded cells—he desperately needs to convince himself and the readers of *Memoirs* that they have to do with an intelligent man whose experiences should be taken with full seriousness. Thus although he himself overtly harbors few doubts, Schreber requires his readers' conviction for full vindication of his suffering; lacking that he becomes a prophet without following, the very picture of futility.

Finally, Schreber's courtship of his readers take other forms when he writes about his unmanning. Because this represents the most potentially scandalous aspect of *Memoirs,* Schreber assures us above all that he is the very personification of rectitude. His education was uncompromising:

> Few people have been brought up according to such strict moral principles as I, and have throughout life practiced such moderation especially in matters of sex, as I venture to claim for myself. Mere low sensuousness can therefore not be considered a motive in my case; were satisfaction of my manly pride still possible, I would naturally much prefer it; nor would I ever betray any sexual lust in contact with other people. (M, 208)

Of course he does stubbornly resist the first signs of his unmanning. Even when the transformation seemed imminent, all but accomplished, he yet "resolutely set [his] will against it, still following the stirring of [his] sense of manly honor" (M, 148).

However, as long as Schreber upholds the community's standards he hardly risks losing his readers' respect. The rhetorical test comes when he must relate his subsequent resolve to embrace wholeheartedly his apparently increasing feminization. This is no personal predilection, he protests, no dissolute search for unmitigated enjoyment. No, through some dazzling sophistry he transforms soul-voluptuousness from a perversion to a moral imperative, makes of it the very obligation it previously seemed to abrogate. Cultivation of soul-voluptuousness has been "forced upon" an obliging Schreber: "It is [his] duty to provide Him with [constant enjoyment] in the form of highly developed soul-voluptuousness" (M, 209). Thus for Schreber the *"moral limits to voluptuousness"* that bind others *"no longer exist, indeed in a certain sense the reverse applies"* (M,

208). (In this context we might recall that Schreber supposes that the Eternal Jew, God's chosen bride, was selected to maintain the species perhaps because he is the "relatively most moral" [M, 73] of men.)

In any event, I perceive that Schreber is going to some lengths to secure our respect. We must not think him dissolute or mad; rather, he cultivates a self-image that has him the paragon of rationality, a persistent, long-suffering servant of right—he dutifully fulfills his obligations as he finds them, however personally odious they may in fact be. I think we see here one reason that Schreber now blunts his hostility. Verbal assaults might jar the image he cultivates, make him appear unreasonable; whereas his repeated disavowal of malicious intent makes him seem magnanimous, not a bitter, vindictive madman. That is, the covert hostility is but a part of an assiduously cultivated campaign to curry our favor.

The very persistence of this silent plea for our approval makes me suspicious. If someone is not angry, why must he deny it so often? More generally, if someone respects himself, why need he so arduously insist that he is worthy of others' respect? I suggest that narrator Schreber's pleas for our approval derive from bad faith; that is, that he needs our respect because he doubts his own worth. We are to provide the confirmation he cannot always give himself. (Obviously, I am describing phenomena that mirror what psychoanalysts call projection.) *Memoirs* eloquently documents Schreber's extreme sensitivity to slights, a sensitivity that parallels his sensitivity to infringements of his autonomy. Of course God and the tested souls daily affront Schreber's dignity. We find evidence that this sensitivity too precedes this illness, for Schreber reports that even in his treatment for the earlier breakdown Professor Flechsig offered insult by telling his patient *"white lies."* They might be appropriate in some cases, but not his own; Flechsig "must soon have realized that in [Schreber] he was dealing with a human being of high intellect, of uncommon keenness of understanding and acute powers of observation" (M, 62). Like his concern with autonomy, therefore, Schreber's immense need for external confirmation of his worth seems of long duration. Likewise, just as the very fragility of his autonomy makes him guard it all the more vigorously, Schreber's uneasy self-respect makes our respect all the more necessary to him. In other words, I suggest that a corrosive doubt shadowed Schreber's accomplishments, that he could never quite trust his own worth.

Faced with this poverty of inner affirmation Schreber overcompensates. He does so, first, by touchily insisting that all those in his environment—Professor Flechsig, the attendants, his colleagues on the Superior Court, among whom he had "to achieve first of all the necessary respect" (M, 63)—affirm his worth. In writing *Memoirs* Schreber draws us within his circle; he pleads too for our respect in a show of his worthiness. This movement culminates in his megalomania, which makes him the center of earthly life. These last are the signs of desperation, the last, most glorious resources of Schreber's determined effort to clothe himself in more than tattered dignity. Their very extremity suggests Schreber's own; they issue from a need too intense for everyday satisfactions.

We can glimpse the durability of such concerns by focusing on Schreber's behavior and opinions before and after he accedes to his unmanning in late 1895. Before that critical turning Schreber felt the unmanning to be an affront to his manly honor. He consistently followed a course of action set down as early as the onset of his breakdown, when he "would have rejected with indignation if fully awake" the dreamed suggestion "that it really must be rather pleasant to be a woman succumbing to intercourse" (M, 63). (The word "succumbing" has held my attention from the first, for it reflects the issues of domination and submission with which Schreber views sexuality.) These suggestions of feminization and submission so horrified Schreber that he even contemplated suicide as the only recourse to preserve his "whole sense of manliness and manly honor" (M, 76). This seems also to be the period during which Schreber articulated his hostility most clearly; he verbally abused God and physically resisted his attendants. With his conversion Schreber's entire attitude shifts. He now consciously collaborates with the unmanning. Not merely does he no longer contemplate suicide, but he now suspects he might be immortal (M, 212). Finally, although his aggressiveness does not cease, he mutes it, rendering it more covert than open. In a certain sense, his attitude toward sensuousness and his aggressiveness change places after 1895; where the former was suppressed and the latter enacted previously, now the reverse is true.

Obviously this sudden shift is of some moment. It eases Schreber's dilemma, lets him come to terms with himself and his world to an extent he had not achieved at least since late 1893. Despite all these manifest alterations, however, between and within them runs a profound, unbroken continuity. Schreber is still as excessively concerned with earning respect as he was when he assumed his position as *Senatspräsident*. And he wants to earn it through the same means, namely, his intelligence and his high moral character. He recognizes that the revelations in *Memoirs* may cast doubt upon both, so he goes to extraordinary lengths to convince us that his reason remains intact and his rectitude uncompromised. He is still angry, but he masks his hostility ever so lightly, at once permitting it expression and shunting it aside. This delusional Schreber is still very much the judge, still concerned with demarcating between right and wrong; however, now he is both judge and claimant, resolving issues in terms of the Order of the World rather than the more humble German law.

No, this is no new Schreber emerging from the ashes of the old. I suggest, rather, that this sudden reversal represents a costly, delusional accommodation between a sense of his rectitude and a desire for rest and some momentary easement of the strains of accomplishment. We have seen how Schreber paradoxically strives for easement. He struggles to maintain rigid immobility during his catatonic phase, to achieve sleep, later to cultivate his sensuality; miracles even prohibit him from "thinking nothing." An all or nothing logic operates here. Either Schreber is an upright citizen who fulfills his duty or he is a degenerate, worthy only of our (and his own) contempt. The casual or frivolous are strictly prohibited. Schreber then ingeniously finds his duty elsewhere; that is, he converts the very easement once denied him into a sacred duty and thus transcends the merely earthly obligations against which he had fretted. Now he has it both ways: he partakes of a cosmic rectitude, yet attains the easements previously denied.

But he protests too much; Schreber is now a prophet who cannot quite believe his own good fortune. This doubt about his new vocation translates itself into the solicitousness of the tone of *Memoirs*. That is, just as denials mask his anger, the cosmology masks Schreber's bad conscience. He can never free himself altogether from doubt about his divine mission and shame about his behavior. If he could, there would be no need to curry our favor, he could independently resolve upon a course of action. This dependence upon us, his readers, brings us full circle, for in Schreber's very sensitivity to issues of dominance and submission I located the open sores of his hostility. Schreber's reasonable quest for easement finally drives this most rational man within the ulcerated circle that he makes his uneasy home for the final two decades of his life.

From the very first, however, I suspect he doubted his worthiness for whatever mission was then at hand. This corrosive doubt—not of his existence, but of his fitness, a very different issue—seems a shadow he could never put far behind him, regardless of his considerable worldly accomplishments, regardless of his grandiose delusions. In fact, his worldly success may have been more detrimental than anything. Each success may have proved momentary, for in the end each accomplishment only increased the stakes, made easement less likely, made the expectations higher, the disappointments—and the anticipation of them—more devastating. The record preserved in *Memoirs of My Nervous Illness* does not permit a definitive location of the precipitating causes of the breakdown it records. Perhaps the frustrations of his childless marriage contribute; perhaps the strain of fulfilling yet another heavy obligation as *Senatspräsident* nudged him; or more likely there was no single traumatic event. Rather, an entire series of trials in which he vainly sought to meet expectations, his own and those of others, likely culminated in an event that, though apart from this series might have appeared trifling, nonetheless suggested to him that the trials were unending, and that an affirmative verdict was never more than temporary. We can be confident, however, that—whatever the circumstances—they involved affronts to his sense of worth that affected him deeply because he felt they were true. I suggest, in other words, that the entire odyssey of Schreber's life—from his rectitude, to his profession, to his manifest worldly success, and finally to his delusions—involves his futile struggle to undo a wounded sense of worth, to soothe an anguish at expectations left unfulfilled.

A Polemical Epilogue

If this entire book derives from a continuing reflection on the rationality of interpretation in psychoanalysis, I want to conclude by reflecting on the reinterpretation of Schreber's *Memoirs of My Nervous Illness* offered in the preceding chapter. The reading offered there differs dramatically from those previously made by William Neiderland, Mark Kanzer, Morton Schatzman, and, yes, Freud himself. A brief review of some of these differences and a reiteration of the principles that led to them should crystallize several of the issues to which I hope this book makes a contribution.

First, because I believe that the realms of interpretive and theoretical discourse within psychoanalysis are radically discontinuous, "The Unsure Prophet Remembers" eschews a theoretical vocabulary. Theoretical discourse takes as its object some range of shared mental functioning; that range can include anything from mankind generally (as when the object is the structure of the unconscious) to the quite narrow (as when the object is the nature of perversion); its bias is genetic; its vocabulary properly abstract, technical. Interpretive discourse, on the other hand, has an individual as its object; its bias is thematic; its vocabulary ideally derived from that of the individual under consideration. Aside from the recent work of Roy Schafer, this divide has not been the object of scrutiny within the psychoanalytic community. Nor need it have been. Except for the occasional excursion beyond the clinician's immediate purview, almost all the extant literature in psychoanalysis is theoretical in the sense that I am using the term. Of course, most books and articles, no doubt following Freud's example, contain abbreviated case histories and clinical vignettes, but these are merely instantiations of the particular theoretical point under discussion; they make no claim to understanding in any systematic way the individual life. Freud's canonical case histories, despite the remarkable density of his depictions of his subjects, are all instances of theoretical discourse, for in each (with the possible exception of Rat Man), the commentary upon the individual is subservient to a more embracing theoretical argument. We might even say that within clinical psychoanalysis a public form of interpretive discourse does not exist; a place awaits it, its nature is clear, but it remains secreted within the relative privacy and informality of the consulting rooms, of the halls and libraries of the various institutes, within the "shop talk" of the psychoanalysts.

A public form of interpretive discourse only appears when analysts and others push psychoanalysis out of the consulting room to find a larger utility for it. Much of what we might call applied psychoanalysis, be it psychohistory or psychoanalytic criticism, has as its objective the understanding of some segment of an individual's life. It may take the form of a thorough biography, concerned with the entire life, or it may have a more focused intent—the individual's participation in some particular historical event, or the writing of some single text. Be that as it may, the task involves understanding an individual's actions and desires. Rarely, however, do such studies recognize the extent to which this newly public object demands a departure from the usual public language of psychoanalysis. Too often when the interpretive realm emerges into public view it remains mystified as to its own nature; it comes garbed in the language of theoretical discourse, a language that is both unnecessary and inappropriate. However suitable for elucidating general issues in psychology, a theoretical or technical vocabulary elides the issue in interpretive discourse—understanding the singular life in its density. The mere presence of such a vocabulary testifies to a confusion of realms. Often it suggests that the author labors under the false assumption that psychoanalytic interpretations are derived by placing the material in question under the authority of some "covering law," as if a simple correlation of initial conditions and theoretical principles constituted the interpretive process. As we saw in chapter three, such is not the case. Just as frequently, the use of a technical vocabulary represents little more than a crutch or appeal for authority; it tends to proliferate at precisely those junctures of the exposition most in need of authority, that is, where it is weakest, as if its mere presence could patch over the difficulty at hand. It may initially demonstrate the author's own authority, his command of psychoanalytic theory, and may signal the intellectual tradition in which he works, but that language finally testifies more to the author's confusion regarding the nature of the process in which he is ostensibly engaged. Interpretations are not simply derived from psychological principles. A general law of mental functioning might suggest certain features of an interpretation to the interpreter; it might, for instance, suggest the relevance of issues that initially seemed marginal or the lines along which several issues might be related. At no time, however, does the validity of either entail that of the other: adequate interpretations might be suggested by inadequate theories and vice versa. The interpretive process, as we have seen, is relentlessly contextual and holistic; consistency, coherence, and comprehension are the criteria it uses for evaluation, and only in the last instance are they enlarged to include consistency with what is known of mental functioning generally. Therefore not only is a theoretical vocabulary unnecessary, but its presence in so much applied psychoanalysis—that is, in that portion of applied psychoanalysis concerned primarily with the understanding of the singular life or an event of that life—may be pernicious as well: insofar as it claims an undue authority, or mystifies the nature of the interpretive process, that language retards the development of interpretive discourse.

The results for interpretive discourse of this argument resemble those of Roy Schafer's quite different argument in *A New Language for Psychoanalysis,* and, more recently, in *Language and Insight.*[1] He too thinks that interpretations can and should eschew a technical vocabulary, that they can use a variant of everyday speech; but he seems to think also that psychoanalytic theory is by its nature fantasmic, bizarre, and thoroughly mystified. I would disagree. If most of the psychoanalytic literature blurs the distinction between theoretical and interpretive discourse by collapsing the latter into the former, Schafer, in rightly addressing the problem, simply reciprocates—he would collapse them in the other direction. That is, although I agree with Schafer that something akin to his "action language" is appropriate to interpretive discourse, I would not follow him when he suggests the reformulation of psychoanalytic theory generally into that idiom. To do so would be to ignore the difference of their objects, as well as the directive function of theory within the interpretive process. Thus I think psychoanalytic theory has its place and its vocabulary, and its necessary role, but I—like Schafer—think that place and that role do not belong in interpretive discourse.[2]

Besides what could seem the merely cosmetic eschewal of a technical vocabulary, I have also constructed an interpretation of *Memoirs* that lacks the historical or genetic constructions in which most psychoanalytic readings, clinical and applied, often traffic. Specifically, I have not followed Freud in locating the influence of generative earlier relations with his elder brother and his father behind Schreber's delusional tested souls and God. Neiderland and, especially, Schatzman follow this course; they devote themselves to excavating the aetiology of Schreber's delusions. Thus they commonly elucidate one or another of the miracles Schreber discusses by setting it beside, and considering it derivative from, one of Schreber's father's grotesque educational devices. Of course the work of Neiderland and Schatzman is more elaborate and data-bound than Freud's initial speculative construction, but in each case it leads beyond *Memoirs* in search of a more secure, less volatile ground upon which to base interpretation. In a word, such procedures seek the Real. As I argue in chapters three and four, however, the radical power of psychoanalysis necessarily compromises the Real insofar as it is thought of as the hard and fast facticity of particular events, persons, and objects. For psychoanalysis the Real is a construct, a reading—if you will, an interpretation; apprehending it is not merely a matter of collecting data, nor of devising strategies for peeling away accretions to reveal an essential core. Moreover, because psychoanalysis demonstrates that the present shapes the past as relentlessly as the past figures the present, there is no theoretical necessity to excavate that problematic past. The present—be it a text or clinical situation—alone suffices, if we could but see it properly. Understood this way, psychoanalytic interpretation becomes more the deciphering—or better, the reading—of patterns of intention and meaning than exercises in the construction of causal chains.

One consequence of the omission of genetic constructions may seem especially curious: nowhere does my interpretation of Schreber's *Memoirs* make reference to his supposed homosexuality. Freud, you recall, puts homosexuality in an antecedent, causal relation to paranoia; the latter arises out of a strenuous denial of the former. In one sense the lack of reference represents the continuation of a more pervasive theoretical trend that has increasingly attenuated and cast suspicion upon the inner necessity of the linkage between homosexuality and paranoia.[3] In a more fundamental sense, my insistence upon the distinction between theoretical and interpretive discourse, and consequently upon the superfluity of historical constructions for the latter, itself renders any reference to homosexuality at once inappropriate and unnecessary. Finally, however, the basic interpretive move of psychoanalysis, the assumption of a totalizing identity, transforms homosexuality, like paranoia itself, into a secondary phenomenon, one among many lasting possibilities inherent within the cohesive life, but not a determinant of it. Of course, neither homosexuality nor paranoia are irrelevant to the thematic concerns I find in *Memoirs;* both are possible alternative elaborations of them. I would insist, however, that these themes have priority over them; they articulate issues that are at once both more basic and more pervasive than what can be grasped by either of these manifestly more theoretical terms. And this situation is paradigmatic for applied psychoanalysis: insofar as they are necessarily partial and secondary, such nosological categories are inadequate to the task at hand.

Because I believe the thematic concerns I have isolated in *Memoirs* necessarily pervaded Schreber's life, I would like to think that the interpretation offered in the fifth chapter in principle possesses the historical scope sought by Freud, Neiderland, and others, despite the explicit disregard of historical constructions. The assumption of the radical continuity of an individual's life legitimates this ambition, for it suggests that if the central issues informative of *Memoirs* have been formulated at the proper level, they should likewise inform other phases of his life. On the one hand I have related Schreber's preoccupations with autonomy and justice to his vocation; on the other I have suggested how his actions regarding his tutelage, both the suit for its removal and his subsequent slowness in actually departing from Sonnenstein, reflect these same concerns. Of course, this represents a most modest beginning. Nonetheless, I am convinced that had Schreber provided more information about other phases of his life, or had the third chapter of *Memoirs* not been suppressed, this process could have been greatly extended; other interpreters might already be able to do so. Thus the history that was banished in one form, the construction of causal chains, reemerges within interpretive discourse in another, the continuity of the associative chain.

Thus far I have stressed the consequences of severing interpretive discourse from theoretical discourse. It is not set altogether free, left to drift aimlessly; psychoanalytic theory performs several crucial directive roles. Foremost among them, it defines the nature of the object of interpretive discourse; that is, when psychoanalytic theory defines the human subject as a precipitate of relationships, or, alternatively, as the embodiment of an associative chain, it suggests the nature of the object with which interpretive discourse must deal and the locus of the cohesion it must make manifest.

Another segment of psychoanalytic theory served as a series of pointers to potentially relevant issues and information in my writing of the fifth chapter. For instance once I perceived the crucial role of autonomy in *Memoirs of My Nervous Illness,* Erikson's developmental scheme suggested possible corollary concerns, such as shame and doubt.[4] One might say that to some extent Erikson's developmental recasting of psychoanalysis guided my reading after a certain point, preparing me for some issues, suggesting the likely irrelevance of others. To a somewhat lesser extent, Robert Waelder's classic essay, "The Structure of Paranoid Ideas," and David Shapiro's fine "The Paranoid Style" performed a similar directive function, as did, of course, Freud's theories of paranoia as outlined in the second chapter.[5] Despite their obvious importance to my work, at no time do I invoke their real authority to buttress my interpretation of *Memoirs.* There were moments when I was severely tempted, when I felt the rhetorical need of their authority, but I resisted. Such resistance implies little grandiosity; it merely reflects my recognition that their correctness on the level of theory cannot, alas, insure my own in this or any particular interpretation.

Once I had tentatively constructed an interpretation of *Memoirs,* a third use of psychoanalytic theory came into play. Although theory cannot unilaterally validate any particular interpretation, to the extent that a comprehensive and coherent interpretation complies with that theory, the interpretation is *weakly* confirmed. Even here, however, the issues of comprehension and coherence have priority. I can readily provide an example of this confirming function. I was initially somewhat distraught when I recognized myself lodging the issue of autonomy at the matrix of my interpretation. I had presumed that other, more basic issues must be at the core of so severe a disorder. Thus it was with considerable comfort that I saw first Erikson implicitly associate autonomy and the *"principle of law and order,"* both so manifestly crucial to Schreber, with paranoia, and then saw David Shapiro do so, even more emphatically.[6] Thus the theoretical formulations of both Erikson and Shapiro weakly confirm my interpretation; or perhaps more accurately, neither theory explicitly falsifies it.

In turn, my reading of *Memoirs* provides a very modest confirmation of their theoretical linking of paranoia and preoccupation with autonomy, and it does so despite the fact that I do not employ the historical constructions implicit in Erikson's epigenetic scheme.

In fact, although it is beyond the scope of this essay and my competence, this weak confirmation might initiate theoretical work leading to the revision of the conceptualization of paranoia. As far as I know, only Erikson and Shapiro have mentioned this linkage, and Erikson does so in the most glancing manner. One consequence of such work might be the situating of paranoia nosologically between depression and obsession, thus removing it from its more customary immediate proximity to schizophrenia. Only John Rickman, a British psychoanalyst, curently locates paranoia here, but this classification is at least implicit in Erikson and Shapiro, as well as in my reading of *Memoirs of My Nervous Illness.*[7] Thus, although the relations between theoretical and interpretive discourse are tenuous and nowhere nearly so direct as often thought, that does not mean that such relations are nonexistent, nor that developments in one do not eventually impinge upon the other, nor that this impingement occurs in only one direction.

If we somewhat reformulate this confirmatory function of theory we can glimpse its more experiential side. In my attempt to get at the particular rationality of psychoanalytic interpretation, its necessary logic, I have systematically neglected the no less crucial experiential dynamic, but the two momentarily merge when the interpreter must evaluate a tentative interpretation.[8] Quite simply, the theory can provide a check upon the interpreter's subjectivity. Of course, theory is not sacrosanct; the cacophonous present state of psychoanalytic theory stands as a monument to its very pliability in the hands of its various practitioners. The communal status of theory can nevertheless help facilitate a fruitful collaboration between the interpreter's concerns and those immanent in the subject at hand; conversely, it strongly suggests error when a particular interpretation cannot find any theoretical groundings. I have already mentioned my retrospective discomfort at finding the issue of autonomy at play in Schreber's *Memoirs.* I find derivatives of that issue far too widely not to recognize its recurrent prominence as a comment about me as much as the topic at hand. Versions of autonomy are my hobbyhorse. Hence my especial pleasure at finding it related to paranoia by Erikson, Shapiro, Rickman, and others. Although these correlations alone cannot confirm my interpretation, they do at least hold out the possibility that it can be validated. Had I lacked even such weak encouragement in the theoretical literature this book would no doubt have suffered the terminal fate of much else that I have written only to discard later. In sum, theory can help us triangulate the interpretive situation, can provide a therapeutic self-reflexiveness at the very moment we collaborate most intimately with the subject at hand, trying to lift it and ourselves to new levels of understanding.

I have sought in this book to clarify the internal relations between therapeutic and interpretive discourse within psychoanalysis; I hope also to have gone some way toward clarifying the more external relations between the disciplines of psychoanalysis and literary studies. As I understand them, these external affiliations take a form comparable to those between theoretical and interpretive discourse. A long series of figures, beginning with Freud himself, has intuited the existence of such relations; we are by now the heirs to a dispiriting heritage of conflicting claims as to their real nature. The heritage takes many forms. A large strand of this scholarship, especially of that written by psychoanalysts, turns to literature simply for exemplifications of one or another theoretical issue within psychoanalysis. We can set such work aside; however appropriate the examples located, such work does not truly engage the question of the affiliations between literary studies and psychoanalysis. It turns to the literary archive merely as a convenience, as the public counterpart to the case history or clinical vignette; the discourse in which these examples are embedded is narrowly theoretical. A second, more interesting strand of the heritage takes up the question of creativity. Literary and psychoanalytic concerns truly coincide in such work, but the activity is again theoretical, since the object of attention is a general process or processes. Although at this time the results of such labors must register disappointment, the activities themselves seem proper and potentially fruitful.

It is with the third strand of this heritage that I am most concerned, for in it the affiliations between psychoanalysis and literary studies become most confused. Works in this prolific tradition deploy psychoanalysis in the service of assisting in the interpretation of discrete texts and canons. Their secret wish seems to be to stabilize what is perceived as the capriciousness of the interpretive act in literary criticism—to give it the respectability of the sciences. It commonly seeks to achieve this end by a liberal and direct use of psychoanalytic terminology. By this point my quarrel with such work should be obvious: it collapses the discontinuity within psychoanalysis proper between interpretive and theoretical discourse, it mystifies the nature of the interpretive act. Although such work advances beyond most literary criticism in its explicit recognition of the necessity of psychological theory for the effective conduct of the interpretive act, it mistakes the nature of the contribution psychology can make. The theoretical discourse of psychoanalysis can serve interpretive discourse within literary studies precisely as it serves that within psychoanalysis. Although it cannot simply dictate interpretations, it can perform a directive role within the interpretive process, suggesting the possible relevance of some issues and the likely irrelevance of others; it can provide—after the standards of comprehension, consistency, and coherence have been applied—tertiary confirmation of tentative interpretations. Perhaps these are modest benefits; surely they are more niggardly than those frequently sought, but they are nonetheless benefits psychoanalysts enjoy to our elected exclusion.

One might say that the problem with most of the extant efforts to align psychoanalysis and literary studies is that they perceive the benefits that accrue from the enterprise as falling solely in one direction: literary studies apparently bring no dowry. Literary interpretation will be normalized, made a respectable consort of the social sciences. Actually, in this view interpretation is not so much normalized as done away with; it evaporates within the deductive regularities of science. One can understand the appeal of such a vision without giving way to its vainglories. By our time, the allure of science has become nigh irresistible; one after another of the humanistic disciplines—and I number psychoanalysis among them—have abdicated before it. Thus in most of the previous investigations of the relations between psychoanalysis and literary studies the former, already thoroughly scientized, intervenes therapeutically into the slightly déclassé goings-on of the latter. When these are the terms of the relationship, the results are as much infection as health. We witness yet again the illusion of the Real, now in the guise of psychological theory, being called upon to dispel the anxiety of interpretation. In actuality, as we saw in the third chapter, at the level of the interpretive act the distance between psychoanalysis and literary studies narrows. Indeed, insofar as literary studies retain an explicit awareness of the nature of their interpretive processes, they can restore to psychoanalysis knowledge of its proper nature. That is, if psychoanalysis can contribute to literary studies the substantial benefits of its psychological theory, literary studies can reciprocate by lending the former the benefits of their recognition of the linguistic nature of their evidence. Even standard literary handbooks, such as Brooks and

Warren's *Understanding Poetry* or Aristotle's *Rhetoric*, contain reflections that cannot but assist the psychoanalyst in the daily conduct of his practice. In sum, benefits would accrue to both parties if a dialogue between these disciplines could be properly joined.

The ambition to which this entire book is addressed is precisely that the immanent relations between the two disciplines be actualized. Literary studies could assist the return to psychoanalysis of Freud's immense sensitivity to the vagaries of language and thereby realign it with the other hermeneutic disciplines; psychoanalysis, on the other hand, could share with literary studies the hard-won benefits of its psychological theory. In such a coming together psychoanalysts and literary critics would commemorate again that altogether prescient recognition of their affiliation, the awarding to Freud in 1930 of the Goethe Prize. Only in such a cooperative spirit can either discipline flourish; only once joined can they achieve their separate ends.

Notes

Although many of the books I repeatedly cite were published in England, for the sake of consistency, I have Americanized all spellings.

Introduction: Contexts and Problems

1. Daniel Paul Schreber, *Memoirs of My Nervous Illness,* trans. Ida Macalpine and Richard A. Hunter (London: Dawson, 1955), p. 41. All subsequent references are to this edition and will be incorporated into the text, preceded by M.

2. Macalpine and Hunter, "Introduction," *Memoirs,* p. 8.

3. Sigmund Freud, "Psychoanalytic Notes on an Autobiographical Account of a Case of Paranoia (Dementia Paranoides)," in *The Standard Edition of the Psychological Works of Sigmund Freud,* trans. James Strachey et al. (London: Hogarth, 1958–74), 12:9. All subsequent references to Freud's works are to this edition and will be incorporated into the text, preceded by SE and the volume number. Note that Freud's assertion in this passage implies a radical extension of psychoanalysis's explanatory power; this is a point to which I shall return.

4. David W. Swanson, Philip J. Bohnert, and Jackson A. Smith, *The Paranoid* (Boston: Little, Brown, 1970), p. 257.

5. Obviously a precise understanding of the relationship of an individual to his or her language would be required were I to attempt a full accounting of these interpretive similarities. However, psychoanalysis has just begun to appreciate the extent to which its domain is linguistic, and none of the work to date seems to me adequate. Therefore, although I acknowledge their extreme importance, I must leave such considerations to one side. For examples of current thinking, see John Henry Clippinger, *Meaning and Discourse: A Computer Model of Psychoanalytic Speech and Cognition* (Baltimore: The Johns Hopkins University Press, 1977); Marshall Edelson, "Language and Dreams: *The Interpretation of Dreams* Revisited," *Psychoanalytic Study of the Child* 27 (1972): 203–82, and *Language and Interpretation in Psychoanalysis* (New Haven: Yale University Press, 1975); William Labov and David Fanshel, *Therapeutic Discourse: Psychotherapy as Conversation* (New York: Academic Press, 1976); and Victor Rosen, *Style, Character and Language* (New York: Jason Aronson, 1977).

6. For Lacan's own work, see Jacques Lacan, *Ecrits: A Selection,* trans. Alan Sheridan (New York: Norton, 1977); *The Four Fundamental Concepts of Psychoanalysis,* ed. Jacques-Alain Miller, trans. Alan Sheridan, The International Psychoanalytic Library, no. 106 (London: Hogarth Press, 1977); and *The Language of the Self,* trans. Anthony Wilden (Baltimore: The Johns Hopkins University Press, 1968). An indication of what his work generates by way of literary studies can conveniently be seen in two special

issues of *Yale French Studies*, no. 48 (1972), and nos. 55–56 (1978). The most sustained commentary on Lacanian psychoanalysis is Anika Lemaire, *Jacques Lacan*, trans. David Macey (London: Routledge and Kegan Paul, 1977); see also Stanley Leavy, "The Significance of Jacques Lacan," *Psychoanalytic Quarterly* 46 (1977): 201–19; Eugen Bär, "Understanding Lacan," *Psychoanalysis and Contemporary Science* 3 (1974): 473–544; Sherry Turkle, *Psychoanalytic Politics: Freud's French Revolution* (New York: Basic Books, 1978); and Richard Wollheim's incisive "The Cabinet of Dr. Lacan," *New York Review of Books*, 25 January 1979, pp. 36–45.

7. This passage is taken from a footnote apparently added to the manuscript sometime after Schreber's court victory, several months after the body of the postscript was written. In his "Grounds of Appeal," dated from Sonnenstein, 23 July 1901, he mentions to the court such revisions as a future possibility: "This is an indication that I will, in the eventuality of my *Memoirs* being printed, first check the content whether some parts could not be cut out without detracting from the whole or some expressions rendered more mildly, etc." (M, 308). We can be confident that one form such revisions took was the addition of ancillary footnotes that qualify, amplify, or cross-reference the body of the text (M, 124 n, 139 n, 166 n, 171 n, 189 n). Schreber dates one such note as having been written in March 1903, several months after the presumed completion of the manuscript (M, 171 n).

8. This is often discussed by literary critics when they approach autobiography; see, for instance, Robert F. Sayre, *The Examined Self: Benjamin Franklin, Henry Adams, Henry James* (Princeton: Princeton University Press, 1964). Psychoanalysts, on the other hand, have not appreciated its significance in their discussions of Schreber's *Memoirs;* this seems to me a curious and revelatory omission from work supposedly done within the discipline that gives us "transference" and "deferred action" *(Nachträglichkeit).* In any event, this appears to be an instance in which psychoanalysis has something to learn from literary criticism.

9. This discontinuity could be a factor in the extreme difficulty psychologists experience in diagnosing paranoid personalities; see Frank A. Dinello, "Psychological Testing of the Paranoid Patient," in Swanson, Bohnert, and Smith, *The Paranoid*, pp. 169–94.

10. The editors of *The Standard Edition* make a similar observation while commenting on the difficulties of rendering an adequate translation of *Memoirs:* "One of the remarkable features of the original," they write, "is the contrast it perpetually offers between the involved and elaborate sentences of official academic nineteenth-century German and the *outré* extravagances of the psychotic events which they describe" (SE, 12:8).

11. But see Anthony Wilden's "Translator's Introduction" to Jacques Lacan, *The Language of the Self*, p. xviii; and Jeffrey Mehlman's "Translator's Introduction" to Jean Laplanche, *Life and Death in Psychoanalysis* (Baltimore: The Johns Hopkins University Press, 1976), p. x.

1 : Schreber and His *Memoirs*

1. Thus Schreber first says that all souls revel in voluptuousness, then limits it to females, a state inferior to the male, which he never describes further. However, if his initial assertion holds, the implication is that *all* souls are female. I sense that Schreber is

trying to have it both ways here; in any event, this is just another of *Memoirs*'s internal contradictions.

2. The records of University Clinic for Nervous Diseases in Leipzig for Schreber's first hospitalization in 1884 mention two miscarriages; quoted in Franz Baumeyer, "The Schreber Case," *International Journal of Psychoanalysis* 37 (1956): 61. Subsequent research demonstrates that Mrs. Schreber suffered four more miscarriages between 1885 and 1893; see Robert B. White, "The Schreber Case Reconsidered in the Light of Psychosocial Concepts," *International Journal of Psychoanalysis* 44 (1963): 215.

3. In the act of writing *Memoirs* Schreber comes to quite another reading of God's involvement: ". . . only while writing this essay did it become quite clear to me, that God Himself must have known of the plan, if indeed He was not the instigator, to commit soul murder on me, and to hand over my body in the manner of a female harlot" (M, 77). This change is consistent with the gradual diminishment of Flechsig's role in Schreber's difficulties.

4. We are told that the use of *nerve-language* was begun by Flechsig, but was soon employed also by innumerable other "tested souls" and by God Himself (M, 72). The voices are incessant and, at the time of writing, still present: ". . . since the beginning of my contact with God . . . that is to say for almost seven years—except during sleep—*I have never had a single moment in which I did not hear voices.* They accompany me to every place and at all times . . ." (M, 225). We may note in passing that Schreber's emphasis in the passage quoted in the text upon the phrase *"from without"*—that is, that his nerves were constantly subject to external stimulation—would seem to mark an especially noxious aspect of *nerve-language.* However, in the first sentence of the first chapter he suggests that such is the nature of nerves: "the total mental life of a human being rests on [the nerves'] excitability by external forces" (M, 45).

5. It is unclear how much Schreber's inability to elaborate further is due to his own ignorance and how much to some moral scruples. The next sentence begins, "One might only add," but is immediately broken off with the notation that the remainder was found "unfit for publication" (M, 58), presumably by the same agent who suppressed chapter three.

2 : Freud and Schreber's *Memoirs*

1. This and the following quotations are from Freud's correspondence with Jung; the first from a letter dated 22 April 1910; the second from one written while on holiday in Rome, dated 24 September 1910; see *The Freud/Jung Letters: The Correspondence Between Sigmund Freud and C. G. Jung,* ed. William McGuire, and trans. Ralph Manheim and R. F. C. Hull, Bollingen Series, no. 94 (Princeton: Princeton University Press, 1974), pp. 311, 353.

2. From a letter from Freud to Sandor Ferenczi, dated 6 October 1910; quoted in Ernest Jones, *The Life and Works of Sigmund Freud* (New York: Basic Books, 1957), 2:83.

3. This concern also appears in a letter written to Jung during the time Freud was writing "Psychoanalytic Notes": "During my trip I was able to amplify this theory [i.e., "that paranoics are unable to prevent the re-cathexis of their homosexual leaning"] a little, and now I mean to test my progress against Schreber's case history and various other publications on paranoia. Still, measured by my original design, the whole thing is so incomplete that I do not know when I shall be able to publish it or how long it will

be. In any case the outcome will be a study of Schreber and people will think I designed my theory with the book in mind" (*The Freud/Jung Letters*, p. 358).

4. Sigmund Freud, *The Origins of Psychoanalysis, Letters to Wilhelm Fliess, Drafts and Notes: 1887–1902*, eds. Maria Bonaparte, Anna Freud, and Ernst Kris (New York: Basic Books, 1954), p. 109.

5. The dating must remain imprecise, but a letter to Sandor Ferenczi locates the recognition prior to early 1908: "From a theoretical point of view the case confirmed what I already know, that in these varieties of paranoia it is a matter of the libido being detached from the homosexual component." The letter is quoted in Jones, *The Life*, 2:438.

6. Freud, *Origins*, p. 111–12. At this point Freud had apparently not made a connection between homosexual fantasies and paranoia.

7. Robert Waelder's fine essay, "The Structure of Paranoid Ideas," has influenced my discussion; see *International Journal of Psychoanalysis* 32 (1951): 167–77.

8. On 21 November 1906 Freud briefly presented to the Vienna Psychoanalytic Society the case of a female patient that vaguely takes this form. See *Minutes of the Vienna Psychoanalytic Society*, ed. Herman Nunberg and Ernst Federn (New York: International Universities Press, 1962), 1:57–59.

9. It also explicitly introduces contradictions latent elsewhere. Specifically, Freud first posits a withdrawal from the external world, then this excessive sensitivity to it. Something seems amiss, but we must leave such considerations to one side.

10. These behaviors must also produce another sense in which the paranoid is always right. His extreme distrust and suspiciousness surely make those around him uncomfortable, often causing them to move off if at all possible. Thus the paranoid's behavior can cause the very signs he looks for, locking him in a circle of self-fulfilling prophecies.

11. Biographical information on Dr. Daniel Gottlob Moritz Schreber can be found in the following publications: Franz Baumeyer, "The Schreber Case," *International Journal of Psychoanalysis* 37 (1956): 61–74; William Neiderland, "Schreber: Father and Son," *Psychoanalytic Quarterly* 28 (1959): 151–69, and "Schreber's Father," *Journal of the American Psychoanalytic Association* 8 (1960): 492–99 (both reprinted in his *The Schreber Case: Psychoanalytic Profile of a Paranoid Personality* [New York: Quadrangle, 1974]); and Morton Schatzman, *Soul Murder: Persecution in the Family* (New York: Random House, 1973). I discuss Schreber's father and the various treatments of him in chapter three.

12. In case some may now consider the gulf between human and divine too wide to cross, Freud reminds us that such was not always the case. "The gods of the peoples of antiquity stood in a closer human relationship to them" (SE, 12:52), and indeed the border between them was constantly crossed. Freud often makes recourse to such historical information, presumably to improve the probability of a psychoanalytic interpretation.

13. Cf. "Don't forget that Schreber's father was—a doctor. As such he performed miracles, he miracled. In other words, the delightful characterization of God—that he knows how to deal only with corpses and has no idea of living people—and the absurd miracles that are performed on him are a bitter satire on his father's medical art. In other words, the same use of absurdity as in dreams" (*The Freud/Jung Letters*, p. 369).

14. Freud adduces as other evidence of this, first, the accusations of voluptuous excess made by the voices, and second, the fear of losing his sanity, which, he says, "is a reaction (with which we are also familiar in other cases) to the threat of losing one's

reason as a result of indulging in sexual practices and especially in masturbation" (SE, 12:56).

3 : Psychoanalysis as Literary Criticism/ Literary Criticism as Psychoanalysis

1. Sigmund Freud, "The Question of Lay Analysis" (1926), SE 20:246.

2. Jacques Lacan, "The Function and Field of Speech and Language in Psychoanalysis," *Ecrits: A Selection,* trans. Alan Sheridan (New York: Norton, 1977), p. 76.

3. I say "almost exclusively"; in a letter to Jung dated 1 October 1910, Freud asked if he should write to Schreber for further information: "Since the man is still alive, I was thinking of asking him for certain information (e.g., when he got married) and for permission to work on his story. But perhaps that would be risky" (*The Freud/Jung Letters,* p. 358). Apparently nothing came of this thought (note that it already occurs in the past tense), for in a letter of 31 October he comments that he was "still waiting for Stegman [an analyst in Dresden] to send me news of our Daniel Paul" (*The Freud/Jung Letters,* p. 369). We cannot be sure what information Stegman provided; Freud apparently utilized only Schreber's age at the time of his second illness and the fact that he had an elder brother (SE, 12:46, 50). In any event neither piece of information seems crucial; the essay could well have been written without either.

4. *The Freud/Jung Letters,* p. 358.

5. Edelson, *Language and Interpretation in Psychoanalysis,* p. 53.

6. Sherwood, *The Logic of Explanation in Psychoanalysis* (New York: Academic Press, 1969), p. 244. See his entire analysis of "psychoanalytic narratives as explanations," pp. 220–44. This gap relates to another, that between theory and therapy; that is, there is no necessary reciprocal relation between their validities. A good theory can lead to an ineffectual therapy and vice versa; see Sherwood, p. 250; and Perry London, *The Modes and Morals of Psychotherapy* (New York: Rinehart and Winston, 1964), pp. 28–29.

7. Obviously the indiscriminate deployment of a technical vocabulary is not limited to psychoanalytic criticism; it bedevils much interdisciplinary activity. Jonathan Culler comments on the problem among certain structuralists: "[the] prestige of linguistics may lead the critic to believe that simply applying linguistic labels to aspects of the text is necessarily a worthwhile activity, but of course when used metaphorically or in isolation such terms enjoy no privileged status and are not necessarily more revealing than other concepts which the critic might import or create" (*Structuralist Poetics: Structuralism, Linguistics and the Study of Literature* [Ithaca: Cornell University Press, 1975], p. 109).

8. Erikson, *Gandhi's Truth* (New York: Norton, 1969), p. 98. See also Erik H. Erikson, *Young Man Luther* (New York: Norton, 1958), p. 18.

9. Carroll, "Freud and the Myth of Origins," *New Literary History* 6 (1975): 523. Psychoanalysts themselves frequently seem less aware of these implications; but see Stanley A. Leavy, "Psychoanalytic Interpretation," *Psychoanalytic Study of the Child* 28 (1973): 305–30; and Ernst Kris, "The Recovery of Childhood Memories in Psychoanalysis," in *The Selected Papers of Ernst Kris,* ed. Lottie Newman (New Haven: Yale University Press, 1975), pp. 301–40.

10. Ezriel, "Experimentation within the Psychoanalytic Session," *British Journal for the Philosophy of Science,* no. 25 (1956), pp. 32–33. A few pages later Ezriel demon-

strates how the genetic interests of many analysts obscure the implications of their theory for grasping the texture of the present.

11. J. G. Schimek, "The Interpretations of the Past: Childhood Trauma, Psychical Reality, and Historical Truth," *Journal of the American Psychoanalytic Association* 23 (1975): 862. The reference to Freud is to the essay "Screen Memories," SE, 3:301–22. This issue of the journal graphically illustrates the current uncertainty within psychoanalysis as to the truth-value of historical constructions; in the same issue in which Schimek in the final essay questions their accuracy, the lead essay, Phyllis Greenacre's "On Reconstruction," asserts the possibility of a total and accurate recall.

12. I have discussed the character of biographical interpretations further in my "Couching Clio: The Nature of Biographical Understanding," *Diacritics* 7, no. 1 (1977): 78–86.

13. Schatzman, *Soul Murder*, pp. 10, 11, 106. Of course, we can never know with any certainty why Freud remains silent here. However, one possibility strongly suggests itself—discretion, professional confidentiality at one remove. While Schreber's publication of *Memoirs* freed Freud from the necessity of rendering his material anonymous, it at the same time prohibited him from extensive discussion of Schreber's family, members of which were still alive, without violating their privacy. Precisely because *Memoirs* was in the public domain there was no way to immunize others; that the family censored portions of the text most potentially revelatory of them indicates their sensitivity to this issue.

14. Schatzman, *Soul Murder*, p. 46. He quotes from the elder Schreber's *Kallipädae oder Erziehung zur Schönheit durch naturgetreue gleichmässige Förderung normaler Körperbildung* (Leipzig: Fleischer, 1858), pp. 203, 204.

15. Schatzman, *Soul Murder*, p. x.

16. There is another danger here, or at least another version of the historical infinite regress. Historical reconstructions encourage a rigid determinism: the present is prey to the past. Thus we can come to see Schreber as the victim of his father's crazed child-rearing practices; the father persecutes the son, whose subsequent delusions simply reproduce his earlier experiences. In essence, Schatzman comes to this position. The problem is that in empathizing with Schreber, Schatzman withholds sympathetic understanding from the father. He thus fails to recognize that empathic understanding and contempt are *functions of the present points of view, not* inherent attributes of the objects or persons under study; we can always elect to exculpate through understanding but we do not always so choose. Put another way, we can extend this explanatory process infinitely far down the generational chain and our location of a primal villain, short of Adam, must always be arbitrary, for he too has antecedents. William Neiderland, another of the researchers into Schreber's childhood, recognizes this situation; see his *The Schreber Case*, p. 109.

17. Cf. "Nor is it merely the *number* of data accounted for in this way that lends support to the original contention; it is also, and perhaps especially, the oddness, the inconsistency, or the 'improbability' (from the point of view of information-theory) of the observations thus covered which matters" (Neil M. Cheshire, *The Nature of Psychodynamic Interpretation* [New York: Wiley, 1975], p. 155). See also G. Davies and V. O'Farrell, "The Logic of Transference Interpretation," *International Review of Psychoanalysis* 3 (1976): 55–64; and Leavy, "Psychoanalytic Interpretation," p. 311.

18. This has been questioned; see, for example, Schatzman, *Soul Murder*, pp.

110–11. However, the validity of this particular segment of Freud's interpretation is not germane to my argument. I am interested only in how Freud evaluates any interpretation and the appropriateness of this particular interpretation is quite beside the point.

19. W. W. Meissner, "Freud's Methodology," *Journal of the American Psychoanalytic Association* 19 (1971): 306.

20. W. W. Meissner, "The Operational Principle and Meaning in Psychoanalysis," *Psychoanalytic Quarterly* 35 (1966): 249, 251.

21. Sherwood, *The Logic of Explanation*, p. 190.

22. Meissner, "Freud's Methodology," p. 301.

23. Cf. Edelson's third chapter, "Interpretation and Explanation in Psychoanalysis," in *Language and Interpretation*, pp. 45–61.

24. "The number of symbols met with in practice is extraordinarily high, and can certainly be counted by thousands. In astonishing contrast with this stands the curious fact that the number of ideas thus symbolized is very limited indeed, so that in the interpretation of them the complaint of monotony is naturally often heard" (Ernest Jones, "The Theory of Symbolism" [1916], in *Papers on Psychoanalysis*, 5th ed. (1948; reprint ed., Boston: Beacon Press, 1961), p. 102). Cf. John Forrester, *Language and the Origins of Psychoanalysis* (New York: Columbia University Press, 1980), pp. 63–130.

25. My discussion in this paragraph is largely derived from Sherwood; see *Logic of Explanation*, pp. 244–57,

26. Ibid., p. 190.

27. Hirsch, *Validity in Interpretation* (New Haven: Yale University Press, 1967), p. 172. Hirsch reformulates his theory somewhat in his *The Aims of Interpretation* (Chicago: University of Chicago Press, 1976). Of course, the classic statement of the hermeneutic situation in literary studies is surely Leo Spitzer's description of the "philological circle"; see his *Linguistics and Literary History: Essays in Stylistics* (Princeton: Princeton University Press, 1948).

28. Ellis, *The Theory of Literary Criticism: A Logical Analysis* (Berkeley: University of California Press, 1974), p. 184; see his entire sixth chapter, pp. 155–210.

29. Sherwood, *The Logic of Explanation*, p. 245; Hirsch, *Validity in Interpretation*, pp. 17–73.

30. But see Norman N. Holland, "A Touching of Literary and Psychiatric Education," *Seminars in Psychiatry* 5 (1973): 287–99.

31. Piaget, *Genetic Epistemology*, trans. Eleanor Duckworth, Woodbridge Lectures, no. 8 (New York: Columbia University Press, 1970), p. 8. Peter Gay makes a similar argument for the necessity of an adequate psychological theory for history; see his *Art and Act: On Causes in History—Manet, Gropius, Mondrian* (New York: Harper and Row, 1976), pp. 1–32.

4 : Groundings in Theory: The Cohesive Life, The Whole Story

1. Sigmund Freud, "On Beginning the Treatment" (1913), SE, 12:135.

2. Sigmund Freud, "Group Psychology and the Analysis of the Ego" (1921), SE, 18:69.

3. Karl Marx, "Economic and Philosophical Manuscripts of 1844," in *Early Writings*, trans. Rodney Livingstone and Gregor Benton, The Marx Library (New York: Vintage Books, 1975), p. 350.

4. Carol Shields, *Small Ceremonies* (Toronto: McGraw-Hill, Ryerson, 1976), p. 51.

5. Cf. chapter nine, "Knowing," in Norman H. Holland's *Five Readers Reading* (New Haven: Yale University Press, 1975), pp. 250–91. It seems to me that Holland weakens his otherwise admirable discussion of the holistic method by not explicitly grounding it in psychoanalytic theory.

6. Claude Lévi-Strauss, *Tristes Tropiques*, trans. John Weightman and Doreen Weightman (London: Jonathan Cape, 1973), p. 58.

7. Michel Foucault, *The Order of Things: An Archaeology of the Human Sciences* (New York: Random House, 1971), pp. 386–87.

8. See, for example, chapter five, "The Rise and Decline of the Individual," in Max Horkheimer, *Eclipse of Reason* (1947; reprint ed. New York: Seabury Press, 1974), pp. 128–61.

9. Fredric Jameson, "On Goffman's Frame Analysis," *Theory and Society* 3 (1976): 130–31.

10. Victor Tausk, "On the Origin of the 'Influencing Machine' in Schizophrenia" (1919), *Psychoanalytic Quarterly* 2 (1933): 519–56. My authority for this attribution is Edith Jacobson, *The Self and the Object World*, Journal of the American Psychoanalytic Association Monograph Series, no. 2 (New York: International Universities Press, 1964), p. xi n.

11. Erikson, *Identity and the Life Cycle*, Psychological Issues, no. 1 (New York: International Universities Press, 1959), p. 102. This monograph collects several of Erikson's earlier papers; they have appeared again, now greatly revised, as part of his *Identity, Youth and Crisis* (New York: Norton, 1968). Unless otherwise indicated, all citations will be to the earlier, I think more trenchant, versions of *Identity and the Life Cycle*. I am solely concerned here with Erikson's concept of identity, thus his over-all transformation of psychoanalytic theory will be only introduced where necessary. Erikson's best description of his general theory is still *Childhood and Society*, 2nd ed. (New York: Norton, 1963); convenient summaries may be found in Robert Coles, *Erik H. Erikson: The Growth of His Work* (Boston: Little, Brown, 1970), pp. 118–58; E. Pumpian-Mindlin, "Anna Freud and Erik H. Erikson," *Science and Psychoanalysis* 7 (1964): 1–16; and Paul Roazen, *Erik H. Erikson: The Power and Limits of His Vision* (New York: Free Press, 1976).

12. I say this despite the fact Erikson himself says, "such 'senses' pervade surface and depth, consciousness and unconscious" (56). A careful reading of *Identity and the Life Cycle* suggests that more often than not such locutions refer to conscious phenomena.

13. Erikson, *Identity, Youth and Crisis*, p. 23.

14. Cf. Coles, *Erik H. Erikson*, p. 177.

15. Erikson, *Identity, Youth and Crisis*, p. 22.

16. Erikson, *Young Man Luther* (New York: Norton, 1958), p. 22 (my emphasis).

17. Erikson appears to preempt the possibility that "newly added identity elements" could merely be assimilated to the preexistent configuration. This is perhaps a necessary pratfall of his epigenetic orientation, but it nonetheless involves him in a logical fallacy. Moreover, his analysis here conflicts with his observation on therapeutic objectives: "Therapy and guidance may attempt to substitute more desirable identifications for undesirable ones, but the total configuration of the ego identity remains unalterable" (26).

18. Willy Baranger, a Uruguayan analyst, has come to much the same formulation, apparently without being influenced by Erikson. He writes: "Ideology partly controls the relationship between the ego, the id, the superego and reality. . . . Ideology seems to be an attempt on the part of the ego to assume consciously the task of reconciling the demands of the superego with those of the id as far as they may be expressed in reality" ("The Ego and the Function of Ideology," *International Journal of Psychoanalysis* 39 [1958]: 194. Also of interest in this regard is the work of Lucian Pye, who has applied Erikson's concept of ideology to the understanding of developing nations; see his "Personal Identity and Political Ideology," *Behavioral Science* 6 (1961): 205–21; reprinted in Bruce Mazlish, ed., *Psychoanalysis and History,* rev. ed. (New York: Grosset, 1971), 150–73.

19. For a cogent analysis of the neo-Freudian efforts, see Russell Jacoby, *Social Amnesia: A Critique of Contemporary Psychology from Adler to Laing* (Boston: Beacon Press, 1975).

20. Of course, others have also called attention to the cultural formation of the ego. Says Theodor Adorno, for instance: "The separation of the ego and super-ego, which the analytical topology insists upon, is a dubious affair; genetically, both of them lead equally to the internalization of the father image. The analytical theories about the super-ego, however bold their beginnings, will therefore flag in short order, lest they be obliged to spread to the coddled ego" (*Negative Dialectics,* trans. E. B. Ashton [New York: Seabury Press, 1973], p. 273).

21. Nonetheless, I do not think the extent to which Erikson's thought aspires to be (and, in fact, is) fully dialectical has been properly appreciated and this omission has been the source of serious misperceptions of his work. In fact, I sometimes entertain the notion that he is our modern Hegel. Of course, he comes to us as a psychoanalyst, not as a philosopher, but that is only appropriate in the Age of Psychological Man. Let me extend the analogy: both Hegel and Erikson see history as progress; both understand that progress as a process of sublation, in which later phases incorporate and make over earlier ones; the bureaucratic Germany of the one gives way to the adopted United States of the other; the Spirit to the Species and so on. Erikson's triad of biology, culture, and ego even functions in a way comparable to those of Hegel, in that the third term arises from the interplay of the first two. Obviously, the analogy is not complete, but it nonetheless suggests some of the strengths as well as weaknesses of Erikson's work.

22. Lichtenstein, "Identity and Sexuality: A Study of Their Interrelationship in Man," *Journal of the American Psychoanalytic Association* 9 (1961): 184. Subsequent references to this article will be incorporated into the text, the title indicated simply as IS. Cf. Holland, *Five Readers Reading,* pp. 56–61, 223–25.

23. Lichtenstein develops this idea again in his "Changing Implications of the Concept of Psychosexual Development," *Journal of the American Psychoanalytic Association* 18 (1970): 300–318.

24. Cf. Heinz Lichtenstein, "The Role of Narcissism in the Emergence of Maintenance of a Primary Identity," *International Journal of Psychoanalysis* 46 (1965): 49–56, esp. p. 53.

25. Ibid., p. 51. Compare Lichtenstein's comments upon "metamorphosis," in "Identity and Sexuality," pp. 227–28; and in his lengthy review-article, "The Dilemma of Human Identity: Notes of Self-Transformation, Self-Objectivation, and Metamor-

phosis," *Journal of the American Psychoanalytic Association* 11 (1963): 173–223, esp. pp. 213–15.

26. Lichtenstein, "Towards a Metapsychological Definition of the Concept of Self," *International Journal of Psychoanalysis* 46 (1965): 125. Cf. D. C. Levin, "The Self: A Contribution to Its Place in Theory and Technique," *International Journal of Psychoanalysis* 50 (1969): 209–20.

27. Lichtenstein, "The Concept of Self," p. 126.

28. Lichtenstein's formulations bear some obvious resemblances to those of Jacques Lacan; see, for instance, the latter's "Of Structure as an Inmixing of an Otherness Prerequisite to Any Subject Whatever," in *The Languages of Criticism and the Sciences of Man,* ed., Richard Macksey and Eugenio Donato (Baltimore: The Johns Hopkins University Press, 1970), pp. 186–95; and "The Field of the Other and Back to Transference," in his *The Four Fundamental Concepts of Psychoanalysis,* pp. 201–60. I find Lichtenstein's formulations more useful.

29. I have done so elsewhere; see my ". . . Reading Readers Reading Readers Reading . . . ," *Diacritics* 5, no. 3 (1975): 24–31.

30. I am strongly tempted to see this as more than a figure; that is, I would like to think that these processes replicate one another and that the process at the individual level provides the missing explanation for it at the level of culture.

31. Cf. D. W. Winnicott's concept of "potential space," developed most fully in "The Location of Cultural Experience" and "The Place Where We Live," both collected in his *Playing and Reality* (London: Tavistock, 1971), pp. 95–110. I have not directly appropriated Winnicott's analysis because it strikes me as preserving an irreducible opposition between subject and object even as it tries to overcome the distance between them. But see Murray Schwartz, "Where Is Literature?," *College English* 36 (1975): 756–65.

32. Compare the following from chapter seven of *Interpretation:* "If the first account given me by a patient of a dream is too hard to follow I ask him to repeat it. In doing so he rarely uses the same words. But the parts of the dream which he describes in different terms are by that fact revealed to me as the weak spot in the dream's disguise: they serve my purpose just as Hagen's was served by the embroidered mark on Siegfried's cloak. That is the point at which the interpretation of the dream can be started. My request to the patient to repeat his account of the dream has warned him that I was proposing to take special pains in solving it; under the pressure of the resistance, therefore, he hastily covers the weak spots in the dream's disguise by replacing any expressions that threaten to betray its meaning by other less revealing ones. In this way he draws my attention to the expression which he has dropped out. The trouble taken by the dreamer in preventing the solution of the dream gives me a basis for estimating the care with which its cloak has been woven" (SE, 5:515).

33. Freud initially extends the series when he notes that all the dreams that occur during a single night themselves form an interrelated series (SE, 4:333–34).

34. We can be somewhat more precise about the location of this point; it is the point at which the so-called day's residues are insinuated into this latticework.

35. And: "At least once in the course of every analysis a moment comes when the patient obstinately maintains that just now positively nothing whatever occurs to his mind. His free associations come to a stop and the usual incentives for putting them in motion fail in their effect. If the analyst insists, the patient is at last induced to admit that he is thinking of the view from the consulting-room window, of the wall-paper

that he sees before him, or of the gas-lamp hanging from the ceiling. Then one knows at once that he has gone off into the transference and that he is engaged upon what are still unconscious thoughts relating to the physician; and one sees the stoppage in the patient's associations disappear, as soon as he has been given this explanation" (SE, 18:126 n).

36. The remainder of the paragraph is also of interest: "Some of these transferences have a content which differs from that of their model in no respect whatever except for the substitution. These then—to keep to the same metaphor—are merely new impressions or reprints. Others are more ingeniously constructed; their content has been subjected to a moderating influence—to *sublimation,* as I call it—and they may even become conscious, by cleverly taking advantage of some real peculiarity in the physician's person or circumstances and attaching themselves to that. These, then, will no longer be new impressions, but revised editions" (SE, 7:116).

37. Cf. "Classically, the transference is acknowledged to be the terrain on which all the basic problems of a given analysis play themselves out: the establishment, the modalities, interpretation and resolution of the transference are in fact what define the cure" (Jean Laplanche and J.-B. Pontalis, *The Language of Psychoanalysis,* trans. Donald Nicholson-Smith [New York: Norton, 1973], p. 455). Laplanche and Pontalis anticipate much of the preceding in their condensed entry on transference.

38. As he reflects back in the *Introductory Lectures* upon the history of analytic therapy, including his early reliance on hypnosis, Freud comments: "And it must dawn on us that in our technique we have abandoned hypnosis only to rediscover suggestion in the form of transference" (SE, 16:446).

39. See also his passing comments in both the Clark Lectures (SE, 11:55) and *Introductory Lectures* (SE, 16:446). I should add that with few exceptions contemporary psychoanalysts generally resist this extension of the concept, but it is precisely this more inclusive usage of the term that is crucial to my argument; see, for instance, Arthur F. Valenstein's report, "Panel on 'Transference,'" *International Journal of Psychoanalysis* 55 (1974): 311–21. For an important exception to this tendency, see the second chapter, "Transference and Love," of Hans Loewald, *Psychoanalysis and the History of the Individual,* The Freud Lectures at Yale (New Haven: Yale University Press, 1978), pp. 29–51.

40. See SE, 2:302 and SE, 12:143, respectively.

41. I base this hypothesis upon Freud's discussion of the relationship between love and transference-love; see his "Observations on Transference-Love," SE, 12:168–69.

42. Just as, on another theoretical level, Freud defines the ego in *The Ego and the Id* (1923): "It may be that by this introjection, which is a kind of regression to the mechanisms of the oral phase, the ego makes it easier for the object to be given up or renders that process possible. It may be that this identification is the sole condition under which the id can give up its objects. At any rate the process, especially in the early phases of development, is a very frequent one, and it makes it possible to suppose that *the character of the ego is a precipitate of abandoned object-cathexes and that it contains the history of those object-choices*" (SE, 19:29, my emphasis). This passage bears obvious importance for the entire argument of this chapter.

43. Sherwood, *The Logic of Explanation,* p. 190.

44. "In the traditional case history . . . the patient's residence, ethnic background, and occupations are the first items to be radically altered when it is necessary to dis-

guise his personal identity. The essence of the inner dynamics of a case, it is judged, is thereby left intact. The exact nature, then, of the values common to the patient's background are considered to be so close to the 'surface' that they are not necessarily of 'psychoanalytic' interest. I will not now discuss the rationale for such neglect but merely offer observations from my notebook which seem to indicate that contemporary social models are both clinically and theoretically relevant and cannot be shunted off by brief and patronizing tributes to the role 'also' played by 'social factors' " (Erikson, *Identity, Youth and Crisis,* pp. 44–45).

5 : The Unsure Prophet Remembers

1. Wallace Stevens, "Adagia," *Opus Posthumous,* ed. Samuel French Morse (New York: Knopf, 1957), p. 164.

2. Robert Creeley, "The Immoral Proposition," *For Love: Poems, 1950–1960* (New York: Scribner's, 1962), p. 31.

3. Shengold, "Soul Murder," *International Journal of Psychoanalytic Psychotherapy* 3 (1975): 366–73.

4. Schreber repeatedly employs the indefinite pronoun "one" to refer to God, especially when being, directly or indirectly, critical. I perceive such usages as further examples of the overall strategy of muting his anger, making its expression covert.

5. Leonard Shengold apparently defines soul murder as "the extinction of a person's individuality" ("Soul Murder," p. 366); although this obviously approximates my own reading, I think it claims too much, for it aligns it directly with schizoid phenomena, but obscures its manifold connections with other developmental issues.

6. We should recall in this context that insomnia was among Schreber's presenting symptoms when he first sought out Professor Flechsig in 1893.

7. Note that this is the same word Schreber uses to relate the sexual experience in the repugnant early dream. Thus just as Schreber succumbs like a woman to intercourse in the dream, now God succumbs to the attractiveness of Schreber's nerves. Who, then, is the woman now? In any event, issues of mastery and submission are paramount here, not those of genital sexuality per se.

8. See Franz Baumeyer, "The Schreber Case," pp. 61–74.

A Polemical Epilogue

1. Schafer, *A New Language for Psychoanalysis* (New Haven: Yale University Press, 1976); and *Language and Insight,* The Sigmund Freud Memorial Lectures, 1975–76, University College, London (New Haven: Yale University Press, 1978).

2. I have characterized "ideal types" of interpretive and theoretical discourse; in actual practice they could both appear within a single essay, as when, for instance, an interpretive crux generates theoretical speculation. Nonetheless, the possibility of such joint appearances does not alter the nature of either. For a somewhat different critique of Schafer, see W. W. Meissner, "Methodological Critique of the Action Language in Psychoanalysis," *Journal of the American Psychoanalytic Association* 27 (1979): 79–105.

3. See, for instance, Arthur C. Carr, "Observations on Paranoia and their Relationship to the Schreber Case," *International Journal of Psychoanalysis* 44 (1963): 195–200;

L. Ovesey, "Pseudo-homosexuality, the Paranoid Mechanism and Paranoia," *Psychiatry* 18 (1955): 163–73; and the review of the relevant literature in W. W. Meissner, "Schreber and the Paranoid Process," *Annual of Psychoanalysis* 4 (1976): 3–40, esp. pp. 19–21.

4. See Erikson, *Childhood and Society*, pp. 80–85, 251–54.

5. Robert Waelder, "The Structure of Paranoid Ideas," pp. 167–77; and David Shapiro, *Neurotic Styles*, Austen Riggs Center Monograph Series, no. 5 (New York: Basic Books, 1965), pp. 54–107.

6. Erikson, *Childhood and Society*, p. 254; Shapiro, *Neurotic Styles*, esp. pp. 104–7.

7. See the graph appended to the end of Rickman, *Selected Contributions to Psychoanalysis*, The International Psychoanalytic Library, no. 52 (London: Hogarth Press, 1957). There is a sense in which Rickman's formulations represent a continuation of a tradition begun by Karl Abraham, and developed most fully by Melanie Klein; see Abraham, "A Short Study of the Development of the Libido" (1924), in *Selected Papers* (New York: Basic Books, 1954), pp. 418–501; and Klein, *Contributions to Psychoanalysis: 1921–1945* (New York: McGraw-Hill, 1964).

8. The best discussion of the experiential dynamic of interpretation with which I am familiar can be found in Stanley Leavy, "Psychoanalytic Interpretation," pp. 305–30; see also his *The Psychoanalytic Dialogue* (New Haven: Yale University Press, 1980).

Bibliography

Abraham, Karl. "A Short Study of the Development of the Libido.' In *Selected Papers.* New York: Basic Books, 1954, pp. 418–501.

Adorno, Theodor. *Negative Dialectics.* Translated by E. B. Ashton. New York: Seabury Press, 1973.

Bär, Eugen. "Understanding Lacan." *Psychoanalysis and Contemporary Science* 3 (1974): 473–544.

Baranger, Willy. "The Ego and the Function of Ideology." *International Journal of Psychoanalysis* 39 (1958): 191–95.

Baumeyer, Franz. "The Schreber Case." *International Journal of Psychoanalysis* 37 (1956): 61–74.

Carr, Arthur C. "Observations on Paranoia and their Relationship to the Schreber Case." *International Journal of Psychoanalysis* 44 (1963): 195–200.

Carroll, David. "Freud and the Myth of Origins." *New Literary History* 6 (1975): 513–28.

Chabot, C. Barry. "Couching Clio: The Nature of Biographical Understanding." *Diacritics* 7, no. 1 (1977): 78–86.

———. ". . . Reading Readers Reading Readers Reading. . ." *Diacritics* 5, no. 3 (1975): 24–31.

Cheshire, Neil M. *The Nature of Psychodynamic Interpretation.* New York: Wiley, 1975.

Clippinger, John Henry. *Meaning and Discourse: A Computer Model of Psychoanalytic Speech and Cognition.* Baltimore: The Johns Hopkins University Press, 1977.

Cody, John. *After Great Pain: The Inner Life of Emily Dickinson.* Cambridge: Harvard University Press, 1971.

Coles, Robert. *Erik H. Erikson: The Growth of His Work.* Boston: Little, Brown, 1970.

Crews, Frederick. *The Sins of the Fathers: Hawthorne's Psychological Themes.* New York: Oxford University Press, 1966.

Culler, Jonathan. *Structuralist Poetics: Structuralism and the Study of Literature.* Ithaca: Cornell University Press, 1975.

Davies, G., and V. O'Farrell. "The Logic of Transference Interpretation." *International Review of Psychoanalysis* 3 (1976): 55–64.

Edelson, Marshall. "Language and Dreams: *The Interpretation of Dreams* Revisited." *The Psychoanalytic Study of the Child* 27 (1972): 203–82.

———. *Language and Interpretation in Psychoanalysis.* New Haven: Yale University Press, 1975.

Ellis, John. *The Theory of Literary Criticism: A Logical Analysis.* Berkeley: University of California Press, 1974.

Erikson, Erik H. *Childhood and Society,* 2nd ed. New York: Norton, 1963.

———. *Gandhi's Truth.* New York: Norton, 1969.

———. *Identity and the Life Cycle.* Psychological Issues, no. 1. New York: International Universities Press, 1959.

———. *Identity, Youth and Crisis.* New York: Norton, 1968.

———. *Young Man Luther.* New York: Norton, 1958.

Ezriel, Henry. "Experimentation within the Psychoanalytic Session." *British Journal for the Philosophy of Science,* no. 25 (1956), pp. 29–48.

Forrester, John. *Language and the Origins of Psychoanalysis.* New York: Columbia University Press, 1980.

Foucault, Michel. *The Order of Things: An Archaeology of the Human Sciences.* New York: Random House, 1971.

Freud, Sigmund. *The Freud/Jung Letters: The Correspondence Between Sigmund Freud and C. G. Jung.* Edited by William McGuire. Translated by Ralph Manheim and R. F. C. Hull. Bollingen Series, no. 94. Princeton: Princeton University Press, 1974.

———. *The Origins of Psychoanalysis, Letters to Wilhelm Fliess, Drafts and Notes: 1887–1902.* Edited by Maria Bonaparte, Anna Freud, and Ernst Kris. New York: Basic Books, 1954.

———. *The Standard Edition of the Psychological Works of Sigmund Freud.* Translated by James Strachey et al. 24 vols. London: Hogarth, 1958–1974.

Gay, Peter. *Art and Act: On Causes in History—Manet, Gropius, Mondrian.* New York: Harper and Row, 1976.

Greenacre, Phyllis. "On Reconstruction." *Journal of the American Psychoanalytic Association* 23 (1975): 693–712.

Hirsch, E. D. *The Aims of Interpretation.* Chicago: University of Chicago Press, 1976.

———. *Validity in Interpretation.* New Haven: Yale University Press, 1967.

Holland, Norman N. "A Touching of Literary and Psychiatric Education." *Seminars in Psychiatry* 5 (1973): 287–99.

———. *Five Readers Reading.* New Haven: Yale University Press, 1975.

Horkheimer, Max. *Eclipse of Reason.* 1947. Reprint. New York: Seabury Press, 1974.

Jacobson, Edith. *The Self and the Object World.* Journal of the American Psychoanalytic Association Monograph Series, no. 2. New York: International Universities Press, 1964.

Jacoby, Russell. *Social Amnesia: A Critique of Contemporary Psychology from Adler to Laing.* Boston: Beacon Press, 1975.

Jameson, Fredric. "On Goffman's Frame Analysis." *Theory and Society* 3 (1976): 119–33.

Jones, Ernest. *Hamlet and Oedipus.* London: V. Gollancz, 1949.

———. *The Life and Works of Sigmund Freud.* 3 vols. New York: Basic Books, 1961.

———. "The Theory of Symbolism." *Papers on Psychoanalysis.* 5th ed. 1948. Reprint. Boston: Beacon Press, 1961, pp. 87–144.

Klein, Melanie. *Contributions to Psychoanalysis: 1921–1945.* New York: McGraw-Hill, 1964.

Kris, Ernst. *Psychoanalytic Explorations in Art.* New York: International Universities Press, 1952.

———. "The Recovery of Childhood Memories in Psychoanalysis." *The Selected Papers of Ernst Kris.* Edited by Lottie Newman. New Haven: Yale University Press, 1975, pp. 301–40.

Labov, William, and David Fanshel. *Therapeutic Discourse: Psychotherapy as Conversation.* New York: Academic Press, 1976.

Lacan, Jacques. *Ecrits: A Selection.* Translated by Alan Sheridan. New York: Norton, 1977.

———. *The Four Fundamental Concepts of Psychoanalysis.* Edited by Jacques-Alain Miller. Translated by Alan Sheridan. The International Psychoanalytic Library, no. 106. London: Hogarth Press, 1977.

———. *The Language of the Self: The Function of Language in Psychoanalysis.* Translated by Anthony Wilden. Baltimore: The Johns Hopkins University Press, 1968.

———. "Of Structure as an Inmixing of an Otherness Prerequisite to Any Subject Whatever." In *The Languages of Criticism and the Sciences of Man: The Structuralist Controversy.* Edited by Richard Macksey and Eugenio Donato. Baltimore: The Johns Hopkins University Press, 1970, pp. 185–95.

Laplanche, Jean, and J.-B. Pontalis. *The Language of Psychoanalysis.* Translated by Donald Nicholson-Smith. New York: Norton, 1973.

Leavy, Stanley. *The Psychoanalytic Dialogue.* New Haven: Yale University Press, 1980.

———. "Psychoanalytic Interpretation." *Psychoanalytic Study of the Child* 28 (1973): 305–30.

———. "The Significance of Jacques Lacan." *Psychoanalytic Quarterly* 46 (1977): 201–19.

Lemaire, Anika. *Jacques Lacan.* Translated by David Macey. London: Routledge and Kegan Paul, 1977.

Levin, D. C. "The Self: A Contribution to Its Place in Theory and Technique." *International Journal of Psychoanalysis* 50 (1969): 209–20.

Lévi-Strauss, Claude. *Tristes Tropiques.* Translated by John Weightman and Doreen Weightman. London: Jonathan Cape, 1973.

Lichtenstein, Heinz. "Changing Implications of the Concept of Psychosexual Development." *Journal of the American Psychoanalytic Association* 18 (1970): 300–318.

———. "The Dilemma of Human Identity: Notes of Self-Transformation, Self-Objectivation, and Metamorphosis." *Journal of the American Psychoanalytic Association* 11 (1963): 173–223.

———. "Identity and Sexuality: A Study of Their Interrelationship in Man." *Journal of the American Psychoanalytic Association* 9 (1961): 179–260.

———. "The Role of Narcissism in the Emergence of Maintenance of a Primary Identity." *International Journal of Psychoanalysis* 46 (1965): 49–56.

———. "Towards a Metapsychological Definition of the Concept of Self." *International Journal of Psychoanalysis* 46 (1965): 117–28.

Loewald, Hans. *Psychoanalysis and the History of the Individual.* The Freud Lectures at Yale. New Haven: Yale University Press, 1978.

London, Perry. *The Modes and Morals of Psychotherapy.* New York: Rinehart and Winston, 1964.

Mazlish, Bruce, ed. *Psychoanalysis and History.* Rev. ed. New York: Grosset, 1971.

Mehlman, Jeffrey. Translator's Introduction to *Life and Death in Psychoanalysis* by Jean Laplanche. Baltimore: The Johns Hopkins University Press, 1976.

Meissner, W. W. "Freud's Methodology." *Journal of the American Psychoanalytic Association* 19 (1971): 265–308.

———. "Methodological Critique of the Action Language in Psychoanalysis." *Journal of the American Psychoanalytic Association* 27 (1979): 79–105.

———. "The Operational Principle and Meaning in Psychoanalysis." *Psychoanalytic Quarterly* 35 (1966): 233–55.

———. "Schreber and the Paranoid Process." *Annual of Psychoanalysis* 4 (1976): 3–40.

Meyer, Bernard. *Joseph Conrad: A Psychoanalytic Biography.* Princeton: Princeton University Press, 1967.

Milner, Marion. *On Not Being Able to Paint.* 2nd ed. New York: International Universities Press, 1957.

Minutes of the Vienna Psychoanalytic Society. Edited by Herman Numberg and Ernst Federn. New York: International Universities Press, 1962, Vol. I.

Neiderland, William. *The Schreber Case: Psychoanalytic Profile of a Paranoid Personality.* New York: Quadrangle, 1974.

Ovesey, L. "Pseudo-homosexuality, the Paranoid Mechanism and Paranoia." *Psychiatry* 18 (1955): 163–73.

Piaget, Jean. *Genetic Epistemology.* Translated by Eleanor Duckworth. Woodbridge Lectures, no. 8. New York: Columbia University Press, 1970.

Pumpian-Mindlin, E. "Anna Freud and Erik H. Erikson." *Science and Psychoanalysis* 7 (1964): 1–16.

Pye, Lucian. "Personal Identity and Political Ideology." *Behavioral Science* 6 (1961): 205–21.

Rickman, John. *Selected Contributions to Psychoanalysis.* The International Psychoanalytic Library, no. 52. London: Hogarth Press, 1957.

Roazen, Paul. *Erik H. Erikson: The Power and Limits of His Vision.* New York: Free Press, 1976.

Rosen, Victor. *Style, Character and Language.* New York: Jason Aronson, 1977.

Sayre, Robert F. *The Examined Self: Benjamin Franklin, Henry Adams, Henry James.* Princeton: Princeton University Press, 1964.

Schafer, Roy. *Language and Insight.* The Sigmund Freud Memorial Lectures, 1975–1976, University College, London. New Haven: Yale University Press, 1978.

———. *A New Language for Psychoanalysis.* New Haven: Yale University Press, 1976.

Schatzman, Morton. *Soul Murder: Persecution in the Family.* New York: Random House, 1973.

Schimek, J. G. "The Interpretations of the Past: Childhood Trauma, Psychical Reality, and Historical Truth." *Journal of the American Psychoanalytic Association* 23 (1975): 845–65.

Schreber, Daniel Paul. *Memoirs of My Nervous Illness.* Translated by Ida Macalpine and Richard A. Hunter. London: Dawson, 1955.

Schwartz, Murray. "Where is Literature?" *College English* 36 (1975): 756–65.

Shapiro, David. *Neurotic Styles.* Austen Riggs Center Monograph Series, no. 5. New York: Basic Books, 1965.

Shengold, Leonard. "Soul Murder." *International Journal of Psychoanalytic Psychotherapy* 3 (1975): 366–73.

Sherwood, Michael. *The Logic of Explanation in Psychoanalysis.* New York: Academic Press, 1969.

Spitzer, Leo. *Linguistics and Literary History: Essays in Stylistics.* Princeton: Princeton University Press, 1948.

Swanson, David W., Philip J. Bohnert, and Jackson A. Smith. *The Paranoid.* Boston: Little, Brown, 1970.

Tausk, Victor. "On the Origin of the 'Influencing Machine' in Schizophrenia." *Psychoanalytic Quarterly* 2 (1933): 519–56.

Turkle, Sherry. *Psychoanalytic Politics: Freud's French Revolution.* New York: Basic Books, 1978.

Valenstein, Arthur F. "Panel on 'Transference.'" *International Journal of Psychoanalysis* 55 (1974): 311–21.

Waelder, Robert. "The Structure of Paranoid Ideas." *International Journal of Psychoanalysis* 32 (1951): 167–77.

White, Robert B. "The Schreber Case Reconsidered in the Light of Psychosocial Concepts." *International Journal of Psychoanalysis* 44 (1963): 213–21.

Winnicott, D. W. *Playing and Reality.* London: Tavistock, 1971.

Wollheim, Richard. "The Cabinet of Dr. Lacan." *New York Review of Books,* 25 January 1979, pp. 36–45.

Yale French Studies, no. 48 (1972).

Yale French Studies, nos. 55–56 (1978).

Index

Library of Congress Cataloging in Publication Data

Chabot, C. Barry, 1944 –

Freud on Schreber.

Bibliography: p.

Includes index.

1. Psychoanalytic interpretation. 2. Criticism.

3. Psychoanalysis and literature. 4. Freud,

Sigmund, 1856 – 1939. 5. Schreber, Daniel Paul,

1842 – 1911. Denkwürdigkeiten eines Nervenkranken.

I. Title.

BF175.C43 1982 150.19'52 81 – 16476

ISBN 0 – 87023 – 348 – 3 AACR2